Black Geographies

Black Geographies

and the Politics of Place

edited by Katherine McKittrick
and Clyde Woods

Between the Lines
Toronto, Ontario

South End Press
Cambridge, Massachusetts

Black Geographies and the Politics of Place

First published in 2007 by
Between the Lines
720 Bathurst Street, Suite #404
Toronto, Ontario
M5S 2R4
1-800-718-7201
www.btlbooks.com

Published in the U.S.A. by
South End Press
7 Brookline Street, Suite 1
Cambridge, MA 02139
U.S.A.
www.southendpress.org

Library and Archives Canada Cataloguing in Publication

Black geographies and the politics of place / Katherine McKittrick and Clyde Woods, eds.
Includes index and bibliographical references.
ISBN 978-1-897071-23-6

1. African diaspora – History. 2. Blacks – History. I. McKittrick, Katherine II. Woods, Clyde Adrian
DT16.5.B54 2007 909'.0496 C2007-900343-5

Library of Congress Cataloguing-in-Publication Data

Black geographies and the politics of place / Katherine McKittrick and Clyde Woods, eds.
Includes index and bibliographical references.
ISBN 978-0-89608-773-6 (alk. paper)

1. African Americans – Social conditions. 2. African Americans – Race identity. 3. African Americans – Population. 4. Blacks – Canada – Social conditions. 5. Blacks – Canada – Race identity. 6. Blacks – Canada – Population. 7. African diaspora. 8. Human geography – United States. 9. Human geography – Canada. 10. Geography – Psychological aspects.
I. McKittrick, Katherine. II. Woods, Clyde Adrian.
E185.86.B52557 2007 305.896'07–dc22 2007008893

Cover design by Jennifer Tiberio
Cover images: front upper, Jennifer Tiberio; front lower, © iStockphoto.com/Felix Möckel; back, © iStockphoto.com/Brandon Laufenberg
Interior design and page preparation by Steve Izma
Printed in Canada by union labour on 100% post-consumer recycled paper

Between the Lines gratefully acknowledges assistance for its publishing activities from the Government of Ontario through the Ontario Book Publishers Tax Credit program and the Ontario Book Initiative, and from the Government of Canada through the Book Publishing Industry Development Program.

Contents

Acknowledgements

Black Geographies and the Politics of Place is a reflection of our continuing interest in developing and sustaining questions about the intersections between race, blackness, and spatial politics in the diaspora. As editors our shared interests, which address the relational politics of black expressive cultures and uneven geographies, have been challenged and complemented by the contributors to this collection – we thank all of them for thinking and writing about meaningful, new, and interdisciplinary conceptualizations of black geographies.

We also want to thank a group of intellectuals, musicians, and writers who, while not directly involved in this project, have helped us think about the creative and philosophical possibilities of black geographies. These folks are, in no particular order, David "Honeyboy" Edwards, Julio Finn, Michael Baytop, Raymond "Boots" Riley, Barnor Hesse, Sylvia Wynter, Ruthie Gilmore, Marlene Nourbese Philip, Toni Morrison, Nas, Octavia Butler, Alexander Weheliye, Andrea Smith, Ralph Ellison, Dionne Brand, and Edouard Glissant.

We also greatly appreciate the work of the people at Between the Lines Press in Toronto, in particular Paul Eprile, Jennifer Tiberio, Steve Izma, and David Glover, as well as the members of the South End Press collective in Cambridge. Our thanks go to BTL editor Robert Clarke and indexer Martin Boyne for working so closely with the manuscript.

Katherine also thanks Ray Zilli, Dina Georgis, Aaron Kamugisha, Ned Morgan, Minelle Mahtani, Linda Peake, Leslie Sanders, Jennifer McKittrick, and especially M. Jacqui Alexander for her support of things demonic.

Clyde thanks his son Malik, Linda Peake, Laura Pulido, George Lipsitz, Gaye Theresa Johnson, Earl Stewart, Douglas Daniels, Cedric Robinson, Elsa Barkley Brown, Jessica Johnson, and his colleagues at the University of Maryland and University of California, Santa Barbara.

Finally, honour must be given to the noble communities of Louisiana and Mississippi, devastated as they were by the man-made disasters that preceded and followed Hurricane Katrina. Their fight to preserve and create sacred places continues to both inspire the world and shape the future.

Katherine McKittrick and Clyde Woods

1

Katherine McKittrick & Clyde Woods

"No One Knows the Mysteries at the Bottom of the Ocean"

New Orleans, Louisiana, was declared "uninhabitable" on Sunday, August 28, 2005. That same day the National Weather Service office in Slidell, Louisiana, issued a statement describing the impending damage expected from the onslaught of Hurricane Katrina in the area: "Most of the area will be uninhabitable for weeks . . . perhaps longer." Both residential homes and industrial buildings would be threatened, sustaining "major damage." The statement said there might be "widespread" airborne debris, including "heavy items such as household appliances and even light vehicles. Sport utility vehicles and light trucks will be moved." The power outages could last for weeks, and a lack of clean water would "make human suffering incredible by modern standards."[1]

Authorities ordered an evacuation of New Orleans and communities in neighbouring areas, and by the time the full effects of Katrina reached the city and its surrounding suburbs on Monday morning about one million residents had managed to get out. Some of those who were unable to leave sought shelter, at least temporarily, in the city's convention centre and the Superdome sports complex. Others were left behind, stranded or unable to get help. That same morning the mayor of New Orleans described the potential loss of life as "significant." Over the next few days, as Katrina wreaked its havoc on the city, with massive flooding, some of the 50,000 people who remained there did so voluntarily – but in effect most of those left behind were abandoned and left to fend for themselves. In the end some 1,400 to 2,000 residents of Southeastern Louisiana died. They were at the very least the victims of an immense human carelessness, if not inhumanity. They were the victims of the failure of four ineffective, supposedly protective levees and floodwalls established under federal jurisdiction, the victims of dwindling wetlands and barrier islands – which might otherwise have provided a "natural defence" – destroyed by oil, agricultural, and shipping industries. They were the victims of federal abandonment and centuries of racial segregation.

After forming off the coast of Africa, the Atlantic hurricane had gone on to damage and devastate numerous regions from the Bahamas and Cuba through the states of Ohio, Kentucky, Mississippi, and Alabama, and even north to the province of Quebec in Canada. Beyond the immediate effects, in the diaspora created by Katrina the death toll over the following year continued to mount due to stress, a lack of adequate health care, suicides, and family separation. Reconstruction of specific areas of New Orleans was stalled primarily because of the attempt on the part of the city's white economic elite to deny the right of black residents to return. Indeed, as one of us writes in the pages of this book, "Those who built New Orleans over the course of three centuries were instantaneously declared unworthy of returning to their city."[2]

Hurricane Katrina was deemed a "natural disaster," but the language that propped up this supposed naturalness only served to naturalize poor and black agony, distress and death. Indeed, the history of the region provides a different narrative. Given that history's firmly stitched pattern of formal and informal racial segregation, socio-economic differentiation, and long-standing environmental neglect, the human suffering caused by Katrina was hierarchically distributed: the privileged residents of New Orleans, a largely white population, lived higher above sea level, on drier and less polluted lands, and were able to escape the hurricane by using readily available transportation (cars, airlifts); the economically underprivileged residents of New Orleans, largely black and living in areas with insufficient socio-economic services and low-income housing, suffered the brunt of the effects.[3]

The critical politics of the Katrina devastation proved to be vast. They range from continuing governmental neglect and the militarization of the region to racialized media responses and local activisms. These same experiences and narratives indicate how circuits of science, nature, and difference conceal, yet violently situate, non-white communities.[4] In its effects on human geographies, and especially black geographies, Hurricane Katrina reconfigured an already racialized space. While it altered the physicality and demography of New Orleans and other areas, the storm also brought into clear focus, at least momentarily, a legacy of uneven geographies, of those locations long occupied by *les damnés de la terre*/the wretched of the earth: the geographies of the homeless, the jobless, the incarcerated, the invisible labourers, the underdeveloped, the criminalized, the refugee, the kicked about, the impoverished, the abandoned, the unescaped.[5]

That these particular human geographies were briefly emphasized and uncovered during Katrina is significant: the materiality of racial exclusion was visible in the storm-torn bodies and homes of the poor, albeit often through the discourses of the profit-driven, sensationalizing news media. Further, the plight of the unescaped, and their fight to find a safe space within the region, emphasized how processes of normalization – rather than a spontaneous "natural disaster" – are worked out in our geographic system: a broader, and ongoing, history of segregation, violence, and environmental racism, often concealed by partial perspectives and a disregard of the unknowable and unseeable, came clearly into view alongside the spatial, and lived, limits of democracy and citizenship. The politics of citizenship, specifically the rights and protection of those residing in the democratic nation-state of the United States, are clearly not available in some communities, which suggests that the black and poor subjects are disposable precisely because they cannot easily move or escape. The combination of unavailable rights, immovability, and abandoned subjects – those subjects who were, prior to Katrina, forgettable, unseeable, and occupying the underside of democracy, and then, during the storm, catastrophically brought into view – discloses that storm-torn New Orleans, and other locations of *les damné*s, do not simply provide empirical and three-dimensional evidence of injustice. Rather, these locations also prompt us to think hard about the impoverished and neglected areas that were inhabited by those communities prior to the storm. The geography of the region, prior to, during, and after the hurricane devastation, provides a clear picture of how the underside is, for some, not an underside at all, but is, rather, the everyday. Indeed, Katrina cut "deeper the ruts and grooves of social oppression and exploitation."[6]

Submarine Roots: Towards a Reconstruction of the Global Community

While it was above all devastation and death that amplified – in fact, publicized – an existing system of racial and economic neglect, the themes that arise from Katrina provide a way of clarifying how we might critically approach our subject of black geographies. Given that the storm brought into view the ways in which physical geographies are bound up in, rather than simply a backdrop to, social and environmental processes, it follows that the materiality of the environment is racialized by contemporary demographic patterns as shaped by historic precedents. The storm-torn locations of *les damné*s – the unescaped, the abandoned, the immovable, the unseeable – are not anything new. They are disturbing reminders of, but do not twin, other racialized spaces: geographies, for example, occupied by the colonized, the enslaved, the incarcerated, the disposable. Within these past and present human geographies several complexities arise due to the continuing legacy of racial-sexual domination. Often hidden from view, socially distanced from what Audre Lorde calls "a mythical norm," seemingly lacking enlightenment and positivist modes of knowledge while also being rendered conspicuous "objects-in-place," black histories, bodies, and experiences disrupt and underwrite human geographies.[7]

A number of closely related trajectories illustrate how black human geographies are implicated in the production of space. One trajectory consists of the ways in which essentialism situates black subjects and their geopolitical concerns as being elsewhere (on the margin, the underside, outside the normal), a spatial practice that conveniently props up the mythical norm and erases or obscures the daily struggles of particular communities. A second trajectory has to do with how the lives of these subjects demonstrate that "common-sense" workings of modernity and citizenship are worked out, and normalized, through geographies of exclusion, the "literal mappings of power relations and rejections."[8] Finally, although often camouflaged by these same processes, the situated knowledge of these communities and their contributions to both real and imagined human geographies are significant political acts and expressions.[9] Black geographies disclose how the racialized production of space is made possible in the explicit demarcations of the spaces of *les damnés* as invisible/forgettable at the same time as the invisible/forgettable is producing space – always, and in all sorts of ways.

To begin a discussion of black geographies, then, we need to consider how the unknowable figures into the production of space. The title of this introduction – "No One Knows the Mysteries at the Bottom of the Ocean" – takes us in a different direction from, and yet folds into, Hurricane Katrina. Borrowed from theorist M. Jacqui Alexander, the title couples place-making with unknowable mysteries – the oceanic remnants of the middle passage and the transatlantic slave trade. This coupling emphasizes the Atlantic Ocean as a geographic region that can also represent the political histories of the disappeared; the materiality of a body of water prompts a geographic narrative that may not be readily visible on maps or nautical charts. This tension, between the mapped and the unknown, reconfigures knowledge, suggesting that places, experiences, histories, and people that "no one knows" do exist, *within our present geographic order*.[10] In black geographies we find a history of brutal segregation and erasure as these processes inform a different or new approach to the production of space; thus erasure, segregation, marginalization, and mysterious disappearances are geographically available, depending on the vantage point.

Of course, black geographies are not simply oceanic, eternally attached to the middle passage; nor are they always already catastrophic, storm-torn, and demarcating sites in which black communities are abandoned and left to fend for themselves. But these kinds of socio-spatial events, among many others, provide a way in which we can start thinking about how the lives of subaltern subjects are shaped by, and are shaping, the imaginative, three-dimensional, social, and political contours of human geographies.[11] Within and against the grain of dominant modes of power, knowledge, and space, these black geographic narratives and lived experiences need to be taken seriously because they reconfigure classificatory spatial practices. Because we live in and through social systems that reward us for consuming, claiming, and owning things – and in terms of geography this means that we are rewarded for wanting and demarcating "our place" in the same ways that those in power do (often through displacement of others) – we also need to step back and consider how these geographic desires might be bound up in conquest. Inserting black geographies into our worldview and our understanding of spatial liberation and other emancipatory strategies can perhaps move us away from territoriality, the normative practice of staking a claim to place.

This is not to suggest that black subjects are free from espousing dominant modes of geographic thought, but rather that these sites, and those who inhabit them, can also trouble those modes of thought and allow us to consider alternative ways of imagining the world. That which, and those who, "no one knows" might also be a map towards a new or different perspective on the production of space. The storm-torn bodies, those thrown overboard and forgotten, and the many other narratives and experiences that are violently and/or uncomfortably situated within the geography of reason have produced what Edouard Glissant calls "submarine roots": a network of branches, cultures, and relations that position black geographies and the oceanic history of diaspora as integral to and entwining with – rather than outside – what has been called "coloniality's persistence."[12]

Conversely, should the pre-conquest and post-conquest geographic traditions of creating and preserving sacred places be abandoned? Are reclamation, preservation, and remembrance merely a question of re-enacting hegemony, or are these processes a defining feature of regional identity and humanity? The act of making corners, neighbourhoods, communities, cities, rural lands, rivers, and mountains sacred is central to their defence and the defence of the communities that love and cherish them. The people of New Orleans, the people of urban and rural communities that are undergoing gentrification, the prisoners, refugees, and orphans, and all displaced persons from Africa to Africville have different desires for home. They want to build new homes in places that have barred their entry. They also want to explore and reimagine the politics of place. The realization of these desires can transform the world when these visions are based in traditions that see place as the location of co-operation, stewardship, and social justice rather than just sites to be dominated, enclosed, commodified, exploited, and segregated. Black geographies will play a central role in the reconstruction of the global community.

Dilemmas in the Convergence of Race and Space

This book explores these tensions and themes by unravelling the ostensible mysteries that take place when subaltern geographies are theorized, lived, creatively expressed, and socially produced. We take for granted the geographic knowledges that black subjects impart, as well as the long-standing spatial politics – from segregation to incarceration to emancipatory strategies – that inform black lives. While the articles and thoughts included here are certainly limited, and by no means cover a cohesive genealogy of black geographies and black geographic thought, they do at least initiate a discussion of how we might begin to work through the dilemmas that continually come forth when race and space converge with one another and relegate black geographies to bodily, economic/historical materialist, or metaphoric categories of analysis.

Many geographic investigations of black cultures bring into focus empirical evidence based on ethnographic, demographic, or quantitative research. These studies locate where black people live. They bring to light labour-market discrimination, housing patterns, ethnic migrations, and how racialized ghettos contribute to (or defile) the urban environment. While that kind of work does importantly situate the materiality of race and racism, it can also be read as naturalizing racial difference in place.[13] That is, identifying the "where" of blackness in positivist terms can reduce black lives to essential measurable "facts" rather than presenting communities that have struggled, resisted, and significantly contributed to the production of space. In some cultural and social geographic studies, blackness is included in analyses that centralize the scale of the body; indeed, black bodies (rather than a black sense of place) are integrated into many discussions of "difference" in order to briefly point to race and racism, thus reiterating, rather than critically engaging with, the Fanonian predicament of Manichean space.[14] Additionally, while scholars of black studies explore the lived experiences and materiality of racial hierarchies, they shy away from underscoring how human geographies – both real and imagined – are integral to black ways of life. In the humanities, spatial metaphors abound through analyses of black creative texts, yet they are often theorized as detached from concrete three-dimensional geographies.[15]

The dilemmas that arise when we think about space and race often take three very separate approaches (bodily, economic/historical materialist, metaphoric) that result in reducing black geographies to either geographic determinism (black bodies inherently occupying black places), the flesh (the body as the only relevant black geographic scale), or the imagination (metaphoric/creative spaces, which are not represented as concrete, everyday, or lived). Consequently race, or blackness, is not understood as socially produced and shifting but is instead conceptualized as transhistorical, essentially corporeal, or allegorical or symbolic. In this process, which might be called bio-geographic determinism, black geographies disappear – to the margins or to the realm of the unknowable. In short, a black sense of place and black geographic knowledges are both undermined by hegemonic spatial practices (of, say, segregation and neglect) and seemingly unavailable as a worldview.

While not all scholars fall into these traps, we need to recognize the ease with which race and space are two themes in social theory that are fundamentally essentialized (race, specifically non-whiteness, is an ongoing signifier for bodily difference; space just is) and also very difficult to grapple with because they are, in fact, complex analytical categories. This book therefore suggests that black geographies demand an interdisciplinary understanding of space and place-making that enmeshes, rather than separates, different theoretical trajectories and spatial concerns. This approach moves away from singling out the body, the culture of poverty, or the material "lack" implied by spatial metaphors, and it insists on reimagining the subject and place of black geographies by suggesting that there are always many ways of producing and perceiving space. To critically view and imagine black geographies as interdisciplinary sites – from the diaspora and prisons to grassroots activisms and housing patterns – brings into focus networks and relations of power, resistance, histories, and the everyday, rather than locations that are simply subjugated, perpetually ghettoized, or ungeographic.

Space and Place: Local Concerns and Alternative Viewpoints

The articles collected here are interdisciplinary discussions of race and space, with specific reference to black geographies. The geographic and theoretical concerns developed in these pieces draw on regions such as

Canada, the United States, Britain, Africa, and the Caribbean – not as distinct areas or nations, but as overlapping diaspora spaces. We therefore borrow from Carole Boyce Davies and Babacar M'Bow to understand the geopolitics of diaspora as the "dispersal of Africans through *voluntary* migrations (pre-Columbian Atlantic and Indian Ocean trade and exploratory journeys), *forced* migrations (Indian Ocean and transatlantic slavery over at least four centuries in the modern period), and *induced* migrations (the more recent dispersal of African peoples based on world economic imbalances in the twentieth and twenty-first centuries). These migrations have resulted in the relocation and redefinition of African peoples in a range of international locations."[16]

Additionally these overlapping diaspora spaces are inflected with local matters and cultural expressions. Thus, the question of voluntary, forced, and induced movements of black peoples, on a global scale, is understood alongside local struggles and cultural practices that demonstrate migratory experiences and situated knowledges. This conceptualization of diaspora geographies not only is underscored by a long history of racial domination, but also opens up an understanding of space and place that does not replicate hegemonic colonial practices because it brings into focus local concerns, alternative worldviews, and the stakes of being a global black subject. The geographies of the diaspora allow the realms, regions, and subjectivities that "no one knows" to be spatially present "with and through, not despite, difference."[17]

Each of the chapters here can be read separately, or together with another chapter, or in any order. While the central focus of each discussion is geography – as it is articulated through the physical, imaginary, and political concerns of black diasporic subjects – the writing is not meant to replace or identify the limits of existing debates in human geography. Rather, the authors explore how black geographies, and black geographic subjects, can help us to better understand the racialization that has long formed the underpinning for the production of space.

The chapter by Carole Boyce Davies and Babacar M'Bow explores the geographic tenets of the black diaspora in order to redefine our nation-centred approach to citizenship and belonging. The authors outline the diverse and long-standing spatial displacements of black peoples as a way of thinking about forging cross-national and outer-national global rights for black subjects. Indeed, they provocatively challenge our understanding of human geography, and in particular of the modern nation-state, in suggesting that centuries of displacement, migrations, and dispersals necessarily inform a sense of belonging. In other words, they ask a key question: In what ways can induced human scatterings indicate new forms of citizenship wherein the links between ethnicity and place are not essentially bound to one another?

The chapters by Clyde Woods, Angel David Nieves, and Katherine McKittrick explore how diasporic subjects experience this history of displacement through re-narrating the philosophical and activist work and geopolitical commitments imparted by black subjects. Woods considers the music of the blues and black expressive cultures as methodological challenges to human geography, inside and outside the Southern United States. Embedded in the blues, Woods argues, are critiques of hegemonic neo-liberal geographies as well as local activisms that challenge these geographies. In paying close attention to the polyphonic, cartographic, eco-humanist codes implicit in black music, an analyst can understand the creative visions of the dispossessed as ethical spaces of geographic reform. Nieves's chapter on black reparations focuses on the destruction of Africville, Nova Scotia, in the 1960s. He explores what is brought to bear on space and place for those who have been expelled from their communities yet are caught up in the struggle over reparations and development projects meant to memorialize and preserve their losses. Nieves asks us to consider rethinking the "preservation" of racial geographies beyond government guidelines – heritage buildings, plaques, namesakes – and to focus on the specific needs of ethnic communities. In doing this, we can perhaps imagine the everyday and local lives of subaltern communities, and their cultural identifications, as implicit to the past and the presently remembered landscape. McKittrick's chapter explores "the underground." Drawing on the work of Edouard Glissant, Ralph Ellison, and Marlene Nourbese Philip, McKittrick argues that we need to critically assess historically present black geographies – in this case the Underground Railroad – for their future usability. Specifically, she analyzes how many Underground Railroad texts – stories, memorials, landmarks – often position Canada (and the North) as an anachronistic, and completed, site of liberation. In arguing that the Underground Railroad might be theorized as a complex, non-linear, diasporic geography, McKittrick outlines the ways in which black subjects continually articulate different spatial matters from the perspective of struggle.

The chapters by Suzette Spencer, Kimberly Ruffin, and Peter Hudson address the ways in which diasporic migrations and ideologies underwrite black geographies. Using a "transatlantic Maroon" framework, Spencer analyzes the travels of fugitive slave Henry Box Brown to call into question the stasis attached to the bodily, real, and representative geographies of black bondage. She argues for an understanding of resistance that is geopolitically diasporic and thus not anchored to one nation or region. Ruffin's chapter draws on the black diaspora geographies of Ntozake Shange. She explores how Shange's vision of the African diaspora – which Shange often positions as a counternarrative to the nation-state – shapes the phenomena of "work" and "the erotic." Ruffin reimagines the contours of black geographies by bringing into focus the erotic-intellectual labour of food preparation, recipes, music, handicrafts, and non-linear time-space practices.

Hudson's chapter critically maps the black/raced contours of the Canadian province of British Columbia. Hudson outlines the complexities implicit in the idea of B.C. black geographies and follows this with a discussion of Ethel Wilson's 1949 novel *The Innocent Traveller*, which fictionalizes the life of Joe Fortes, a local black man who resided in Vancouver between roughly 1850 and 1922. The story of Fortes – real, fictionalized, memorialized – deepens the racialized production of space by disclosing the underlying workings of racial fear and fantasy in a white settler nation, particularly when British Columbia is imagined and spatialized through a black masculine figure and subject.

The chapters by Jenny Burman, Sonjah Stanley Niaah, James Tyner, and Rinaldo Walcott explore black geographic practices. Burman's discussion examines the legislative linkages between deportees in Montreal and the construction of black femininity. Her chapter introduces what she describes as "spaces of removal" – a series of geopolitical restrictions that come to be embodied by black women. These women are necessary to the production of the nation-state, not as removed but as removeable insiders. Burman examines how Canadian courts and legislation map out patriarchal codes and policies. She suggests that these documents and their attendant social processes not only criminalize black femininity and motherhood but also have a stake in geographic management, thus pushing our understanding of space and race beyond the body. Stanley Niaah's chapter expands her continuing work on the geographies of the dancehall and performance practices. She explores black performance practices such as slave-ship dances, blues geographies, urban ghettoes, and the kwaito music genre in post-apartheid South Africa to delineate the continuities among expressive diaspora cultures.

Tyner examines the geographic strands that underwrite the Black Power movement. Implicitly and explicitly sites of radicalization, politicization, and resistance, black activists and the geopolitics of the Black Power movement itself advanced an understanding of space and place that refused the urban (ghettoized) trappings of the United States a century after slavery. As part of this study Tyner discusses various political visions – from Martin Luther King Jr. to the Black Panthers to Malcolm X – to emphasize how the struggle for black freedom during the Black Power movement was necessarily a spatial project, not rooted in integration but in "communal separatism."

In our final chapter Walcott explores the issues of black queer diasporas and the politics of place-making – outlining in particular how the fashionings of black queer subjects underwrite the production of space. The presence of blackness in queer cultures necessarily reconfigures space through black men's internal critiques of black homophobia and white racism. While black men are relegated to the imaginary and real margins of gay regions, their daily activities and understandings of masculinity offer a new or different local production of racialized (white and non-white) geographies. After examining how black queer men understand and position themselves in what is otherwise considered a white queer space, Walcott suggests that the diasporic identifications and relationalities of black queer cultures have a deep impact upon how we understand, view, and engage with geographies of desire, economy, and difference.

In the end, "no one knows the mysteries" of black geographic thought, but we hope that this book provides a long overdue exploration of the field and contributes to a continuing critical dialogue around the issues. It is the first in a series of books designed to create a global community of scholars. Intellectual traditions within Africa and the African diaspora are undergoing a profound revitalization and historic transformation. They are emerging from the ocean's hidden depths to assume a new role in global society. The shackles of scientific racism and Afro-pessimism are being discarded. The tragedies of New Orleans, Haiti, Darfur, and countless other less well-known sites demand new social visions premised on social justice. It is our hope that this and future books and discussions will contribute to the building not only of new forms of scholarship but also of new societies.

Notes

1 National Weather Service, New Orleans, Louisiana, Aug. 28, 2005: WWUS74 KLIX 281550 NPWLIX. See also <http://www.noaanews.noaa.gov/stories2006/s2656.html>.

2 See chapter 3, p.48.

3 Karen Bakker, "Katrina: The Public Transcript of Disaster," *Environment and Planning D*, 23:6 (2005), pp.796–802.

4 Neil Smith, 'There's No Such Thing as a Natural Disaster," *Understanding Katrina: Perspectives from the Social Sciences* <http://understandingkatrina.ssrc.org/Smith> (accessed August 2006); Bakker, "Katrina: The Public Transcript"; Bruce Braun and James McCarthy, "Hurricane Katrina and Abandoned Being," *Environment and Planning D*, 23:6 (2005), pp.802–9. For a good overview of the linkages between science, nature/natural, geography, and race, see Donald S. Moore, Anand Pandian, and Jake

Kosek, "The Cultural Politics of Race and Nature: Terrains of Power and Practice," in *Race, Nature and the Politics of Difference*, ed. Donald S. Moore, Anand Pandian, and Jake Kosek (Durham, N.C.: Duke University Press, 2000), pp.1–70.

5 Frantz Fanon, *The Wretched of the Earth* (New York: Grove Press, [1961]1963); Sylvia Wynter, "Unsettling the Coloniality of Being/Power/Truth/Freedom: Towards the Human, after Man, Its Overrepresentation – An Argument," *CR: The New Centennial Review*, 3:3 (Fall 2003), p.261; Braun and McCarthy, "Hurricane Katrina and Abandoned Being," p.803.

6 Smith, "There's No Such Thing as a Natural Disaster."

7 Audre Lorde, "Age, Race, Class and Sex: Women Redefining Difference," in *Sister Outsider* (Freedom, Cal.: The Crossing Press, 1984), p.116. Lorde explains: "Somewhere, on the edge of consciousness, there is what I call a *mythical norm*, which each one of us within our hearts knows 'that is not me.' In america, this norm is usually defined as white, thin, male, young, heterosexual, christian, and financially secure." Emphasis in the original; Lorde does not capitalize america, christian.

8 David Sibley, *Geographies of Exclusion: Society and Difference in the West* (New York and London: Routledge, 1995), p.11.

9 Donna Haraway, *Simians, Cyborgs, and Women: The Reinvention of Nature* (New York and London: Routledge, 1991), pp.183–201.

10 M. Jacqui Alexander, *Pedagogies of Crossing: Meditations on Feminism, Sexual Politics, Memory and the Sacred* (Durham, N.C.: Duke University Press, 2005), p.289.

11 Among many others, see, for example: Dionne Brand, *A Map to the Door of No Return: Notes to Belonging* (Toronto: Doubleday, 2001); Marlene Nourbese Philip, *A Genealogy of Resistance and Other Essays* (Toronto: The Mercury Press, 1997); Clyde Woods, *Development Arrested: The Blues and Plantation Power in the Mississippi Delta* (London and New York: Verso, 1998); Linda Tuhiwai Smith, *Decolonizing Methodologies: Research and Indigenous Peoples* (London and New York: Zed Press, 1994); Melvin Dixon, *Ride Out the Wilderness: Geography and Identity in Afro-American Literature* (Urbana and Chicago: University of Illinois Press, 1987); Matthew Sparke, "Mapped Bodies and Disembodied Maps: (Dis)Placing Cartographic Struggle in Canada," in *Places Through the Body*, ed. Heidi J. Nast and Steve Pile (New York and London: Routledge, 1998), pp.305–36; Sylvia Wynter, "On How We Mistook the Map for the Territory, and Re Imprisoned Ourselves in Our Unbearable Wrongness of Being, of Désêtre," in *Not Only the Master's Tools: African American Studies in Theory and Practice*, ed. Lewis R. Gordon and Jane Anna Gordon (London and Boulder, Col.: Paradigm Publishers, 2006), pp.107–69; Ruth Wilson Gilmore, *Golden Gulag: Prisons, Surplus, Crisis and Opposition in Globalizing California* (Berkeley: University of California Press, 2007); Katherine McKittrick, *Demonic Grounds: Black Women and the Cartographies of Struggle* (Minneapolis: University of Minnesota Press, 2006).

12 Edouard Glissant, *Caribbean Discourse: Selected Essays*, trans. J. Michael Dash (Charlottesville and London: University Press of Virginia, 1989), p.67; Greg Thomas, "Coloniality's Persistence," *CR: The New Centennial Review*, 3:3 (2003), p.1–4.

13 Some recent examples of these studies include: Joe T. Darden and Sameh M. Kamel, "Black Residential Segregation in the City and Suburbs of Detroit: Does Socioeconomic Status Matter?" *Journal of Urban Affairs*, 22:1 (2000), pp.1–13; Joseph Mensah, *Black Canadians: History, Experiences, Social Conditions* (Halifax: Fernwood, 2002); John W. Frazier, Florence Margai, and Eugene Tettey Fio, *Race and Place: Equity Issues in Urban America* (Cambridge: Westview Press, 2003); LeeAnn Bishop Lands, "A Reprehensible and Unfriendly Act: Homeowners, Renters and the Bid for Residential Segregation in Atlanta, 1900–1917, *Journal of Planning History*, 3:2 (2004), pp.83–115; Kesh S. Mooer, "What's Class Got to Do with It? Community Development and Racial Identity, *Journal of Urban Affairs*, 27:4 (2005), pp.437–51. The practice of conducting empirical research that locates, counts, and marks black bodies and communities is long-standing with too many sources to list – and is certainly not relegated to the

discipline of geography. For an overview of the representational history of black communities in/and human geography, see Owen Dwyer, "Geographical Research about African Americans: A Survey of Journals, 1911–1995," *Professional Geographer*, 49:4 (1997), pp.441–51. For an overview of the themes that arise from this research in the social sciences, see Joe W. Trotter, Earl Lewis, and Tera Hunter, "Introduction: Connecting African American Urban History, Social Science Research and Policy Debates," in *The African American Urban Experience: Perspectives from the Colonial Period to the Present*, ed. Joe W. Trotter, Earl Lewis, and Tera Hunter (New York: Palgrave Macmillan, 2004), pp.1–20.

14 For a discussion of the body, blackness, and the discipline of human geography, see McKittrick, *Demonic Grounds*. On Manichean space, see Ato Sekyi-Otu, *Fanon's Dialectic of Experience* (Cambridge, Mass.: Harvard University Press, 1996), pp.71–87.

15 For example: Houston A. Baker, Jr., *Blues Ideology and Afro-American Literature: A Vernacular Theory* (Chicago: University of Chicago Press, 1984); Paul Gilroy, *The Black Atlantic: Modernity and Double Consciousness* (Cambridge, Mass.: Harvard University Press, 1993); George Elliot Clarke, "Honouring African Canadian Geography: Mapping Black Presence in Atlantic Canada," *Border/Lines*, 45 (December 1997), pp.35–38; Brian Jarvis, *Postmodern Cartographies: The Geographical Imagination in Contemporary American Culture* (New York: St. Martin's Press, 1993); Dixon, *Ride Out the Wilderness*.

16 See chapter 2, p.14.

17 Stuart Hall, "Cultural Identity and Diaspora," in *Identity: Community, Culture, Difference*, ed. Jonathan Rutherford (London: Lawrence and Wishart, 1990), p.235.

2

Carole Boyce Davies & Babacar M'Bow

Towards African Diaspora Citizenship

Politicizing an Existing Global Geography

The African diaspora – the dispersion of African peoples all over the world – is in effect an already existing globalization of African peoples. Created through centuries of migrations, it preceded, at the level of the demographic, the economic and communications structures now defined as globalization.[1] As a result the African diaspora has a different intent and political identity than has the globalization created for economic oppression. It refers to the dispersal of Africans through *voluntary* migrations (pre-Columbian Atlantic and Indian Ocean trade and exploratory journeys), *forced* migrations (Indian Ocean transatlantic and trans-Saharan slavery over at least four centuries in the modern period), and *induced* migrations (the more recent dispersal of African peoples based on world economic imbalances in the twentieth and twenty-first centuries). These migrations have resulted in the relocation and redefinition of African peoples in a range of international locations.[2]

The work of scholars of the African diaspora has been fundamental in providing a background to the nature of these movements.[3] Gwendolyn Midlo Hall's "Making Invisible Africans Visible: Coasts, Ports, Regions and Ethnicities," in her *Slavery and African Ethnicities in the Americas*, for example, provides a good overview of the various studies of the African diaspora in the Americas and clearly identifies the various movements of African diaspora peoples and their ethnic origins.[4] Additionally, the library of the Schomburg Center for Research in Black Culture in New York has developed "In Motion: The African American Migration Experience," a series mounted by Sylviane Diouf and Howard Dodson, which documents a range of black migrations, largely concentrating on four hundred years of migration to, within, and out of the United States.[5]

Despite this international dispersal that became the African diaspora, to institutionalize its geopolitical reality we still have to develop usable approaches for questioning and transcending the limitations of particular geographies, nation-state boundaries, and ethnic and linguistic differences. This politicization of African diaspora citizenship would put into practice a central intent of pan-Africanist thinkers, which is to create an international network of ideas and practices that can then be positioned as a usable political body for the benefit of common yet separate and dispersed communities. Scholars such as Joseph Harris, whose maps of the African diaspora still function as the guiding historical model for understanding the various movements that created the phenomenon, have already plotted the various time periods of international migrations of African peoples. Out of this work arises questions of diaspora that relate to citizenship, in particular the primary cultural models that have been articulated as well as the various political attempts to counter the various forms of black displacement.

An Already Existing Globalization: African Peoples

The *Constitutive Act of the African Union* (July 2001) begins its preamble with a direct assertion concerning African peoples:

> INSPIRED by the noble ideals that guided the founding fathers of our Continental Organization and generations of Pan-Africanists in their determination to promote unity, solidarity, cohesion and cooperation among the peoples of Africa and the African States.[6]

While not providing a full definition of African peoples, this most important statement invokes generations of pan-Africanists, and thereby the worldwide political leadership community that initiated the major decolonization movements from the 1940s to the 1970s. These pan-Africanists were often African diaspora and African continental peoples with a commitment to working towards the liberation and advancement of the continent and its dispersed peoples. Beginning in 1900 and continuing throughout the century, a range of pan-African activists, thinkers, and strategists from the continent and the African diaspora met repeatedly in Pan-African Congresses to work towards the independence of Africa from colonial rule, to produce independent states, and secure a place for a range of displaced African diaspora peoples. These activists include W.E.B. Du Bois, Anna Julia Cooper, Sylvester Williams, George Padmore, C.L.R.

James, Marcus Garvey, Edgar Wilmot Blyden, J.E. Casely Hayford, Kwame Nkrumah, and others. Du Bois, who was at the first Pan-African Congress, held in 1919, retired to Ghana, where he died and was buried in 1963. George Padmore, an assistant to Kwame Nkrumah of Ghana, was a major architect of pan-Africanism as articulated by Nkrumah. Recalling this history, the African Charter (Banjul) consistently refers to African peoples in the plural, thus presenting the possibility of including a multiplicity of peoples across the continent of Africa and abroad. This definition of African peoples is, in comparison to other ethnic-citizenship categories and geographies, a progressive advancement in the sense that it allows space for a definition of African peoples in both the broad continental and diaspora meanings.

Here we define African peoples as those who have historical origins in Africa irrespective of time period and geographical location. In this way, descendants of those who were displaced from the continent forcibly and voluntarily in the Indian Ocean migrations, and of those who were moved forcibly during the period of transatlantic and trans-Saharan slavery, as well as those who migrated later on for economic, educational, social, and other reasons, all have claims to the status of African peoples. The term African peoples as we use it thus refers to peoples of African origin comprising a variety of African ethnicities, on the continent of Africa and in the international African community that we call the African diaspora.

Historical Background and Citizenship Rights

What we have seen in the twentieth and twenty-first centuries represents the culmination of at least five centuries of mass movements and major human scientific and technological developments. In what has been called the modern period (beginning in roughly the fifteenth century), the creation and redefinition of a range of identities, theories, and concepts occurred. From a series of disparate nation-states, Europe, for example, moved towards regional unification under a single geopolitical entity called the European Union, making that imagined community a political reality.

These changes and mutations have also entailed a redefinition of statuses and structures, particularly the administrative definition of individuals as citizens or subjects with agency. Today citizenship, traditionally defined in the legal field as *jus sanguis* or *jus solis*, is being reconsidered in the context of globalization as also being transnational. The related concept of nationality is part of this discussion. Siegfried Wiessner, in "Blessed Be the Ties That Bind: The Nexus between Nationality and Territory," and subsequently in "The Function of Nationality," indicates: "Contemporary nationality thus is unique in both historical and cross-cultural perspective. Its transnationally commonly recognized features include excessive ultimate access rights to the home state's territory, the prohibition of banishment, participation in at least formally democratic decision-making processes of the community as well as the home state's right to protection."[7]

For our purposes here, we define citizenship not in fixed terms, but broadly in terms of contemporary understandings: as an individual's legal participation in a territory of identification with all the rights and duties associated with that status. The standard definition of a citizen is "a person owing loyalty to and entitled by birth or naturalization to the protection of a particular state."[8] The term "national' is defined as "of, relating to, or belonging to a nation as an organized whole . . . and more directly as a citizen of a specific nation."[9] For Wiessner, the distinction between these two terms is between "status theory," which "maintains that nationality is an original juridical situation independent of rights and duties arising from it," and "relationship theory," which "views nationality as a legal bond between an individual and his home state that encompasses, by necessity, specific rights and duties." In either case, he concludes, "While some states refer to their membership status as 'citizenship,' others use the term 'nationality.' "[10]

The "relationship theory" model therefore seems more relevant to the status of African diaspora peoples, already dispersed in a series of other nation-states. For those African diaspora peoples who were forcibly separated from the continent during a time when the nation-state definitions of today were not in place, the right to a selected, optional state-of-choice identification was a factor in this definitional consideration. Historically, in the nation-state contexts in which they lived, African diaspora peoples were accorded neither the rights nor the protection of those states.

A pre-existing and unresolved issue is that African people uprooted by forced enslavement never did give up their rights to citizenship on the continent of Africa, even though the nation-states that now make up this geopolitical entity did not exist during the time of transatlantic slavery. Throughout black history many emotive narratives and songs have testified to the desire always to return – whether this return be through travel, writings, imagination, or the fostering of political affiliations.[11] In the contemporary context, then, we have to see both continental Africans and African diaspora peoples as also engaging in the redefinition process based on their own historico-social experiences.

The history of Euro-American imperialism's border transgressions and the larger assumption of control of human and physical resources, unlimited space, and movement serve as the countercontextual background for this discussion. The development of triangular trade routes through the middle passage and the economics of slavery and colonialism facilitated the rise of European modernity. Contemporary notions of globalization, we can conclude, have always been economic. The frameworks that ensured European control of the world's resources were put in place with the rise of European modernity.

Even before the period of transatlantic slavery, African dispersals had already occurred through the trans-Saharan passage and trade routes that opened up the circum–Indian Ocean area. Both of these passageways led to a range of African peoples being located in the Mediterranean region and in Asia and South Asia.[12] Joseph Harris, for example, describes the "pre-Atlantic phase of the slave trade," as well as earlier migrations across the Mediterranean Sea, Red Sea, and Indian Ocean, of free and enslaved people from around the sixth century.[13] Later, the long history of forced migration through the transatlantic slave trade – which lasted from the fourteenth to the nineteenth centuries – disrupted the lives and displaced the peoples of numerous intact African nations, locating them in the "New World" for the services of plantation systems. Industrial development from the fifteenth to nineteenth centuries was facilitated through the labour of the enslaved – until slavery was finally, and hesitantly, abolished in various locations in the nineteenth century based on intermittent decisions in the various colonizing centres of power (French, Spanish, English, U.S., Portuguese) between 1838 and 1888.[14]

The result of these processes of free and forced migration was the appearance of Africans in the Americas, Europe, and Asia and the simultaneous re-creation of socio-cultural practices in these various locations, making Africans essentially a global people. Africans thus moved from a range of political formations – specifically from pre-colonial nations, empires, and other smaller ethnic political structures (often misnamed "tribes" by anthropologists) – to these locations beyond the continent. In the Indian Ocean diaspora some Africans, such as Malik Amber, became members of the ruling classes.[15] For the most part, though, this relocation of African peoples to different geographical locations often meant subordination or dispossession, with lives that remained consistently debased. With enslavement in the Americas came the most glaring of inequities; various colonial projects that coincided with and followed transatlantic slavery formally instituted economic, gendered, and raced hierarchies. Some three hundred years later in Africa, political independence, in selected countries, began a process of recognition of the African peoples' rights, both on that continent and in the Americas. Even so, post-independence nation-states were often transformed into neo-colonial systems that were (and are) not reliable protectors of rights because within them were already imposed race-based and class-based hierarchies that subordinated non-white populations.[16] In many countries, African peoples remained disenfranchised under various colonialisms (English, French, Spanish, Portuguese, Dutch, Arab, Asian), with no means to return to their native lands and subject to horrendous conditions that violated every tenet of human rights. These peoples had no other legitimate recourse but to fight for those rights.

In the United States, as late as the 1960s, the *Voting Rights Act* and *Civil Rights Act* had to be passed to ensure the protection of rights of African Americans. In 2006 the *Voting Rights Act* remained political fodder, with African Americans still subject to the whims of the U.S. Congress and Senate on this fundamental citizenship matter. Africans, or African Americans, in the United States have therefore generally not been considered full citizens (the fourteenth amendment to the U.S. Constitution notwithstanding). Instead, they have been subject to the state terrorism of official Jim Crowism (an apartheid-like segregation) and the terrorism of non-state actors such as the Ku Klux Klan and Night Riders. They were the victims of lynchings and property and community destruction (such as the burning of entire towns, as occurred in Rosewood, Florida) well into the mid-twentieth century. Throughout the Americas the abuse of labour, the denial of rights, beatings, and other forms of brutality accompanied the processes of colonialism that succeeded plantation slavery. In India, Africans who describe themselves as Siddis or Habshis still live visibly oppressed by the state and its elites, demarcated as "backward tribes." In 2001 they were accorded the status of "scheduled tribes," with few benefits of citizenship.[17]

The Denial of Citizenship Rights within Nation-States

For many years the status of African diaspora peoples in various nation-states has entailed a recognition that they are always a "deportable subject."[18] Additionally, Africans often did not have access to the basic rights accorded citizens in many locations prior to civil rights and other anti-colonial movements. This ongoing denial of rights speaks most strongly to what the concept of "citizenship" in the United States has meant for black people. As a direct result, this sense of statelessness can have the effect of creating not only a sense of alienation from the nation-state but also an international African identity in the diaspora.[19]

U.S. history reveals glaring examples of the denial of citizenship rights (Constitutional rights) to the black population as a whole. Particular governmental, legal, and political arrangements, such as the *Fugitive Slave Act*, the *Dred Scott* decision, and *Plessey v. Ferguson*, in addition to the need for the thirteenth, fourteenth, and fifteenth amendments, provide examples of how citizenship has intersected with the lives of African Americans. Thus, constitutional objectives such as "All persons born or naturalized in the United States, and subject to the jurisdiction thereof, are citizens of the United States and the states wherein they reside" are understood alongside the fifteenth amendment (1870), which notes, "The right of citizens of the United States to vote shall not be denied or abridged by the United States or by any state on account of race, color, or previous condition of servitude." As critical race theorists have argued, neither of these amendments have undone the escape hatch of imprisonment by which a technical denial of citizenship and slavery remains in effect. Amendment XIII, Section 1 (ratified December 6, 1865), for example, reads: "Neither slavery nor involuntary servitude, except as punishment for crime whereof the party shall have been duly convicted, shall exist within the United States, or any place subject to their jurisdiction."[20] Technically, the United States functioned and continues to function as a "multination state," with African Americans historically being treated worse than recent white foreign immigrants. The high numbers of black men and women incarcerated in the prison-industrial complex is a glaring example of race-based treatment; but so too is the way in which economics, health, and education are underwritten by processes of racialization. African Americans who attempt to put into practice their right to run for high political office continue to face overwhelming difficulties, especially when compared to the success of second-generation European immigrants – or even, as in the case of California governor Arnold Schwarzenegger, a first-generation immigrant (and movie star), who was able to gain access to state power even without fluency in English. The changes in the realm of politics have been slow and painstaking for African Americans, who have an uphill battle for credible support in their candidacies for local, state, and national office.

The combination of black identity and non-U.S. birth – together with historic deportations of non-U.S.-born black radicals such as the Jamaican black nationalist Marcus Garvey and C.L.R. James and Claudia Jones (both originally from Trinidad) – creates a dual sense of not-belonging. Paul Robeson and W.E.B. Du Bois and a range of other African American activists and entertainers had their passports seized, leaving them unable to travel abroad. Some of these same intellectuals and activists, who were born in Caribbean countries, were sometimes not accorded those full rights in the countries of their birth. Stokely Carmichael was denied entry to his birthplace of Trinidad and Tobago. Claudia Jones, who was born in Trinidad in 1915 and moved with her family to Harlem, New York, at the age of eight, was deported to England rather than being allowed to go back to her place of birth.

In the final analysis, these various denials of entry, denials of right to vote, deportation, and incarceration indicate that nation-state citizenship for black people anywhere in the diaspora is a fragile and mutable condition. The political histories of "immigration, racial politics and political repression are not so separate and discrete" as U.S. African Americans often want to make them.[21] U.S. African Americans were often defined as "sojourners," and routinely denied basic "citizenship rights."[22] Indeed, historically the struggle in the United States has involved great, seemingly unending efforts to get those rights. The politics of incarceration and the resulting denial of voting rights (plus the frailty of the *Civil Rights Act* and *Voting Rights Act*) for large proportions of the U.S. African American population as well as the denaturalization clause in the *Patriot Acts* (2001 and 2006) are recent manifestations of this same tendency.[23]

A series of political movements called, variously, civil rights/Black Power struggles in the United States, anti-apartheid movement in South Africa, decolonization and independence movements in Africa, the Caribbean, and India, and Movimento Negro Unificado in Brazil battled for the ending of specific nation-state aggressions and political oppressions. At the policy level a number of United Nations instruments attempted to address some of these issues. The Declaration on the Granting of Independence to Colonial Countries and Peoples (General Assembly Resolution 1514 [XV] of December 14, 1960) addressed the issue of the right to self-determination, stating, "The continued existence of colonialism prevents the development of international economic cooperation, impedes the social, cultural and economic development of dependent peoples and militates against the United Nation's ideal of universal peace." It declares in Item 1, therefore: "The subjection of peoples to alien subjugation, domination and exploitation constitutes a denial of fundamental human rights, is contrary to the charter of the United Nations and is an impediment to the promotion of world peace and cooperation."

Similarly, the United Nations' Declaration on the Elimination of All Forms of Racial Discrimination" (General Assembly Resolution 1904 [XVIII], November 20, 1963) declares in Article 1, "Discrimination between human beings on the ground of race, colour or ethnic origin is an offence to human dignity." The International Convention on the Elimination of All Forms of Racial Discrimination (2106A, ratified December 21, 1965) is more detailed, containing twenty-five articles. Its Article 5 specifically applies to the denial of rights in a range of areas from housing to political rights, education, and access to public facilities. The International Convention on the Suppression and Punishment of the Crime of Apartheid (3068 [XXVIII], November 30, 1973) addressed the South African phenomenon.

Despite these measures, discrimination continued – formal apartheid in South Africa, for instance, did not end until 1994 – and the legacies of unequal treatment remain. The Declaration on the Rights of Persons Belonging to National or Ethnic, Religious and Linguistic Minorities (General Assembly Resolution 47/135, December 18, 1992), does not go far enough to guarantee the rights that have been lacking for African diaspora peoples. Its nine articles deal largely with strategies for implementing rights. While the intent is to reaffirm and ensure all the prior declarations and conventions, and Article 27 of the International Covenant on Civil and Political Rights (ICCPR), this particular declaration deals largely with participation and not so much with the enforcement of rights. As well, a declaration of the Rights of Indigenous Peoples, which is a bolder declaration and under which some African diaspora peoples, such as Siddis and Habshis in the Indian Ocean diaspora, also fall, has not yet been guaranteed.

Some regional attempts to ensure economic and political rights have also been made. An attempt at a West Indian Federation in the Caribbean region in 1959 failed miserably.[24] The initial intent of decolonization struggles was to create a unified pan-Caribbean, multi-island, nation-state with economic integration and rights of citizenship – and therefore of travel and residence – throughout the area.[25] Instead, the leadership of various Caribbean nations opted for island nation-state independence. Although some attempts at integration – at creating economic and political collaborations – were made in the Eastern Caribbean, the larger nations (Trinidad and Tobago, Jamaica, Guyana) have charted separate courses, adopting regimes of individual passports and individual governmental systems, with only minor inter-island trading. While some individuals have been able to attain residency in various islands outside the countries of their birth, there are no general citizenship rights (as in the European Union). People cannot enter Martinique or Guadeloupe, for example, without going through the French residency requirements, because these places are still defined under colonial structures as "French overseas" territories. The colonially imposed barriers and structures that separate the Caribbean islands remain in place.[26]

The Caribbean is an interesting study for regional integration, however, because, besides the various island locations, the northern countries of South America (including Guyana, Venezuela, and Surinam) and the countries of Central America (such as Belize, Costa Rica, and Nicaragua) have Caribbean relationships that define them as being within the greater Caribbean. A more realistic way of understanding the Caribbean, then, might be to speak of the circum-Caribbean, plus the islands. The Caribbean Community and Common Market (CARICOM) and a variety of related organizations have attempted regional co-operation within the Caribbean region, but their actions are largely economic. Cultural structures, involving exchanges such as the Caribbean common market and CARIFESTA, have been set in place; but as of yet there has been no site of integrated regional action in the "One Caribbean" language through the cross-regional work of cultural artists and activists.

African Diaspora Claims in Relation to Nation-State Sovereignty

African diaspora communities have expressed their common goals as the acquisition of full rights in the nation-states in which they live as well as rights of access to the African countries of origin, of choice, and thereby of the continent.[27] The specific claims related to African diaspora citizenship are:

1. Claims of commonality: that African diaspora peoples, because of their history of origins, have a right to return to the continent and thereby have access claims, defined as legal entry, residency, and citizenship rights in a country of choice.
2. That various governments of countries housing African diaspora populations recognize the access claims of transnational citizenship and thereby allow legally instituted dual citizenship rights.
3. Continuing and enhanced rights in the nation-states in which they have been born or naturalized should be assured.

Historically these claims have been made, at least to some extent, through the political and cultural appeals to the broader community within and outside the continent of Africa, and by establishing nation-state sovereignty.

Political and Cultural Claims to the Diaspora

In the early days of political independence (1950s and 1960s), Kwame Nkrumah of Ghana spearheaded an ideological movement of pan-Africanism, aimed not only at integrating the continent as a political and economic unit, but also at making Africa a potential destination for African diaspora peoples located around the world.[28] The intent of pan-Africanism, as developed in its various congresses from 1919 onward, was to develop strategies for integrating African and African diaspora peoples wherever they may be, and for providing benefits equivalent to citizenship, educational and knowledge exchanges, and the like. The organizational frameworks of the Organization of African Unity (OAU) came out of this post-independence period and politic.

Various African diaspora political movements and organizations have approached the issues and strategies of pan-Africanism in different ways. At times pan-Africanists have developed emotive or romanticized stratagems; other tactics have been politically directed and assertive. Marcus Garvey's Back to Africa movement, launched in the early twentieth century and expressed through his UNIA (Universal Negro Improvement Association), was intended to encourage both an emotional and a physical return to the continent. The Kouyaté/Padmore collaboration, spanning the anglophone and francophone African diaspora, was another version of this type of decolonizing activism.[29] These efforts provided only the beginning points for the assertion of African diaspora citizenship claims. Pan-Africanism as a particular claim of political membership therefore asserts the right not only to return to an ancestral homeland but also to claim a common identity from a series of dispersed locations, even if this remains an ideal not actualized.

African diaspora cultural claims also assert the right for dispersed Africans to enjoy cultural and religious traditions in the nation-states in which they live, without oppression from the state apparatuses. Following years of resistance against Euro-colonial and neo-colonial state suppression, these claims, in a variety of fields such as religion, music, carnival, dance, physical adornment, hairstyles, and clothing, have been perhaps more easily exercised in the contemporary period. In some cases the states consigned the claims to the realm of "entertainment" or "folklore," as in Brazil.[30] In other cases the rights of an African diaspora culture are tolerated because cultural and community exchanges do not necessarily always entail the transfer of economic resources. African diaspora citizenship at the level of a cultural connection has therefore been more easily acquired, with the cultural practices at times serving as an equivalent to political African diaspora citizenship. These cultural claims have also kept various connections alive and reconnected a fragmented history among dispersed African subjects.

African diaspora religions have made a number of legal claims, and gains, at the level of cultural citizenship. Discussions and debates regarding religious practices and rituals such as Santeria, Lukumi, Shango, and Candomble are instructive in that they clarify the linkages between culture, ethnicity, displacement, and citizenship.[31] Although there have been legal challenges around self-presentation issues in terms of clothing, hair, music, and basic aspects of personal style and taste within various nation-states, African diaspora religions have been the most formally co-ordinated in asserting African diaspora claims at the cultural level. While some versions use Catholic saints and liturgical practices as the mask for the practice of more traditional African-based religious belief systems, in other versions the African spiritual entities are represented on their own without the mask of syncretism. Trinidad, for instance, has instituted a National Orisha Day, thereby accepting the place of African Orisha practice as a religious holiday on a par with Easter, Rosh Hashanah, or Eid ul-Fitr. Its council of elders has been identified as a legitimizing body. Further, in Trinidad, the government has moved to recognize marital unions performed under Orisha rights.[32]

African traditional religious practices are central to the lives of people in many New World communities, operating as a parallel system of belief. They regulate healing practices, well-being, relationship to ancestors and elders, community, extended family, agriculture, and nature in general.[33] The U.S. Supreme Court case of *Church of Lukumi Babalu Aye v. City of Hialeah,* 508 U.S. 520 (1993), argued November 4, 1992, and decided June 11, 1993, made a significant assertion of these rights. In this case the Church of Lukumi Babalu Aye had to detail the nature of its religious structure.[34] A fundamental feature in this religious practice is the sacrificing of animals; its successfully argued case has to be taken as a standard for other related cases. Given this case, in Miami the Hialeah Orisha community was able to be officially recognized on the basis that the four ordinances enacted by the City of Hialeah were found to suppress the church's religious freedom because they violated first amendment freedoms, particularly the "Free Exercise" clause. This legal victory, in a major country like the United States, provided an important usable model of an African religious practice being legitimated in a national context.

Religion and spirituality have provided a principal means by which African diaspora communities have been able to sustain themselves, and a series of conferences have in turn provided dispersed communities with a means of exchanging strategies for asserting religious rights. The International Council of Orisha Religious Practices, for example, has established an African diaspora structure outside of the various nation-states in which the practitioners live. Additionally, a local systemizing of these practices has begun to occur: Oyetunji Village in South Carolina describes itself as a land space that has a religious identity apart from that which exists in the rest of the country. This, alongside the formalizing of an Orisha Day in Trinidad, the acceptance by the government of Cuba that *lucumi* is a central feature of the country's social-religious structure, and the preponderance of *terrereiros* in Brazil, gives a land-based existence to the practical features of Orisha. These examples illustrate the various ways in which African diaspora citizenship claims are asserted at the cultural level. The cultural practices and histories tend to be differentially systematized across the diaspora – albeit under different names – but provide a clear identification of an African presence in the New World.

Nation-State Sovereignty Claims

The history of earlier attempts to resituate African peoples on the continent clarifies nation-state sovereignty claims. The situation of Africans returning to the then-colonial states of Sierra Leone and Liberia can be described as an experiment that resulted in the displacement of local inhabitants in both places. On a smaller scale, even as this return migration granted the right of citizenship to Africans formerly displaced by the transatlantic slave trade, the location of a new population installed an unending crisis that would emerge later on as these two groups – the returned and the locally displaced – had different cultural and political tendencies. These conflicts in the end produced the conditions for violent internecine struggles, which, in part, culminated in the wars in Liberia and Sierra Leone. Still, the potential and actual situations of conflict between returning Africans and those locally displaced could be pre-empted by appropriate negotiated relationships, in particular because the continent has numerous states and possibilities.

A way of moving beyond conflict situations may be to learn from the past and the nature of the process of resituating with regard to these two diaspora nation-states. The mistake in this case was the colonial nature of the project, which dated back to plans first proposed in the eighteenth century. At the heart of these plans were arguments about the impossibility of Africans getting justice in the United States and the need for them to stay and fight against slavery and for full legal rights. Another argument concerned the role that black American colonists could play in "Christianizing" and "civilizing" Africa. However, the paramount motive in the resituating, which goes to the heart of our argument for African diaspora citizenship, was the rationale for the process. Indeed, the American Colonization Society (ACS) was formed in 1817 to send free African Americans to Africa as an alternative to working towards emancipation in the United States. In 1822 the Society established, on the west coast of Africa, a colony that in 1847 became the independent nation of Liberia. By 1867 the Society had resituated more than 13,000 emigrants in Liberia. Hence African diaspora citizenship was symbolically embedded in the dynamic of the creation of the nation-state.

The Christianizing and civilizing mission embedded in the early debates may certainly have had something to do with the tensions between resituated and local Africans that culminated in attacks on local African villages by resituated militiamen, which led to a November 1835 treaty. The irony in the situation of Liberia was that the resituated, people who were fleeing oppression, reproduced this same oppression in stiff and sometimes violent opposition against indigenous Africans, who were excluded from citizenship in the new republic until 1904. Sierra Leone, which was also repopulated by Africans from the Caribbean, became another version of this tendency, with similar results, as witnessed by the practices of the Sierra Leone Creoles in relation to the local populations.

The largest obstacle to African diaspora citizenship claims, but paradoxically the greatest opportunity for the exercising of domestic human rights, thus exists in the sovereignty claims of the nation-state in which a number of diaspora peoples reside. Independence from colonialism, in the Caribbean from the 1950s onward, brought island nation-state assertions of sovereignty. In the Charter of the Organization of African Unity, Addis Ababa (1963), issues of sovereignty were also tied to freedom from colonialism and therefore accompanied by nation-state assertions: "Determined to safeguard and consolidate the hard-won independence as well as the sovereignty and territorial integrity of our states, and to fight against neocolonialism in all its forms." The charter goes on to further develop this nation-state assertion:

> The Member States, in pursuit of the purposes stated in Article II solemnly affirm and declare their adherence to the following principles:
>
> 1. the sovereign equality of all Member States.
> 2. non-interference in the internal affairs of States.
> 3. respect for the sovereignty and territorial integrity of each State and for its inalienable right to independent existence.

Included as well was an absolute dedication to the total emancipation of all the African countries that were still under colonial rule, and the condemnation of attacks by one state on another and the reaffirmation of a policy of non-alignment.[35] The principle of sovereignty, while it does operate as a conflicting claim as far as citizenship is concerned, does not necessarily foreclose the question of rights,[36] particularly if we see a model of African diaspora citizenship not as a substitute for national citizenship as nationality, but as an international relationship of belonging to a larger polity.

The Caribbean region, which has a large demographic representation of African diaspora peoples inhabiting varying island nation-states, has similarly had to address this issue of sovereignty, on the one hand, and the recognition of migration and multiple location of peoples on the other. Still, there have been consistent attempts at some form of regional integration.[37] And in Brazil and other countries throughout South America, African peoples' lives have been subordinated to nation-state narratives of "racial democracy" and *mestizaje* (the process of cultural mixing that came to constitute a "national" character and multicultural pluralism). In the Caribbean, for example, issues of integration have been at the heart of the ongoing development of policies through CARICOM. In Brazil and Latin America, new political geographies are constantly being instituted, the most recent being the leftist geographies and connections of Venezuela, Cuba, and to a lesser degree Brazil. The recent political declarations on the history, conditions, and political desires of Afro-descended peoples in Latin America, prior to and after the 2001 World Conference against Racism in Durban, South Africa, are examples that again cross national borders.

As for Africa, at the Berlin Conference of 1888 various European countries took it upon themselves to divide up the continent, drawing up borders and claiming and creating nations and thereby destroying pre-existing geographical and cultural and natural boundaries. The entire continent was thrown into confusion as people tried to navigate their lives in imposed nation-state geographies and foreign political and economic systems. A number of regional attempts were made to ameliorate this situation. For example, ECOWAS (Economic Community of West African States) allowed for economic integration, educational examination councils, and travel across member states. In "The Role of African Regional and Sub-Regional Organisations in Conflict Prevention and Resolution," Abiodun Alao concludes that many of the "existing structures in some of the organisations are weak" and that there would have to be more concrete ways of "harmonising their activities" because they tend to avoid "multiple initiatives."[38]

In general, then, a series of regional political movements have tried to harness political power and more fully represent populations subordinated in various nation-states. The movement for an African diaspora citizenship can benefit and learn from these processes.

From Political to Legal African Diaspora Citizenship: Recent Advances

The African Diaspora and the African Union

The African Union, which on its establishment in 1999 accepted the political framework of its predecessor, the Organization of African Unity, began by asserting a pan-Africanist orientation, beginning with a continental assumption, but moved rapidly to shape a growing recognition of the claims of African diaspora peoples outside of the continent. Still, for its members, the need for a strong and economically solid continental Africa is a laudable goal and is perhaps the first leg in any pursuit of African diaspora rights. Thus they insist on a new path of socio-economic growth:

> CONSCIOUS of the fact that the scourge of conflicts in Africa constitutes a major impediment to the socio-economic development of the continent and of the need to promote peace, security and stability as a prerequisite for the implementation of our development and integration agenda.

In its *Constitutive Act* the African Union took into consideration the Lusaka Summit Decision of 2001 on the "establishment of a strategic framework for a Policy of Migration in Africa," therefore gesturing towards the development of a future relationship with the African diaspora:

> The Lusaka Summit Decision encourages Member States to work towards the development of a strategic framework for migration policy in Africa that could contribute to addressing the challenges posed by migration, but also to make effective use of the opportunity presented by the phenomenon and thereby ensuring the integration of migration and related issues into their national and regional agenda for security, stability, development and cooperation. (African Union Program Summary, Addis Ababa, Ethiopia, CM/Dec. 614 [LXCIV])

In addition an African Union Diaspora Conference, held in Washington, D.C., in December 2002 took as two of its objectives the development of "capacity building projects by Diaspora civil society organizations in the Western Hemisphere Diaspora" and the devising of a "plan of ongoing collaboration with the African Union, including a plan of action and a hemisphere steering committee."[39] One of the conference's most important resolutions, accepted unanimously, called for the creation of a co-ordinating body for the African Union Western Hemisphere diaspora. This body has as one of its initiatives a proposal for the establishment of an African diaspora component to the African Union and its representative bodies, particularly the Pan-African Parliament (Article 17) and the Commission of the Union (Article 20 of the *Constitutive Act* of the African Union).[40]

In the years since the African Union has taken significant steps towards including the African diaspora within its framework. In its third extraordinary session, held in Sun City, South Africa, May 21–24, 2003, the Executive Council decided, for instance, to support the Commission's initiative to convene a workshop that would elaborate a framework and make recommendations on the relationship between the African Union and the diaspora. The proposed workshop would address a number of issues: the definition of the diaspora; the role of the diaspora in reversing a perceived African brain drain; the creation of a diaspora fund for investment and development in Africa; the development of scientific and technical networks to channel the repatriation of scientific knowledge from the diaspora to Africa, and the establishment of co-operation between those abroad and at home; and the establishment of a diaspora database to promote and facilitate networking and collaboration between experts in their respective countries of origin and those in the diaspora. The Executive Council also suggested that the Commission "respond speedily to proposals from the African diaspora to help the AU and the Continent and provide moral and diplomatic support for diaspora initiatives aimed at effectively assisting the Continent." It asked the Commission "to work out modalities for mutual cooperation between the African Union and CARICOM and other existing formations such as Western Hemisphere Diaspora Network (WHADN)," while stressing "the need for the AU to show political concern for, and respond to issues and developments that affect the lives and well being of the Africans in the Diaspora." It encouraged not only its member states and African leaders "to respond positively to initiatives aimed at promoting relations and cooperation between the Diaspora and Africa," but also the African diplomatic missions outside Africa "to maintain close relations with the representatives of the Diaspora in their countries of accreditation."[41]

Ethiopia and Rastafari Rights to Return

Rastafari has its roots, in part, in the teachings of Marcus Garvey, who in the 1930s preached a message of black self-empowerment and initiated a "Back to Africa" movement. The legacy of Garvey's teachings was to be the idea of an emotional, cultural, and physical return of dispersed African peoples to an African homeland. For Rastafarians this location was specified as Ethiopia. "Look to Africa when a black king shall be crowned, for the day of deliverance is near."[42] In 1930 Ras Tafari was crowned Emperor Haile Selassie I of Ethiopia and proclaimed "King of Kings, Lord of Lords, and the conquering lion of the Tribe of Judah."[43] Haile Selassie claimed to be a direct descendant of King David, and the 225th ruler in an unbroken line of Ethiopian kings from the time of Solomon and Sheba. For most Rastafari, though, the return has been mostly psychic. It revolves around the development of African cultural sites in the New World and has involved the separation of their communities from the dominant nation-state's practices.

Although Rastafari operates largely as an African diaspora movement in which its adherents accept the premise of the practice of Africanity in the New World – even as it links historically with Ras Tafari and the imagined and real community of Ethiopia – the practical execution of a physical return has also occurred, but not without struggle against nation-state and local community dynamics. On June 27, 2001, the Rastafari Community of Shashamane wrote a letter to UN Secretary General Kofi Annan indicating the need to formalize their existence in Ethiopia legally. They stated, "Shashamane is the gift land granted to the Black people of the world wishing to return to Africa by His Imperial Majesty Emperor Haile Selassie I in 1931."[44] (See Appendix.) Given the earlier and emotive or romanticized visions of Africa and the actual experience of physical return, the citizenship rights assumed under one administration are less easily obtainable based on changes in political will. Clearly, in this case there was a group, the Oromos, living in the space granted to the Rastafari community, and the Oromos were indicating that they had prior land rights. From all accounts, the land granted to the Rastafarians by Haile Selassie – while the move appeared to be a humanitarian act made on behalf of the Rastafarians – was identified internally as springing from a monarchical right to use and assign property at will. The letter to Kofi Annan seems to assert a supra-nation-state identification, similar, for instance, to a proposal made by a group of African Americans to identify themselves as an internally oppressed nation within the United States and thus assert a case directly to the United Nations for protection. Precedents for this example have existed in other situations, such as the Quilombo Palmares in Brazil, a community of former enslaved Africans who took up arms in their defence in the sixteenth and seventeenth centuries, left their various plantations, and attempted to negotiate separate agreements for their existence with foreign governments.

One of the major conclusions of the Shashamane situation – and this is also similar to the Liberia and Sierra Leone situations – is that in the relocation of peoples who have been formally displaced, the rights of the people occupying the site of that geographical relocation also have to be taken into consideration. Otherwise we face perpetual struggles of the type waged by the Palestinians against the Israelis, or the native people against the Americo-Liberians or the Sierra Leonean Creoles. Some negotiated co-existence with the local community has to be seen as part of the conditions of this return.

In 2002 the Government of Ethiopia drew up a draft proclamation aimed at giving foreign nationals rights in their home country. The proclamation stated its objective as "identifying foreign nationals of Ethiopian

Origin who have acquired Foreign nationality due to their life circumstances or other factors." Also, "by lifting the legal restrictions imposed on them when they lost their Ethiopian nationality," the government would "entitle them to various rights and privileges." It would also hypothetically "create a legal framework whereby persons of Ethiopian Origin fulfill their contribution to the development and prosperity of their country of origin."

The document also established "Rights and Responsibilities of the Holder of the Identification Card of Foreign Nationals of Ethiopian Origin":

1. He shall not be required to have an entry visa or residence permit to live in Ethiopia.
2. Without prejudice to Article 6(2) of this Proclamation, he shall have the right to be employed in Ethiopia without a work permit.
3. He shall not be subjected to the exclusion that applies to foreign nationals regarding coverage of pension scheme under the relevant pension law.
4. Without prejudice to Article 40(3) of the Constitution, the provisions of Article 390–393 of the Civil Code shall not apply to persons of Ethiopian origin holding the Identification Card.
5. He shall have the right to be considered as domestic investor to invest in Ethiopia under Investment law.
6. Restrictions imposed on foreign nationals regarding the utilization of Economic, Social, and Administrative Services shall not be applicable to foreign nationals of Ethiopian origin holding the Identification Card.[45]

While this document applies largely to the second-level African diaspora of the mid-to-late-twentieth-century migrations, the approach carries implications for issues of African diaspora citizenship and reflects questions that are at the heart of the African Union's definitions of the African diaspora. It also carries implications for other African diaspora groups and their interest in claiming residence in Ethiopia.

African Nation-State Abode Rights – The Ghana Example

The recent and hopeful examples of the African Union and Ethiopian experience allow us to see African diaspora citizenship as a possibility. The state-specific plans to accommodate the exiles and children of their dispersed post-independence nation-states, and to mitigate the brain drain that has resulted from that dispersal, also have implications for the descendants of the earlier transatlantic migrations. The Ghanaian Right to Abode was clearly documented in Ghana's *Immigration Act, 2000*, which was passed in November 2001 and became law in March 2002. The new Immigration

Regulations, 2001, offers Africans born in the diaspora the right to reside in Africa, in this case in Ghana. Applicants who want to be considered for the "right to abode" have to submit an application "to the Minister through the Director." The legislation spells out the details:

> 13(2) A Ghanaian national who by the acquisition of another nationality cannot hold a Ghanaian nationality because of the laws governing the acquired nationality and who wishes to be granted right of abode shall not be required to produce documentary evidence of financial standing.
>
> 13(3) A person of African descent in the diaspora who wishes to be considered for the grant of right of abode, shall be subject to a verification process which requires among other things:
>
> (a) an attestation by two Ghanaians who are notaries public, lawyers, senior public officers or other class of persons approved by the Minister to the effect that the applicant is of good character and that they have known the applicant personally for a period of at least five years;
>
> (b) a declaration by the applicant to the effect that the applicant has not been convicted of any criminal offence and been sentenced to imprisonment for a term of twelve months or more;
>
> (c) production by the applicant of documentary evidence of financial standing;
>
> (d) the applicant satisfying the Minister that the applicant is capable of making a substantial contribution to the development of Ghana; and
>
> (e) the applicant has attained at least the age of eighteen years. . . .
>
> 13(5) For the purposes of verification under sub-regulation (3) the applicant must have resided in the country
>
> (a) throughout the period of twenty-four months immediately preceding the date of the application, and
>
> (b) during the seven years immediately preceding the period of twenty-four months referred to in paragraph (a), for a period amounting in the aggregate to not less than five years.

The *Dual Citizenship Act*, which allows Ghanaians and foreigners to acquire dual citizenship, was launched in Accra on July 3, 2002. A report from Info-Ghana stated:

> The Ghana Immigration Service (GIS) will from next month begin implementing the new laws on Right of Abode, Indefinite Stay and Dual Nationality for citizens who wish to take advantage of the regulation.
>
> Under the law, a person may decide to acquire the citizenship of another nation in addition to his citizenship, and thereby become a dual citizen, if the citizenship laws of that nation would permit him to retain his existing citizenship.[46]

The Right to Abode as identified in the Ghana constitution demonstrates early formations of diaspora citizenship and in effect uses "dual citizenship" clauses to facilitate this policy. The examples of the decisions of Du Bois and Padmore, and Garvey's vision, to exercise African diaspora citizenship rights resonate here. Du Bois deliberately migrated to Africa at the end of his life, proving the efficacy of a U.S. national activating a physical location outside the boundaries of the United States. This move has been emulated by a series of U.S. pan-Africanists such as Dhoruba Bin Wahad (Richard Moore), formerly of the Black Panther Party, who as a victim of COINTELPRO prefers to live in Ghana. Padmore in many ways activated Garvey's dream of return by serving as a major advisor to Nkrumah in the early days of Ghana's independence. In effect he helped to lay the groundwork for Ghana's ability as a state to now exercise leadership in the realm of African diaspora citizenship.

Nation-State Diasporas

A recent trend within the larger African diaspora framework has been the development of structures to take advantage of the growing phenomenon of nation-state diasporas – a phenomenon springing from post-slave, postcolonial migrations from and connections with post-independence states in Africa and the Caribbean. Nation-state diasporas thus consider how the political boundaries after independence might instigate migratory and disaporic cultures. Thus, each country that has a migrant population abroad technically has a nation-state diaspora. Caribbean communities in North America, for example, are beginning to claim, directly and indirectly, political allegiances in two regions: their nation of relocation and their "home" land.

Jamaica and Haiti have had to account for their large diasporas because tangible political and economic connections necessarily have to be maintained for the nation's well-being. The Haitian diaspora has had a major impact on the political developments in the home island because issues of exile have been a fundamental aspect of the island's leadership.

Additionally, given U.S. involvement in the politics of Haiti, leadership has been created and nurtured in the diaspora. Jamaica has also begun to operate similarly, creating an official Jamaican diaspora conference and political mechanisms to allow the dispersed people to have an impact on the political and economic life of their country. Indeed, a first foreign visit to the South Florida area by the new woman prime minister, Portia Simpson Miller, in June 2006, was meant to acknowledge this Jamaican diaspora support.

A range of other nation-state diasporas are either acting similarly or working towards these dual recognitions. This approach is mutually beneficial both to the leadership of these countries and to the diaspora communities that are seeking to preserve a tangible connection with their home countries' developments. People living outside of their home countries who maintain responsibilities at home often have clear priorities of helping their families there via remittances, as well as wanting to ensure the interests and well-being of their home countries to sustain their own general sense of personal well-being.

Contemporary transnational relocations and movement mean that many states now have to recognize that a number of their nationals who live abroad have to be ensured rights. Mexico, for instance, provides citizens living abroad with voting rights; and the often negative role of the Cuban exile community and its larger diaspora are well known in their tendencies to seek to have an impact on U.S. attempts to undo the Cuban revolution, from 1959 to the present. These cases offer at the microlevel a model of a possible assertion of an African diaspora citizenship through the existence of nation-state diasporas. In the final analysis, many Africans will prefer to express their nation-state diaspora citizenship not through imagining their geographies as distinct, nation-bound sites, but rather as spatial articulations of the layered identities of African peoples in the diaspora.

The right to vote in the nation-state of birth has become one of the most important demands of citizens of the nation-state diaspora; it means that people with dual citizenship can have an impact on the political futures of their home states. Another right is that of owning and maintaining property in one's home nation-state and thereby establishing a tangible identification of belonging to that country and having a stake in what happens there. The transmittal of financial resources is a critical component of these two points – for they are often linked both to family obligations and to securing a future place in one's homeland.

African countries such as Ghana and Nigeria have had to come to terms with the meaning of diaspora in various ways. The loss of a great deal of their educated citizenry through the brain drains indicates that more aggressive harnessing of these human resources has to be part of the citizenship framework, which leads to a new set of geographical indicators in considering the contours of the nation-state. Likewise, an examination of the Chinese diaspora suggests:

> Diasporic activities imply some form of border-crossing expansion of social space, resulting in issues of dual state membership. This refers to the fact of being a citizen in two states, with allowances of having a less privileged form in either one. . . . The significance comes when one starts to consider the emigration country government's interest and policies towards their emigrants.[47]

In the case of India, the government there issued the *Citizen Act* in 2003 (*Overseas Indian Citizenship*) under which persons of Indian origin are eligible to apply for overseas citizenship. The act, under section 7A (1), specifies: "Any persons of Indian origin of full age and capacity who are citizens of a specified country or who have obtained the citizenship of a specified country on or after the commencement of the Citizenship Act 2003 i.e. on 07.01.2004 and who were citizens of India immediately before such commencement under section 7A(1)(b). The minors of persons mentioned above are also eligible for Overseas Citizenship."[48]

African Diaspora Citizenship as Transnational Citizenship: "Complementing and not Replacing National Citizenship"

A developing body of literature argues for transnational citizenship. Much of this work has come from the initiatives of Chicano legal scholars such as Maria L. Ontiveros in California.[49] This transnational citizenship refers to the ability of large communities of people from a given nation, residing elsewhere, to have rights in both locations and in effect creates a more capable diasporic political community. A number of states have already instituted this right through dual citizenship laws. Indeed, Mexico's former president Vicente Fox, in major public addresses, spoke of Mexican citizenship as transnational. Scholars of Latin American migration quoted in the *Miami Herald* of May 27, 2001, asserted that the phenomenon of "transnational citizens" would alter "the nature of U.S.–Latin American relations."

> While recent U.S. census figures showing a record 34 million Hispanics in the United States surpassed the boldest demographic projections, the most interesting phenomenon is the changing nature of this ethnic group: Increasingly, it is made up of Latin American-born migrants who go back and forth

between their two homelands. . . . "Transnationalism is becoming a reality for today's migrants," said Susan F. Martin, head of Georgetown University's Institute for the Study of International Migration. Cheaper air fares and telephone calls are making it easier to move to another country and keep contact with one's home community, she explained. As has happened in the European Union, this trend is bound to accelerate if planned U.S.–Latin American free trade agreements allow greater migration of managers and professionals. Already, under a little-noticed clause of the 1994 free trade deal between the United States, Canada and Mexico, U.S. immigration authorities will have to remove some restrictions on work visas to Mexican executives, professionals and skilled workers by 2004. Similar provisions are expected in future U.S.–Latin American free trade deals, experts say.

A series of conferences in various locations have pursued this discussion and considered possible areas for policy-making. For example, a conference of the Association of American Geographers, March 7, 2003, identified issues of transnational movement and transnational citizenship, indicating why the transnational citizen has become key in migration studies. Topics included the grounded practice and meanings of transnational citizenship; which transnational migrants can be transnational citizens and why; the role of the state in incorporating or not incorporating transnational citizens in various ways; contemporary developments in transnationalism and citizenship policy; and challenges for policy formulation. According to an announcement on the Conference website:

> Citizenship has outgrown its national dress. On the one hand, nation states are no longer the sole and supreme source for determining citizenship policies. On the other, many citizens have ceased to practice their citizenship in only one national setting. The emergence of transnational dimensions of citizenship poses a critical challenge to today's policy-makers, activists and academics. The principal aim of this session is to conceptualize citizenship in a transnational context and to discuss subsequent policy implications. For this purpose, the session will address critical theoretical and political considerations that are to be illustrated at concrete research findings. In particular, the session will test some of the assumptions of policy makers in regard to dual nationality, access to rights and political engagement in more than one country, multiple loyalties, and issues relating to inclusion and exclusion of ethnic minorities.[50]

The work of scholars engaged in identifying the contours and possibilities of transnational citizenship will have implications for a state's treatment of its citizens at home and abroad. Each nation-state has had to come to terms with how migration patterns result in a large number of its citizens living outside of its geographical boundaries, but still needing access to their countries of origin for cultural and family connections, personal preferences, and other emotive reasons. These discussions will have implications for African diaspora citizenship, which is also a form of transnational citizenship.

The European model may offer a contemporary approach – one already implemented – to this problem of rights and the integration and practicalities of transnational citizenship. The European model is multistate, ensuring all its members residence and citizenship rights in the areas of education, labour, retirement, employment, and travel. While respecting the national identity of member states, the European Union has been able in various ways to ensure common and reciprocal rights of citizenship. The third report from the Commission on Citizenship of the Union (held in Brussels, Sept. 7, 2001) identifies a directive on the right of residence as "the right of citizens of the Union and their family members to move and reside freely within the territory of the Member States, adopted by the commission on 23 May 2001."[51] In this directive, the right to residence in any member state is not subject to any condition and can become permanent: "After four years of uninterrupted residence individuals will acquire a permanent right of residence in the host member state." The EU directive states:

> Citizenship of the Union is hereby established. Every person holding the nationality of a Member State shall be a citizen of the Union. Citizenship of the Union shall complement and not replace national citizenship (Article 17 of the Treaty establishing the European Community).
>
> In concrete terms European citizenship confers four specific rights on all nationals of EU Member States: (1) the right to move freely and to stay in the territory of Member States; (2) the right to vote and to stand as a candidate in local and European Parliament elections in the Member State of residence; (3) entitlement to protection, in a non-EU country in which a citizen's own Member State is not represented, by the diplomatic or consular authorities of any other Member State; (4) the right to petition the European Parliament and to apply to the European Ombudsman.

A massive set of documents, representing a movement still in process, with far-reaching implications, the European Union legislation is one of the most advanced versions of multistate, transnational citizenship rights. It demonstrates the possibilities of African diaspora citizenship for states in

Africa and the New World, which can participate in developing similarly imaginative ways of interpreting citizenship. While the EU continues in various ways to struggle with issues of nationality and sovereignty and individual states' desires, these are problems to be anticipated in any regional, political structure. What is perhaps most important are the strategies set in place to work through and satisfy sovereignty issues and rights.

Towards African Diaspora Citizenship: Implementation Activities

The First Western Hemisphere Diaspora Forum, sponsored by the African Union, was held in Washington, D.C., in December 2002 with the primary goal of establishing linkages between the continent of Africa and the Western Hemisphere, and in particular to develop a structure of diaspora inclusion in the African Union. At this conference a working group entitled Democracy, Governance and the Rule of Law moved that the African diaspora be organized to establish itself for full representation in the African Union.[52] The working group members suggested that members of the diaspora be represented on the basis of regions, with representation coming from Latin America (including Mexico and Central America), the Caribbean, Brazil, the United States, and Canada. As for citizenship questions, an inclusive model was proposed, with each African Union member-state legislating the right of citizenship to members of the diaspora, and the African Union according certain legal, civil, and economic rights to members of the diaspora. The general intent was to develop a mechanism to provide citizenship to people of African descent through the African Union. The final plenary meeting of the Diaspora Forum passed a recommendation that called for the participants to begin to set in place a structure of African Union representation for the African diaspora.

An African Union Technical Workshop on Relations with the Diaspora, held in Trinidad and Tobago in June 2004, provided the next step.[53] Its recommendations ranged from a definition of the African diaspora to the role of the diaspora in reversing the African brain drain in line with the recommendations of NEPAD (New Partnership for Africa's Development). Other themes and visions discussed included the creation of a diaspora fund for investment and development in Africa; the development of scientific and technical networks to channel the repatriation of scientific knowledge from the diaspora to Africa, and the establishment of co-operation between those abroad and those at home; and establishment of a diaspora database to promote and facilitate networking and collaboration between experts in their respective countries of origin and those in the diaspora.

The execution of this plan for African diaspora citizenship made its way slowly through the various administrative systems, with at least two conferences of African intellectuals, in Senegal (2004) and Brazil (2006), discussing the international and local issues related to the process. Indeed, a series of conferences leading to specific resolutions will have to be organized to provide a body for a skeletal frame of entitlements. Various commissions and their administrative structures organized for these purposes will have to set this framework into place.

African diaspora citizenship rights as proposed include reciprocal, dual-state membership with open possibilities for enlargement towards multistate membership. African diaspora citizenship assumes the rights and duties normally accorded to citizens of the African Union. The rights include:

1. **Entitlements**
   a. **Residency** – the ability to live and attain residence in the state of one's choice.
   b. **Land ownership** – the ability to own land in the state of one's choice.
   c. **Movement** – the ability to move freely through those states and across borders with appropriate identification; a possible passport structure. (African Union passport will be available to both AU and qualified African diaspora members.)
   d. **Trade** – the development of trade and economic relationships for the circulation of goods, products, and resources (human and natural) within and across member states and in support of various member states for the economic well-being of all.
   e. **Educational exchanges** – the ability of students to acquire education in member states of choice and the development of African diaspora studies in African universities.
   f. **Retirement** – the securing of retirement communities in the state of choice for members of the African diaspora.
   g. **Workers' rights** – the rights to work in member states as qualified.
   h. **Refugee rights** – the rights of people desiring or seeking another life possibility to move freely to co-operating member states.

Revisiting the Geography of the African Diaspora

While the proposals for citizenship entitlement may seem idealistic or utopian, we believe that almost all the various national and regional economic declarations began with some sort of imaginative schematizing. After all, as popular Caribbean common-sense articulation of unequal exchange would say, "Why should we give up a continent in exchange for an island?" It is in the global common interest of African diaspora peoples that we begin a process of realizing African diaspora citizenship. Current trends in the development of transnational citizenship rights – particularly as represented by the European Union – indicate that with the developments in communication and a range of other processes of globalization in the contemporary era, states can, and must, work collaboratively to ensure the advancement of their well-being and the rights of their citizens. Given that the African diaspora is a pre-existing demographic and cultural condition of globalization, what remains for us is to activate its various economic and political components into an effective political and economic structure – into a model that would ensure that basic categories of human rights can begin to be achieved.

The language of "African peoples" in the AU *Constitutive Act* already allows for the possibility of a wide-ranging participation. As the Lusaka Summit Decision declares, African peoples include peoples of African descent in the diaspora as well as on the continent. In its Article 3, "Objectives," the *Constitutive Act* specifies as a primary goal "to achieve greater unity and solidarity between the African countries and the peoples of Africa" and also to "promote and defend African common positions on issues of interest to the continent and its peoples." Article 4, paragraph C, similarly calls for the "participation of the African peoples in the activities of the Union."[54]

If we understand African peoples to include African peoples outside of the continent, then in this era of economic globalization African peoples globally dispersed will have to transform their own situated geographies – the limited geographies of their nation-states – not only to achieve more integrated benefits in their homes but also to navigate the larger global reaches of the African diaspora.

Notes

1 Lawrence M. Friedman, "Erewhon: The Coming Global Legal Order," *Stanford Journal of International Law* 27 (2001); IMF, "Globalization: Threat or Opportunity?" *International Monetary Fund: Issues Brief 2001/2000* <http://www.imf.org/external/np/exr/ib/2000/041200.htm> (accessed 2006); Saskia Sassen, *Globalization and Its Discontents: Essays on the New Mobility of People and Money* (New York: The New Press, 1999).

2 For a useful study of some of the theories of African diaspora, see Maggie M. Morehouse, "The African Diaspora: An Investigation of the Theories Employed When Categorizing and Identifying Transnational Communities" <http://ist-socrates.berkeley/˜african/morehouse.pdf> (accessed 2006).

3 Brent Hayes Edwards, *The Practice of Diaspora: Literature, Translation, and the Rise of Black Internationalism* (Cambridge, Mass.: Harvard University Press, 2003); Michael

Angelo Gomez, *Reversing Sail: A History of the African Diaspora, New Approaches to African History* (Cambridge and New York: Cambridge University Press, 2005); Joseph Harris, ed., *Global Dimensions of the African Diaspora* (Washington, D.C.: Howard University Press, 1993); Sidney Lemelle and Robin D.G. Kelley, *Imagining Home: Class, Culture and Nationalism in the African Diaspora* (London: Verso, 1994); Isidore Okpewho, Carole Boyce Davies, and Ali A. Mazrui, *The African Diaspora: African Origins and New World Identities* (Bloomington: Indiana University Press, 1999); Tiffany Patterson and Robin D.G. Kelley, "Unfinished Migrations: Reflections on the African Diaspora and the Making of the Modern World," *African Studies Review*, April 2000. See also the essays by Joseph Harris, Joseph Inikori, and Colin Palmer in Alusine Jalloh, ed., *The African Diaspora* (Walter Prescott Webb Memorial Lectures) (Texas: A & M Press, 1996).

4 Gwendolyn Midlo Hall, *Slavery and African Ethnicities in the Americas: Restoring the Links* (Chapel Hill: University of North Carolina Press, 2005).

5 Sylviane A. Diouf and Howard Dodson, *In Motion: The African American Migration Experience*, Schomburg Center for Research in Black Culture, 2005 <http://www.inmotionaame.org/> (accessed 2006).

6 See African Union website <www.african-union.org>.

7 Siegfried Wiessner, *Die Funktion Der Staatsangehörigkeit* [function of nationality] (Tübingen: Tübingen University Press, 1989), pp.396–97; Siegfried Wiessner, "Blessed Be the Ties That Bind: The Nexus between Nationality and Territory," *56 MISS. L.J.* (1988), pp.447–55. A point of contrast is offered by Peter H. Schuck, "The Re-Evaluation of American Citizenship," which refers to a "positive concept of citizenship" defined as "a relationship between individuals and the polity in which citizens owe allegiance to their polity . . . while the polity owes its citizens the fullest measure of protection that its laws affords, including the right to vote." Peter H. Schuck, "The Re-Evaluation of American Citizenship," in *Challenge to the Nation State: Immigration to Western Europe and the United States*, ed. Christian Joppke (Oxford: Oxford University Press: 1998), p.191.

8 "Citizen," in *Webster's II New College Dictionary* (1995), p.204.

9 "National," in *Webster's II New College Dictionary* (1995), p.728.

10 Wiessner, "Blessed Be the Ties That Bind," pp.448–49.

11 The narrative of Ibo Landing, a narrative of returning Africans, is captured in Paule Marshall, *Praisesong for the Widow* (New York: E.P. Dutton, 1984); Edward (Kamau) Brathwaite, *The Arrivants: A New World Trilogy* (Oxford University Press, 1867); a range of songs, poems, and narratives of return such as the "Flying Back" genres of stories are examples. More recently, works such as Carole Boyce Davies and Molara Ogundipe-Leslie, *Moving Beyond Boundaries* (Washington Square, N.Y.: New York University Press, 1995); Bob Marley, *Exodus* (Island Records, 1977); Marlene Nourbese Philip, *Caribana: African Roots and Continuities: Race, Space and the Poetics of Moving* (Toronto: Poui Publications, 1996).

12 A. Fitzroy Baptiste, "African Presence in India (1 and 2)," *African Quarterly*, 38: 2 (1998); Joseph Harris, "Expanding the Scope of African Diaspora Studies: The Middle East and India, a Research Agenda," *Radical History Review*, 87 (2003); Runoko Rashidi and Ivan Van Sertima, eds., *African Presence in Early Asia* (New Brunswick: Transaction Publishers, 1999); Kenneth X. Robbins and John McLeod, eds., *African Elites in India: Habshi Amarat* (Ahmedabad, India: Mapin Publishing, 2006); Benigna Zimba, Edward Alpers, and Allen Isaacman, eds., *Slave Routes and Oral Tradition in Southeastern Africa* (Maputo, Mozambique: Filsom Entertainment 2005). A recent contribution in this area is "The African Diaspora in Asia," a conference held in Goa, India, in January 2006.

13 Harris, "Expanding the Scope of African Diaspora Studies," p.157.

14 Gomez, *Reversing Sail*; Hall, *Slavery and African Ethnicities*; Jalloh, ed., *African Diaspora*.

15 Cheikh Anta Diop, *Precolonial Black Africa: A Comparative Study of the Political and Social Systems of Europe and Black Africa, from Antiquity to the Formation of Modern States* (Westport, Conn.: Lawrence Hill, 1987); Chancellor Williams, *The Destruction of Black Civilization: Great Issues of a Race from 4500 B.C. to 2000 A.D* (Chicago: Third World Press, 1987). For a substantial discussion and presentation of artistic representations of some of these Africans in various social roles in India, see Robbins and McLeod, eds., *African Elites in India: Habshi Amarat*.

16 Examples of the most egregious of these include apartheid in South Africa, U.S. segregation laws, and in Brazil official processes of "racial democracy" that still function to disenfranchise the majority African-derived populations.

17 Amy Caitlin-Jairazbhoy and Edward Alpers, eds., *Siddis and Scholars: Essays on African Indians* (Trenton, N.J. and India: Red Sea Press and Rainbow Publishers, 2004); Kiran Kamal Prasad, *In Search of an Identity: An Ethnographic Study of the Siddas in Karnataka* (Bangladore: Jana Jagrati Prakashana, 2005).

18 Carole Boyce Davies, "Deportable Subjects: U.S. Immigration Laws and the Criminalizing of Communism," *South Atlantic Quarterly*, 100: 4 (2001).

19 See "Declaration and Plan of Action: Africans and African Descendants," April 2001.

20 *The Declaration of Independence, the Constitution of the United States of America (with Amendments), and Other Important American Documents*, ed. Thomas Jefferson, Digireads.com, 2005.

21 Boyce Davies, "Deportable Subjects," p.955.

22 Michael Hanchard, "The Color of Subversion: Racial Politics and Immigration Policy in the United States," Northwestern University, Evanston, Ill., unpublished manuscript made available to the authors, 2006.

23 Other manifestations are the *Indian Removal Act*, the *Chinese Exclusion Act*, and, as far back as 1790, the *Naturalization Act*, which identified people who could be defined as proper citizens. The history of Puerto Rican "citizenship" rights is also worth considering here.

24 Franklin W. Knight and Colin A. Palmer, *The Modern Caribbean* (Chapel Hill: University of North Carolina Press, 1989); Karen Fog Olwig, *Small Islands, Large Questions: Society, Culture, and Resistance in the Post-Emancipation Caribbean*, *Studies in Slave and Post-Slave Societies and Cultures* (London and Portland, Ore.: F. Cass, 1995).

25 Interview with Billy Strachan by Carole Boyce Davies, London, 1997.

26 For a discussion of attempts at integration, see Patsy Lewis, *Surviving Small Size: Regional Integration in Caribbean Ministates* (Kingston, Jamaica: University of the West Indies Press, 2002).

27 A growing body of literature by historians charts, via documentary and oral history, the origins of African diaspora peoples to specific locations in Africa. See, for example, the documentary work of Gwendolyn Midlo Hall and the oral history of Alex Haley, which produced *Roots*. Alex Haley, *Roots* (Garden City, N.Y.: Doubleday, 1976); Hall, *Slavery and African Ethnicities*. A range of other projects of genealogy have allowed Africans in the New World to reclaim their family, kin-groups, and communities of origin – real or imagined. The recent DNA projects have also reproduced this discourse in a more technical way, via precollected DNA from African communities. The scientific validity of this approach is still being questioned; nevertheless it is one of the steps along the way towards some sort of direct location of African diaspora peoples in their African communities of origin, beyond facial resemblances and other physiognomic identifications, language and family oral history, and long and painstaking genealogical work.

28 P. Olisanwuche Esedebe, *Pan-Africanism: The Idea and Movement, 1776–1963* (Washington, D.C.: Howard University Press, 1982); Tony Martin, "Pan-Africanism," in *Encyclopedia of the African Diaspora*, ed. Carole Boyce Davies (Oxford: ABC-CLIO, forthcoming, 2007).

29 Edwards, *Practice of Diaspora*, pp.241–305. The Kouyaté/Padmore strategy involved

anti-imperialist writings and activism (newspapers, coalitions, collectives, congresses) in the United States, Britain, and parts of Africa and the Caribbean.

30 See for example, Abdias do Nascimento, *Brazil: Mixture or Massacre* (Dover, Mass.: The Majority Press, 1979); Michael Hanchard, *Orpheus and Power* (Princeton, N.J.: Princeton University Press, 1994); Kim D Butler, *Freedoms Given, Freedoms Won: Afro-Brazilians in Post-Abolition Sao Paulo and Salvador* (Chapel Hill, N.C.: Rutgers University Press, 1998). A series of other reports such as the most recent 2005 UN report and the earlier "Afro-Brazilians: Time for Recognition," a Minority Rights Group International Report written by Darien J. Davis, London, 1999, are sources for information on this issue.

31 For an overview of these debates, see Jacob Olupona, ed., *African Traditional Religions in Contemporary Society* (New York: International Religious Foundation and Paragon House, 1991).

32 Funso Aiyejina, "Orisha Cultures in Trinidad and Tobago," *Encyclopedia of the African Diaspora* (Oxford: ABC/CLIO, forthcoming, 2007).

33 For an extended reading list, "African Religions in the Americas," see <http://sparta.rice.edu/~maryc/Bibliography.html>. The Globalization of Yoruba Religious Culture conference, Florida International University, 1999, held as a joint project of African–New World Studies and the Department of Religious Studies, explored many of these issues. Videotapes are available through the program and an edited collection by Jacob Olupona and Terry Rey is being prepared. See also Olupona, ed., *African Traditional Religions in Contemporary Society*.

34 *Church of Lukumi Babalu Aye V. City of Hialeah, 508 U.S. 520*, 1993 <http://userwww.sfsu.edu/~biella/santeria/dec1.html>.

35 *Charter of the Organization of African Unity*, 479 U.N.T.S. 39, entered into force Sept. 13, 1963 <http://www1.umn.edu/humanrts/africa/OAU_Charter_1993.html> (accessed 2006).

36 Danielle S Petito, "Sovereignty and Globalization: Fallacies, Truth and Perception," *New York Law School Journal of Human Rights*, 17:1 (2001).

37 Brian Meeks, *Narratives of Resistance: Jamaica, Trinidad, the Caribbean* (Kingston: University of the West Indies Press, 2000), pp.155–73.

38 Abiodun Alao, "The Role of African Regional and Sub-Regional Organisations in Conflict Prevention and Resolution," *Working Paper No. 23*, African Security Unit, King's College, University of London, July 2000, p.29.

39 See <http://democracy-africa.org/articles/diaspora02.html>.

40 See <www.au2002.gov.za/docs/key_oau/au_act.pdf>.

41 See <http://www.whadn.org/>.

42 See M.G. Smith, Roy Augier, and Rex Nettleford, "Report on the Rastafari Movement in Kingston, Jamaica," ISER, University of the West Indies, Mona, Jamaica, 1960, p.5.

43 A number of studies provide this historical information on the birth of Rastafari as a movement in the Caribbean. See, for example, Horace Campbell, *Rasta and Resistance: From Marcus Garvey to Walter Rodney* (London: Hansib, 1985); Barry Chevannes, *Rastafari: Roots and Ideology*, *Utopianism and Communitarianism* (Syracuse, N.Y.: Syracuse University Press, 1994).

44 See Sandrine Desroses, "Shashamane, terre rasta en Ethiopie: Une communauté pas très appréciée par la population," Feb. 4, 2005 <http://www.afrik.com/article8094.html> (accessed January 2007). The actual letter (see Appendix) is no longer online.

45 See <http://www.ethiopianembassy.org/proclamation.shtml>.

46 The *Republic of Ghana (Amendment) Act 1996*, which repealed Article Eight of the 1992 Constitution. See <www.info-ghana.com/Dual%20citizenship>.

47 Sek Pei Lim, "The Question of Diaspora in International Relations: A Case Study of Chinese Diaspora in Malaysia," M.A. dissertation, University of Sussex, 2000.

48 See <http://www.mha.nic.in/oci/intro.pdf>. Of particular interest in this document is:

"4. A person registered as OCI is eligible to apply for grant of Indian citizenship under section 5(1)(g) of the Citizenship Act, 1955 if he/she is registered as OCI for five years and has been residing in India for one year out of the five years before making the application."

49 Maria L. Ontiveros, "Forging Our Identity: Transformative Resistance in the Areas of Work, Class, and the Law, *U.C. Davis Law Review*, 33:1057 (2000), pp.1062–71, which argues that "farmworkers, like many other immigrants today, refuse to choose between an identity that is defined as being based solely in Mexico or in the United States." See also Paul Johnston, "Citizens of the Future: the Emergence of Transnational Citizenship among Mexican Immigrants in California <http://www.newcitizen.org>.

50 Workshop 26: Contemporary Developments in Transnationalism and Citizenship Policy, Wednesday, Nov. 28, 2001.

51 Europa, the official website of the Europe Union, contains relevant documents <http://europa.eu/treaties/Index_en.htm>.

52 Both writers were part of this working group. See the Africa Union website, in particular <www.africa-union.org/Special_Programs/CSSDCA/cssdca-firstau-forum.pdf> (accessed January 2007) for a report on the meeting.

53 <http://www.africa-union.org/organs/ecosocc/Workshop%20>.

54 See <http://www.africa-union.org/root/au/Documents/decisions.htm>.

3

Clyde Woods

"Sittin' on Top of the World"

The Challenges of Blues and Hip Hop Geography

Worked all the summer, worked all the fall,
Had to work Christmas in my overalls
But now she's gone, and I don't worry,
Because I'm sittin' on top of the world.
— Mississippi Sheiks, 1930[1]

When the Chatmon brothers and their band, the Mississippi Sheiks, recorded the blues classic "Sittin' on Top of the World" in 1930, the Mississippi Delta was already in the devastating grip of the Great Depression, well before this economic downturn undermined the United States as a whole. Although the systems of debt peonage and sharecropping would soon be transformed, hunger, evictions, and terror would haunt the region for another four decades. We must ask how could someone trapped in this web of social destruction assume the supernatural position, the superimposition, of "sittin' on top of the world"? Was the author gripped by madness, or was he rooted in an intellectual tradition that inherently enabled destitute African Americans to traverse multiple scales of consciousness and space? Many present-day social theorists continue to bemoan the lack of humility among impoverished African Americans; but these scholars have yet to understand the global epistemological stance of "self-made and Blues rich."[2]

Numerous scholars have argued that the current system of neo-liberal global governance rests on idealized versions of cosmopolitanism and free markets that are bereft of a critical understanding of the history, geography, anthropology, and ecology of other nations. According to Anwar Shaikh, the practice of neo-liberalism is justified by a set of theoretical claims rooted in standard economic theory. Markets are represented as optimal and self-regulating social structures. It is claimed that if markets are allowed to function without restraint, they would optimally serve all economic needs, efficiently utilize all economic resources, and automatically generate full employment for all persons who truly wish to work.[3]

According to geographer and social theorist David Harvey, an inadequate understanding of the spatial contexts and histories emphasized within the discipline of human geography

> makes it too easy for the US to portray itself as the bearer of universal principles of justice, democracy and goodness while in practice operating in an intensely discriminatory way. The easy way in which various spaces in the global economy can be "demonized" in public opinion . . . illustrates all too well how geographical knowledge of a certain sort is mobilized for political purposes while sustaining a belief in the US as the bearer of a global ethic.[4]

Harvey goes on to ask several questions. What would a socially just cosmopolitan ethic look like? How can "geographical knowledges be reconstituted to meet the needs of a democratic and ethical system of global governance? Finally, what "kinds of geographical knowledges are presently available" to accomplish this task?[5]

This chapter explores several potential answers to these queries, focusing in particular on three intertwining concerns: the regional, and plantation, socio-economic history of the Southern United States; the long-standing socio-spatial demonization of African Americans and other subaltern groups; and the imagined ethical possibilities of the blues epistemology. We must start with the unique set of regional relations that gave rise to North American neo-liberalism. Many of the roots of this system were nourished by the reaction to the modern civil rights movement. A campaign of massive resistance slowly reorganized the political and intellectual institutions of the United States. The Southern pillars of racial supremacy and an anti-union low-wage economy effectively eviscerated the welfare state. The neo-plantation epistemology was used to manufacture campaigns against supposed black moral deviancy and criminality in order to both devolve the federal state and marginalize the most progressive sector of the body politic.

Yet much of the literature on neo-liberalism and globalization conveniently ignores the literature on the historic "Southern Strategy" institutional realignment in the United States. Scant attention is given to the relationship between this hegemonic discourse and the regional conditions and social movements that spawned it over forty years ago. Ignoring the transformation of regional and racial regimes allows proponents and critics of neo-liberalism to also freely ignore their own complicity in a wide variety of domestic racial projects that undermine democratic institutions and constituencies: massive social spending cuts, segregated education, welfare reform, gentrification, the prison-industrial complex, employment discrimination, and electoral disenfranchisement, among others.

Another strategy for discovering social justice ethics requires an examination of the genealogy and processes of socio-spatial demonization in the United States. As part of this review, it would be necessary to simply ask, what are the social ethics of the groups most consistently demonized by hegemonic discourse? During Hurricane Katrina, hegemonic neo-liberal discourse seamlessly deployed plantation and white supremacist representations to define African Americans as cannibals, looters, rapists, and insurgents. Those who built New Orleans over the course of three centuries were instantaneously declared unworthy of returning to their city. In the face of public opinion, overt demonization was quickly followed by the equally repulsive dance of deniability. Post-racial rhetoric is one of the pillars of neo-liberalism. It is the glue that binds the dominant economic powers with the billions who are still suffering the effects of historic racialized colonialism and modern forms of marginalization and demonization.[6]

Neo-liberalism is not simply producing and normalizing new forms of inequality. It also represents a decay of the Keynesian regime: its leadership, institutions, economic architecture, and discourse on social progress. The welfare state has been replaced by older forms of essentialisms and dependencies.[7] An expansive study of the discourse on African American conditions and social movements would seem to be an obvious starting point because of the four-century-long campaign of those movements to secure social, economic, and cultural justice.[8] Yet the scholarship on neo-liberalism is peculiarly silent on the global significance of the forms of hegemony that have been worked out in the United States. Internal racial regimes can no longer be treated as incidental to global processes. For example, the end of the First and Second Reconstructions – the periods after the U.S. Civil War and the Second World War, both of which coincided with the black struggle for civil rights – were accompanied by attacks on the domestic social welfare state, the reordering of international markets, and the diminution of the meaning of sovereignty. Which methods provide the tools necessary to understand this intersection?[9]

Scholars who launch investigations regarding the racial workings of neo-liberalism will eventually encounter the blues tradition.[10] In addition to being a musical tradition, the blues is a knowledge system indigenous to the United States that is expressed through an ever-expanding variety of cultural, economic, political, and social traditions. Embedded within the blues tradition are highly developed and institutionalized forms of philosophy, political economy, social theory and practice, and geographic knowledge that are dedicated to the realization of global social justice.

Several principles shape what I call "blues geography." First presented at a 2000 conference of geographers in Seoul, Harvey's essay "Cartographic Identities: Geographical Knowledges under Globalization" is particularly useful as an aid to organizing a cursory examination of the production and structure of geographic knowledge within the blues tradition.[11] This initial investigation is part of a larger project designed to recover and expand indigenous African American forms of consciousness, social investigation, community development, and democratic governance.

"Standing Here Lookin' One Thousand Miles Away": Sites for the Production of Geographic Knowledge[12]

The disciplinary crisis facing geography and the other social sciences has created racial, class, and nationalist panics among those who feel that pseudo-knowledge, pseudo-scholars, and pseudo-students are besieging the academy. Simultaneously, comparative research on multiple forms of knowledge has reached the stage where it can inform a fundamental transformation of academic intellectual organization and production. The blues tradition will continue to play a central role in this crisis.

During the course of the twentieth century innumerable debates occurred over the meaning of the blues. This intellectual tradition has been defined in several ways: as a form of entertainment; as ontology; as a dead musical genre; as an evolving aesthetic movement; as the ultimate expression of individualism; and as a core African American institution. One of the first academic blues scholars, white Southern sociologist Howard Odum, referred to this intellectual and musical tradition as "openly descriptive of the grossest immorality and susceptible of unspeakable thought and actions rotten with filth . . . the superlative of the repulsive." Must the blues musician, he asked, "continue as the embodiment of fiendish filth incarnated in the tabernacle of the soul?"[13]

Sam "Lightnin'" Hopkins once remarked that the "Blues is like death" and noted that "it's hard to understand" because both are inevitable.[14] Implicit in this debate over marginality and centrality is the refusal to acknowledge even the remote possibility that working-class African Americans in the nineteenth-century rural South could develop an approach to equitable sustainable development informed by their own philosophical system. That such a philosophy, fostered by black musicians, would circle the globe repeatedly through numerous revivalist intellectual movements remains incomprehensible to those who view the production of knowledge through narrow racial, ethnic, class, gender, or institutional lenses. The construction of a university system within the blues tradition occurred through prolonged, intense, and deadly debates and experimentation in the South on social theory, political economy, aesthetics, methodology, and socio-spatial praxis.

Despite notable efforts to integrate different texts and ideas into university curriculums and philosophical frameworks, social research disciplines appear to be ontologically incapable of systematically incorporating new and older forms of social justice–centred indigenous, and subaltern, knowledge. Due to the growth of racial and economic elitism within the academy, combined with the radical celebration of positivism and pragmatism, many social research disciplines have fallen into crisis. The neat conflation of people and places embedded in the globalization discourse has been countered by the exponential reassertion of ethno-regional, class, and gendered forms of consciousness and community.

Harvey's concern with the fate of geography is justifiable: many disciplines show a generalized sense of intellectual exhaustion on the question of social explanation. Yet the long-marginalized intellectual traditions are asked to put aside their further development, while the hegemonic disciplines search for a new mission, a new social order, and a new social-spatial fix. Critical race studies, gender studies, African American studies, ethnic studies, indigenous studies, environmental studies, labour studies, regional studies, and queer studies are being devalued exactly at the moment in which they are poised to produce new multidisciplinary forms of geographic thought and action, while also imagining a new world.

This intellectual exhaustion calls forth renewed efforts to deepen the development of these historically marginalized traditions. There is an expansive literature implicitly, and explicitly, exploring many forms of African American landscapes and geographic thought. However, many of these studies proceed from hegemonic discourses on African American failure, criminality, and deviancy.[15] By definition, these works exclude the possibility of indigenous intellectual traditions. Projects that choose to recognize, and present, African American voices and movements often fall back upon disciplinary forms of interpretation that claim to be transhistorical, transnational, and "universal." Another tendency recognizes the possibility of indigenous knowledge systems but treats them as epiphenomenal. Denied is the presence of indigenous institutions, the multiple meanings of aesthetic movements, multiple forms of historical continuity, class-based intellectual production, and the possibility of interregional dispersion of intellectual movements. While racial formation theory provides valuable insights into the workings of movement-led social transformations, it awaits the insertion of theories of intersectionality, regional differentiation, indigenous knowledge systems, and aesthetic politics.[16]

As a theoretical and methodological intervention, studies organized around consideration of the intersection of race, ethnicity, class, and gender provide an opportunity to fundamentally reconsider the relationship between voice and social structures. However, further advancement in this tradition requires several interventions, particularly in the area of geography, time-space, place, and region: a coherent set of theories on the relationship between time and space, a discourse on the social construction and transformation of places, theories of the intertextuality of regional life, formulations on the role of hegemonic and counterhegemonic movements in shaping place-specific knowledge; a theory of institutional and network knowledges; a theory of the formation of regional alliances that crosses class, race, ethnic, and gender boundaries; a theory of regionally specific social practices and trajectories; a theory of interregional relations; a discourse on sustainable community development; a discourse on indigenous pedagogy; and an expanded discourse on the transformation of scientific inquiry.[17]

Inextricably tied to working-class daily life, the blues epistemology and other partially articulated geographic knowledge systems can embody all of these dimensions. Yet the imperial disciplinary boundaries of existing geography, sociology, political science, and economics operate to fragment and conceal epistemological movements premised upon comprehensive forms of interdisciplinarity. Fragmenting the social-spatial grid possibilities that interdisciplinary investigations open up defeats attempts to produce polyphonal forms of knowledge and knowledge-making. At the same time, new interdisciplinary projects have embedded in them implicit silencing strategies.

For example, in his effort to provide a social spatial fix for the crisis affecting the academic discipline of human geography, Harvey, in the vein of Michel Foucault, argues that there is a powerful link between knowledge, power, and institutions. Certain institutions and their specific forms of knowledge are said to be critical to the discipline of geography: state identity and reproduction; military power; supranational institutions; nongovernmental organizations; corporate and commercial interests; media, entertainment, and tourism industries; and education and research institutions. The discipline of geography is considered to be a contested site that weakly refracts these institutionalized discourses; a "servant of dominant or superior institutions."[18]

As a curative to increased fragmentation within the discipline, Harvey argues that the survival of geography, as a meaningful political discipline, is dependent upon the adoption of a new mission. The new goal is to enrich the conversation on global governance by translating and integrating radically divergent institutional forms of geographic knowledge. The search for "unities" and "strong geographical ideas" will carve out a special place for the discipline in the discourse on global justice. To reach this goal geography and geographers must first formally acknowledge the presence of the institutional knowledges that shape the discipline. Therefore, human geographers must formally recognize the particular role that the state plays in shaping the discipline. According to Harvey, "The 'hidden geography' of geographical knowledges has rarely been addressed except elliptically and occasionally."[19]

The institutionalized geographical knowledges are particularly important to geography as an academic discipline. But far wider and more general kinds of geographic knowledge are embedded in language, local ways of life, the local symbiosis achieved between nature, economy, and culture, local mythologies and diverse cultural practices and forms, common-sense prescriptions, and dynamic socio-linguistic traditions. Specialized geographical knowledges abound (everything from the urban knowledge of the taxi driver to the particular knowledge of amateur ornithologists or local antiquarians).[20] Once thrown into this hodgepodge, major epistemological movements are further devalued because they are said to be narrow, emotionally driven, and incapable of possessing or providing global ethics:

> Local knowledges, for example, often amount to relatively complete geographical descriptions albeit structured from a certain parochialist perspective. Local and regional identities, conversely, are themselves built (as in the nation state) around the formation and articulation of certain kinds of geographical (often strongly colored by environmentalist sentiments) understandings. Geographers (along with anthropologists) have traditionally paid close attention to these localised "structures of feeling" and ways of life and in doing so have helped frequently to highlight the conflict between institutionalized knowledges directed toward governmentality and localized knowledges that guide affective loyalties and socio-environmental identities.[21]

These historically evolved, and regionally distinct, pre- and post-capitalist indigenous epistemologies are conflated and relegated into the narrowly defined category of "local knowledges." They are viewed as being incapable of producing forward-looking institutions, disciplines, theories, and forms of governance. This conception of knowledge freezes the philosophical work of subaltern communities in a primitive time and place. Harvey argues that these historic traditions might still be useful in the effort to accomplish important objectives. He states that class theory and practices alone will not support sustained efforts to achieve social justice across multiple scales. This "does not entail abandoning class politics for those of the 'new social movements,' but exploring different forms of alliances that can reconstitute and renew class politics."[22]

The blues tradition has consistently served to unite working-class communities across different spatial scales: blocks, neighbourhoods, towns, cities, regions, ethnicities, and nations. In 1960 novelist and activist Richard Wright argued that the unique combination of tragedy, realism, sensuality, and faith fuelled the global expansion of the blues tradition:

> Not only did those Blacks, torn from their tribal moorings in Africa, transported across the Atlantic, survive under hostile conditions of life, but they left a vivid record of their suffering and longings in those astounding religious songs known as the spirituals, and their descendants, freed and cast upon their own in an alien culture, created the blues, a form of exuberantly melancholy folk song that circled the globe. In Buenos Aires, Stockholm, Copenhagen, London, Berlin, Paris, Rome, in fact, in every large city on earth where lonely, disinherited men congregate for pleasure or amusement, the orgiastic wail of the blues, and their strident offspring, jazz, can be heard.
>
> Yet the most astonishing aspect of the blues is that, though replete with a sense of defeat and downheartedness, they are not intrinsically pessimistic; their burden of woe and melancholy is dialectically redeemed through sheer force of sensuality, into an almost exultant affirmation of life, of love, of sex, of movement, of hope. No matter how repressive was the American environment, the Negro never lost faith in or doubted his deeply endemic capacity to live. All blues are a lusty, lyrical realism charged with taut sensibility.[23]

Numerous international studies of various manifestations of the blues tradition, such as Michael Urban's recent study of the blues in Russia and Tony Mitchell's volume on global hip hop, have found that this tradition is considered both an extension of the disparate processes described as Americanization, Westernization, individualism, consumerism, and globalization, on the one hand, and their negation, on the other.[24] Although held up as the epicentre of misogyny, this tradition has emerged from a community whose identity is defined by some of the most profound assaults – both external (slavery and white supremacy) and internal (the movements of black women) – on patriarchy in human history. Although the blues and other similar traditions are often described as parochial and isolated, they have provided theories and practices fostering inter-ethnic co-operation when such ideas were considered subversive by the globally dominant hegemonic regimes. In many parts of the world, including the United States, efforts to create such alliances are still considered subversive. The attempts to disrupt the three-decade-long organizing process that led to the 2001 United Nations' "World Conference against racism, racial discrimination, xenophobia and related intolerance" in Durban, South Africa, is just one example. The disruption of the actual event was not due to the narrow parochialism of the representatives of "local" knowledge systems; rather, it was the parochialism of the sole superpower whose intention was to ban all discussions of racism from the global arena.[25] Just as the denial of racism is a central neo-liberal intellectual pillar, hip hop, reggae, and other traditions have become central intellectual pillars of the counternarrative.

Many of the indigenous knowledge systems that emerged prior to, and after, the creation of capitalism have fundamentally defined the meaning of global social justice during the last century. The First Nations movement, African philosophical explorations, Latin American social experimentations, the World Social Forum, and many other movements signal the beginning of an epoch. The twenty-first century will be marked by their increasing influence upon models of governance, environmental stewardship, and science. Yet some would argue that knowledges that have been violently marginalized for centuries should continue to be sacrificed to preserve the sanctity of the imperial disciplines. To move away from the fear, exhaustion, and philosophical impoverishment that characterize much of the discourse on global social justice, we need to engage in an intensified exploration of the blues and other indigenous knowledge systems within and outside the academy. Another global justice priority should be assisting organic schools of intellectuals in their efforts to study and expand their own disciplines, philosophies, and pedagogies.

"Yuh Can Read My Letters but Yuh Sho Cain't Read My Mind": The Origins of Blues Geographic Knowledge[26]

The blues tradition of investigation and interpretation is one of the central institutions of African American life. It has been used repeatedly by multiple generations to organize communities of consciousness. Many of the subsequent African American musical/aesthetic traditions can be viewed as cultural movements designed to revitalize the blues ethos of social-spatial justice. With all its contradictions, the blues epistemology stands at the centre of a planetary array of the multiple-genre social-aesthetic movements known as jazz, gospel, rhythm and blues, rock and roll, soul, funk, and hip hop. When viewed as a whole, the global reach of this system of explanation is unprecedented. To explain this phenomenon, we must look at the origins of blues geography, and to the theories, methods, practices, and movements that ensured its particular relevancy across time, place, and scale.

The blues as an intellectual, cultural, social, political, and economic movement was launched by the two generations of black Mississippians who witnessed in quick succession secession, slavery, the Civil War, Reconstruction, the violent overthrow of Reconstruction, a "second slavery," and disenfranchisement. During Reconstruction, African Americans attempted to realize a social agenda informed by African philosophies of sustainable development and the lessons of the Americas: genocide, colonization, and slavery. After the Civil War, the Union Leagues played a key role in leading the movement to transform the South. The Leagues membership and support were drawn from the newly established black churches, fraternal organizations, social aid societies, educational groups, and secret societies. In addition, members were recruited from the ranks of black Union army veterans who were also known as the Blues.[27] According to Gerald Jaynes, with a platform of "freedom, free schools, free ballot boxes, free jury boxes, free everything," the Leagues were hatcheries of radical economic experiments.[28] In an 1868 address, Alston Mygatt, the African American president of the Mississippi Union League, presented the organizations' social vision: "Large landed estates shall melt away into small divisions, thus densifying population; cities shall grow, towns spring up, mechanism flourish, agriculture become scientific, internal improvement pushed."[29]

Shared by the vast majority of the newly liberated, this agenda stressed the elimination of hierarchical land-tenure patterns, the reorganization of urban and rural relations, and the placement of science and the state in the service of the dispossessed. The Mississippi League organized and supported electoral campaigns, agrarian reform, militias for self-defence, and mass labour actions. By 1874 the Leagues had been destroyed due to a planter-organized campaign of church and school burnings, the exile and murder of white supporters, the assassination of black political leaders, and the massacre of the organizations' membership. This campaign was followed by coups in Vicksburg and New Orleans in 1874 and Mississippi in 1875.[30] This violent strategy was soon adopted throughout the South. In response to the continued massive resistance of the men and women involved in the League, the Mississippi Delta plantation bloc drafted a new constitution in 1890. The document granted the franchise to all adults except for "idiots," "the insane," Native Americans, and women. It banned biracial education, interracial marriage, and voting by those with criminal convictions. The poll tax as a disenfranchisement tool was reinforced by the layering of dozens of exclusionary practices or traps such as the grandfather clause, and constitutional interpretation requirements. Constant movement, imprisonment, poverty, illiteracy, physical attacks, and fear further reduced the power of black communities. This model of domination also spread outward from Mississippi to the rest of the South. Throughout the twentieth century, Mississippi remained the epicentre of racial and class schism.[31]

Although often described as anathema to enlightened American forms of democracy and capitalism, the Mississippi Delta plantation regime is actually emblematic of a deeply rooted American form of social organization and philosophy that have provided neo-liberalism with its core organizing principles. The creation, and expansion, of plantation and neo-plantation movements, regimes, and ideology are the often overlooked undersides of globalization. The historical and current resonance of the blues tradition is partly due to its role as the antithesis of the plantation tradition and all of its manifestations.

To understand this modern dilemma more fully, we need to revisit recent scholarship that characterizes plantation complexes as a backward and semi-feudal economic form incompatible with capitalism. The historical plantation has been described as both a military form of agriculture and a capitalist institution having extensive land requirements, intensive capital and labour requirements, and internal forms of governance. However, the plantation and state models have numerous permutations that extend beyond agriculture: slavery and sharecropping; enclosures and reserves; industrial estates and mill villages; free-trade and export zones; enterprise and empowerment zones; ghettos and gated communities; suburbanization and gentrification; game preserves and tourist resorts; pine plantations and mines; and migratory and prison labour.[32]

All of these economic forms are designed to reproduce the basic features of plantation capitalism: resource monopoly; extreme ethnic, class, racial, and gender polarization; an export orientation; and the intense regulation of work, family, speech, and thought. Other features include multiple types of regulations, sometimes violently imposed, upon organic institutions, communities, and leadership. A final set of features that have survived the centuries are manifest in the militarized diminution of human rights, labour rights, and democratic forms of governance. The present period is defined by the ever-increasing monopolization and mining of an ever-decreasing supply of viable air, sea, land, subterranean, and communal resources.

Despite major economic transformations in the global economy, plantation blocs continue to extract institutional rents using taxation, infrastructure, environmental, social, and other policies that rigidly control labour, race, ethnic, urban, and rural relations. Today, the fragmented neo-plantation model of governance has been rebuilt and expanded globally based on the privatization of critical state resources, the elimination of state subsistence guarantees, and the devolution of national and local state responsibilities.

In the 1960s, many communities and scholars realized that plantation and neo-plantation forms of regional, economic, state, and intellectual organization were going to survive the human rights, labour, and anti-colonial movements aligned against them. As early as 1972, Jamaican scholar George Beckford looked upon the crisis of the Caribbean and other parts of the recently decolonized "Third World." He and other academics and activists in the plantation studies school concluded that political independence alone would not resolve the problems faced by societies that were still dominated by plantation production, institutions, or ethics. These factors remained able to reproduce deep impoverishment, ethnic strife, and dependency.[33] Around the same time, African American scholars and activists were reaching similar conclusions. For example, Addison Gayle traced the intellectual roots of the neo-plantation backlash of the civil rights movement to an 1830s conflict between the plantation intellectual movement and the transcendental movement:

> The voice of Kant calling upon man to be open minded, to be inquisitive, to approach the complex problems of men in humanitarian terms fell on deaf ears in a nation where prejudice, dogmatism, and simplistic approaches to problems, human and social, were and still are the norm. Given the choice between Platonic idealism and Kantian transcendentalism, the South chose to ally itself with the Greek mind, and thus became the embodiment of the American myth.[34]

The resilience of plantation relations is also embedded in its geography, which contains a number of elements: states and firms that create plantations in other nations; plantation-creating economies (internal); plantation-dominated economies; restructured neo-plantation societies; plantation zones within societies where other sectors and forms dominate; institutional networks; and regional intellectual movements that reify and revive the plantation epistemology. In every instance, these platforms produce and celebrate racism, monopoly, destitution, and social fragmentation. The interlinked global plantation political economy and the equally well travelled plantation epistemology destabilizes social justice everywhere by mandating resource monopolization, export-orientation, undemocratic forms of governance, environmental degradation, and extreme racial schism and economic destitution. Progressive globalization and neo-liberal studies are haunted by their masking of both the resiliency of plantation projects and the social justice agenda of indigenous knowledge systems.

Some forty years after the signing of the *Voting Rights Act* of 1965, rural and urban African American communities continue to be defined by institutionalized spatial impoverishment and the attendant, and perpetual, crises in health care, education, and housing. The response to Hurricane Katrina reveals the consequences of this tradition in all of its infamy. From the 1930s onward, the intellectual and political leadership provided by the Southern neo-plantation blocs and their Northern and Western allies played a central role in the development of policies designed to undermine the Keynesian welfare state, the civil rights movement, the War on Poverty, and a host of social justice movements. The act of omitting these movements from the critical neo-liberal literature becomes a defence of these extremely hierarchical regional blocs, their unique racial projects, and their efforts to marginalize historic blocs that have preserved social justice and sustainability agendas across the centuries. Consequently, the fundamentally flawed historiography and geography embedded in the critiques of neo-liberalism operate to mask and devalue the blues.[35]

The continued relevancy of the blues tradition is partially a product of the range of issues that the tradition has been intimately engaged with over the last century and a half. The blues has addressed some of the most brutal manifestations of gender, class, and racial exploitation. It has functioned in the global economy because the sweat of its adherents greased the wheels of world commerce. Their backs were the foundation of industrial capitalism and their hands were its fuel. Therefore, the blues can be viewed as a permanent countermobilization against the constantly re-emerging plantation blocs of the world and their intellectual fountainhead in the South. Led by cultural rebels from a generation that witnessed the overthrow of the Reconstruction, the blues became the channel through which Southern working-class communities attempted to grasp the reality of a world turned inside out. The surreal nature of these events did not deter those communities from organizing an intellectual/cultural movement that shocked the world with its intensity. The world was also shocked by the fearlessness with which that movement tossed aside Victorian codes once women and men regained partial control over their bodies.[36] In *Blues Legacies and Black Feminism*, Angela Davis describes this as a revolution that redefined the global position of women:

> Through the blues, black women were able to autonomously work out – as audiences and performers – a working-class model of womanhood. This model of womanhood was based on a collective historical memory of what had been previously required of women to cope with slavery. But more important, it revealed that black women and men, the blues audience, could respond to the vastly different circumstances of the postslavery era with notions of gender and sexuality that were, to a certain extent, ideologically independent of the middle-class cult of "true womanhood." In this sense, as Hazel Carby has pointed out, the blues was a privileged site in which women were free to assert themselves publicly as sexual beings.[37]

Other shocks emerged from the emphasis upon veracity in a region where "the truth" was equated with death. As a symbol of freedom, the truth was spoken and sung, even if it was shrouded by metaphors, ever-changing terminology, African American vernacular English, triple entendres, and misdirection. The blues worldview enabled the construction of new communities, institutions, and social practices. This complex allowed the organic intellectuals, and their audiences, to systematically investigate and analyze the world around them. It gave them a constantly evolving language to discuss their freedom dreams, agendas, and plans.[38] Also, created within the blues tradition was a holistic, interdisciplinary, and indigenous approach to scholarship. Sites of specialization within this academic grid included the arts, political economy, history, anthropology, sociology, environmental studies, law, medicine, and geography. Yet, narrowly constructed scholarship continues to label this epistemology and its innovative, seamless, and iterative integration of theory, method, investigation, and practice as folklore, while simultaneously designating hyper-fantastic and mythological constructions of African American life as "social science."

Another reason for continued resistance to the philosophic contributions of the blues is its origins in forced labour. The agonies of the 1870s and the blues are permanently intertwined. The turmoil generated by the overthrow of the Reconstruction governments created homeless families and orphans. The former "slave catchers" now travelled the roads of the South looking for men and boys to kidnap for the levee camps, where a man could be killed for injuring a mule.[39] The levee hollers and those of the fields, prisons, docks, and streets were fully incorporated into the blues, and these hollers and chants are still heard in hip hop. Their very utterance signals both a sense of unity and a determination to push forward.[40]

The blues and the spirituals are not simply mechanistic responses to oppression. They are the conscious recodification of African and African American knowledge systems, soundscapes, spirituality, and social research traditions. This tradition developed numerous ethical stances that became foundations of an unofficial customary African American legal system that emerged in the midst of an officially lawless environment. Many blues songs have been labelled "cautionary folktales," when in actuality they are lessons, codes, and laws designed to uphold traditional values and foster group cohesion though an examination of personal, and collective, experiences, failures, and visions. Instead of adopting Victorian mores, the blues generation chose a form of realism that has since been used by following generations in times of crisis to restore their ethical foundation and historic development goals.

Blues geography places regional schools of working-class organic intellectuals at the centre of the production of geographical knowledge. Therefore, families, events, venues, work sites, travel, neighbourhoods, households, and prisons become critical sites in the construction and revision of theory, method, and praxis. Its pedagogy initially relied heavily upon various performance strategies, including songs, poetry, sermons, dance, music, and the visual and plastic arts. Empirical geographic investigations were passed between individuals, schools, audiences, and communities who often relied upon these insights for their survival. According to Muddy Waters (McKinley Morganfield), the geographical diffusion of the blues epistemology "just came down from nation to nation, you know, from the top of the blues thing that all black people were into."[41] In each new place, blues investigators launched studies of all aspects of daily life: nature, family, community, the state, capital, work, religion, culture, and love. According to Sterling Brown, blues folk poetry explored various African American intellectual traditions, from stoicism to self-pity, using a newly indigenous visual language greatly indebted to African aesthetic principles: "The gain in vividness, in feeling, in substituting the thing seen for the bookish dressing up and sentimentalizing is an obvious one and might tell us a great deal about the Blues."[42]

Legions of organic blues scholars emerged from the Lower Mississippi Valley and East Texas during the last decades of the nineteenth century. As they travelled from town to town, field to field, shack to shack, from cell to cell, and from the country to the city, they spread the blues with a missionary zeal. Living on a plantation near Drew, Mississippi, during the 1910s, Charley Patton was at the centre of a group of local musicians, organic intellectuals, who recodified existing folkloric and musical traditions for the purpose of interpreting, and responding to, new times and conditions. Although many older members were not recorded, the younger members went on to become pillars of black music and world music: Son House, Robert Johnson, Bukka White, Howlin' Wolf (Chester

Burnett), and Roebuck "Pop" Staples. These congregants were part of a regional network; a blues school of artists, social observers, and audiences. They produced musical and poetic dialogues that reaffirmed both the dignity and destiny of their community. This was the first blues university, and many more were to follow. Beginning with the release of Mamie Smith's "Crazy Blues" in 1920, the classic blues women of the black vaudeville circuit, particularly Gertrude "Ma" Rainey and Bessie Smith, built a massive audience.[43] The popularity of their recordings soon began to cross over rigidly enforced national, regional, racial, and ethnic boundaries. Blues literary, artistic, political, and academic schools blossomed from the 1930s to the present.[44]

Hip Hop as a Blues Movement

> Stop the Puerto Ricans and rural blacks from living in the city . . . reverse the role of the city . . . it can no longer be the place of opportunity. . . . Our urban system is based on the theory of taking the peasant and turning him into an industrial worker. Now there are no industrial jobs. Why not keep him a peasant?
>
> — Roger Starr, Director, Housing and Development Administration, City of New York, 1976[45]

Hip hop signalled the emergence of a new school of blues geography. It emerged, politicized, and was expressive of U.S. black and Latino communities whose very survival was threatened by the neo-plantation neo-liberal efforts to dismantle the welfare state. The international growth of hip hop was facilitated by the global expansion of the neo-liberal agenda. In the midst of the mid-1970s fiscal crisis, the New York City government adopted a regimentation program of planned shrinkage. Reductions in fire, police, transit, and sanitation services for impoverished black and Puerto Rican neighbourhoods resulted in a South Bronx that was perpetually on fire due to instances of arson inspired by speculators and landlords seeking to escape taxation. Although housing director Roger Starr was forced to resign, his statement was a clear articulation of a policy organized around the Mississippification of the South Bronx.[46] According to Tricia Rose, the organic intellectuals of the South Bronx and other parts of New York turned their planned isolation into its exact opposite, a global movement:

> Although these visions of loss and futility became defining characteristics, the youngest generation of South Bronx exiles were building creative and aggressive outlets for expression and identification. The new ethnic groups who made the South Bronx their home in the 1970s, while facing social isolation, economic fragility, truncated communication media, and shrinking social service organizations, began building their own cultural networks, which would prove to be resilient and responsive in the age of high technology. North American blacks, Jamaicans, Puerto Ricans and other Caribbean people with roots in other postcolonial contexts reshaped their cultural identities and expressions in a hostile, technologically sophisticated, multiethnic, urban terrain. Although city leaders and the popular press had literally and figuratively condemned the South Bronx neighborhoods and their inhabitants, its youngest black and Hispanic residents answered back.[47]

The generation that launched the blues cultural movement witnessed the transformation of a centuries-old dream of freedom, partially realized during the First Reconstruction, into a nightmare. Hip hop is at the centre of a monumental debate on the nightmare that followed the Second Reconstruction. However, when hip hop emerged in the 1970s, some observers argued both that the blues was dead within the African American community and that the blues had nothing to do with hip hop. Yet the blues has been abandoned, declared dead, and resurrected on so many occasions that the tradition has come to be defined by its generational rebirth. Richard Powell's observations are instructive:

> The term "blues" is an appropriate designation for this idea [humanism] because of its association with one of the most identifiable black American traditions that we know. Perhaps more than any other designation, the idea of a blues aesthetic situates the discourse squarely on: 1) art produced in our time; 2) creative expression that emanates from artists who are emphatic with Afro-American issues and ideals; 3) work that identifies with grassroots, popular, and/or mass black American culture; 4) art that has an affinity with Afro-U.S. derived music and/or rhythms; and artists and/or statements whose raison d'être is humanistic.
>
> Although one could argue that other twentieth century Afro-U.S. musical terms such as ragtime, jazz, boogie-woogie, gospel, swing, bebop, cool, rhythm and blues, doo-wop, soul, funk, go-go, hip-hop, or rap are just as descriptive as "the blues," what "the blues" has over and above them all is a breadth and mutability that allows it to persist and even thrive through this century. From the anonymous songsters of the late nineteenth century who sang about hard labour and unattainable love, to contemporary rappers

> blasting the airwaves with percussive and danceable testimonies, the blues is an affecting, evocative presence, which endures in every artistic overture made toward black American peoples.[48]

First, in a way similar to that of the original blues generation, the founding generation of hip hop witnessed the formal dismantling of a system of disenfranchisement, peonage, segregation, and terror after a four-decade-long national mobilization. However, by 1975, Northern African American, Southern African American, Jamaican, Barbadian, Puerto Rican, and other Caribbean youth found themselves amid the rubble and ruins of the South Bronx. Second, this "freedom generation" was the recipient of the intellectual fruits of the civil rights movement, the Black Power movement, the black arts movement, the anti-Vietnam War movement, and numerous anti-colonial movements. Third, they were also defined by the 1970s crises of war, poverty, recession, urban disinvestment, ghettoization, deindustrialization, and political repression.

The leading intellectuals working in the blues musical tradition critiqued this crisis while youths also responded by making, consuming, and performing hip hop. In 1971 Marvin Gaye recorded "Inner City Blues" ("Make me wanna holler . . . This ain't livin'! This ain't life!"), and the Last Poets recorded "True Blues I" on their historic album *This Is Madness*.[49] By 1973 Gil Scott-Heron had declared it "Winter in America" and Jamaican reggae intellectual Bob Marley had begun his incendiary examination of continued poverty and oppression, "Talkin' Blues," with the classic blues lyric "cold ground was my bed last night and rock was my pillow."[50] The following year, in a musical coup, James Brown proclaimed himself the "Funky President." Brown had been heavily influenced by the jump blues of Louis Jordan, the blues shouter Joe Turner, "Mr. Blues" Wynonie Harris, the gospel blues, and by the rhythm and blues/rock and roll king Little Richard. In the rapping tradition of Louis Jordan, Brown channelled the Union League demands of the First Reconstruction a century earlier. In his "danceable testimony," Brown argued that the black community was going to sink if it did not immediately secure land and factories:

> Stock market going up
> Jobs going down
> And ain't no funking
> Jobs to be found.
>
> Taxes keep going up
> I changed from a glass
> Now I drink out of a paper cup

It's getting bad . . .

People, people
We got to get over
Before we go under

Listen to me
Let's get together and raise
Let's get together
And get some land

Raise our food like the man
Save our money like the Mob
Put up a fight down on the job . . .

Change it![51]

The founding generation of hip hop also witnessed the re-emergence of neo-plantation thought upon the national stage. During the 1960s the Delta-based Citizens Council movement and its campaign of "massive resistance" quickly challenged the Second Reconstruction. This movement eventually led a significant portion of the white Southern electorate out of the Democratic Party. On these foundations arose what has been called "Racial Republicanism." A new national electoral alliance was created using the Southern strategy deployed by presidents Richard Nixon and Ronald Reagan. The regional linchpin was the fear of equality and integration felt by Northern, Western, and Southern whites.[52] Several observers have referred to the social philosophy of this movement as the "Delta writ large" and the "Mississippification" of the United States and the world.

This movement fostered deep racial and class divides, the upward redistribution of wealth, and sustained attempts to break off numerous social contracts: the New Deal; the War on Poverty; the Great Society; affirmative action; union shops; collective bargaining; the minimum wage; welfare; civil rights enforcement; employment programs; urban and rural assistance; social security; and health, safety, and environmental regulations. By the mid-1970s, many African American communities were experiencing severe rates of unemployment and homelessness due to federal disinvestment, deindustrialization, and the growing local fiscal crisis.[53]

The hip hop generation also witnessed brutal attacks on their leaders, organizations, and movements, culminating in the assassination of Reverend Martin Luther King Jr. in 1968 and the subsequent rebellions in more than one hundred cities.[54] This community came of age in a deteriorating human rights situation characterized by police brutality, racial profiling, rising rates of homicide, drug epidemics, draconian sentencing guidelines, felon disenfranchisement, and a rapid increase in the institutionalization of children and adults. Young black men were being described both as an "endangered species" and as predators. Rising rates of unemployment and incarceration, when combined with declining wage rates, led to family instability. All of these factors contributed to a dramatic deterioration in gender relations. Simultaneously, with their intellectual origins firmly planted in antebellum and neo-plantation scholarship, social scientists launched a new wave of black depravity studies. Once again, social theory participated in the renaturalization of white supremacist institutions and movements that simultaneously masked the structures of regional power while denying African American initiative, voice, and vision.[55]

Over the last century and a half, sociologists and historians have repeatedly attempted to label the Mississippi Delta as the national centre of black "primitivism." The 1970s witnessed the placement of this label upon the South Bronx – a community located in New York City, the capital of capital and one of the most urbanized regions of the world. Presidential candidate Jimmy Carter of Georgia toured the area during his 1976 campaign and argued that the community represented the federal abandonment of blacks and Latinos, the poor, urban areas, and the goals of the welfare state. Conversely, Ronald Reagan of California toured the South Bronx during his 1980 presidential campaign and, in classic plantation rhetoric, argued that the area's "primitiveness" demonstrated the need to abandon the welfare state and the communities dependent upon it because they created "welfare queens," criminals, and generalized moral corruption. Despite this confluence of events, several authors have claimed that there is no organic relationship between the blues epistemology, hip hop, and the specific crisis of the Second Reconstruction. One school views hip hop as a wholly new tradition produced to respond to the chaotic conditions of the postmodern, post-industrial, and neo-liberal world. Others argue that hip hop involves the global dispersal of a degenerative African American ethic. Another school argues that hip hop is a syncretic blending of African American and Caribbean traditions. In *The Black Atlantic*, Paul Gilroy suggests that hip hop culture grew out of "the cross-fertilisation of African American vernacular cultures with their Caribbean equivalents rather than [being] fully formed from the entrails of the blues. The immediate catalyst for its development was the relocation of Clive 'Kool DJ Herc' Campbell from Kingston to 168th Street in the Bronx."[56] What Gilroy does not address in this formulation is the intellectual turmoil within the U.S.-based blues tradition. Also unaddressed is the influence of this tradition upon Caribbean communities in the United States and upon the Caribbean itself.

We need a blues geography to understand one of the most pressing questions in the globalization and neo-liberalism debate: How deep are the roots of the blues, and where, if any, are its borders?

Several authors have suggested that due to its geographical and cultural location, the South can best be understood as the Northern Caribbean. Although there have been numerous aesthetic exchanges between Afro-diasporic communities in the Caribbean, the United States, Canada, and the United Kingdom, this process accelerated tremendously during the early decades of the twentieth century. By the 1920s the blues and blues-based musical movements had become intricately intertwined with Jamaican musical movements.[57] According to Steve Barrow, by 1950 big band jazz music on the island was being superceded by smaller bebop and rhythm and blues ensembles:

> Jamaicans, traveling to the States in search of work, caught this changing mood; large and powerful sound systems began playing the new music: [led by] Count Smith the Blues Buster. . . . Such sound systems operated in ghetto areas of Kingston, Jamaica's capital, and took the music to country districts. . . . Wynonie Harris and the New Orleans sound of Fats Domino and others, were among the favorites. During the later part of the 50s a decade-long musical war broke out between two of the most important sound systems: the Sir Coxsone Downbeat group led by Clement Dodd and the Trojan group led by Duke Reid. In an annual competition, the latter won the 1956, 1957, and 1958 title of "King of Sounds and Blues."[58]

Kool Herc fully introduced the mobile sound system of his youth to the South Bronx and played an instrumental role, as DJ, in erecting the rhythmic architecture of hip hop. As a cultural organizer, he facilitated the rise of the beat boys (also known as b-boys and Bronx boys) as an identity and as a social and cultural movement. What is often left out of received hip hop geography is that Kool Herc was thoroughly immersed in the blues tradition before he left Jamaica in 1967:

> Hip-Hop, the whole chemistry of that came from Jamaica, cause I'm West Indian. I was born in Jamaica. I was listening to American music in Jamaica and my favorite artist was James Brown. That's who inspired me. A lot of the records I played were by James Brown. When I came over here I just had to put it in the American style and a drum and bass. So what I did here was go right to the yoke. I cut off all anticipation and played the beats.[59]

The global significance of the aesthetic intervention of Brown and his collaborators is still poorly understood. According to Chuck D of Public Enemy, "Brown single-handedly took a lost and confused musical nation of people and bonded them with a fix of words, music and attitude. Well in this game of rap, the forefathers are Kool Herc, Afrika Bambaata, and Grandmaster Flash, and James Brown is the primary influence for them starting hip-hop in the first place."[60]

The great man tradition of argument, though, often hinders an appreciation of the exact contribution of Caribbean pioneers and of the audiences. For example, Afrika Bambaata helped build the Zulu Nation and hip hop into a fluid university system organized around a community-centred consciousness and the principles of "knowledge, wisdom, understanding, freedom, justice, equality, peace, unity, love, respect, work, fun, overcoming the negative to the positive, economics, mathematics, science, life, truth facts, faith, and the oneness of god."[61] This is not the only creative and intellectual link to the blues tradition and its First and Second Reconstruction agendas that gets excised from hip hop history. Caribbean immigrants share with African Americans a long tradition of plantation, colonial, working-class, and aesthetic criticism. Finally, due to regional biases, the conflated category "black New Yorker" makes invisible the powerful contributions made by black Southern migrants over the course of the nineteenth and twentieth centuries. Additionally, eliminating the contributions of Southern working-class migrants who came into the city during the freedom struggles of the 1950s, 1960s, and 1970s also eliminates the link between hip hop, the South, its social justice ethics, and the blues tradition. The blues and its extension, hip hop, are now defined by an international circuit in which all nations participate. However, the South remains the cultural centre of this tradition and of the central dilemmas that it attempts to address.[62]

Debates over "great men" did not fuel the globalization of hip hop. The children of those communities who worked to overturn segregation and colonialism formed an audience of peers internationally. Like the blues, the concern for global justice was embedded in hip hop early on. Even though some view the emphasis on first person, the "I," in the blues and hip hop as an expression of narcissism, that is not the case. The "I" is an expression of collectivity similar to the Jamaican Rastafarian use of "I and I." This "I is we" statement is prevalent in African and African diaspora philosophies; this expansive concept enabled these traditions to become central to the global dialogue on social justice.[63]

House of the Blues: The Structures of Geographic Knowledge

Settin' in the house with everything on my mind (2x)
Lookin' at the clock and can't even tell the time
Walkin' to my window and lookin' out of my front door (2x)
Wishin' my man would come home once more
Can't eat, can't sleep, so weak I can't walk the floor (2x)
Feel like hollerin' murder, let the police squad get me once more
They woke me up before day with trouble on my mind (2x)
Wringin' my hands and screamin', walkin' the floor hollerin' and cryin'
Catch 'em, don't let them blues in here (2x)
They shakes me in my bed, can't set down in my chair
Oh, the blues has got me on the go (2x)
They run around my house, in and out of my front door.
— Bessie Smith, "In the House Blues"[64]

Our discussion so far has focused on the organization of blues geography, its response to change, and its core ethics. The brief exploration that follows will examine this organic discipline in light of the four pillars of geographic knowledge outlined by David Harvey. First, cartography is a central foundation of geography and it is concerned with "locating, identifying, and bounding phenomena within a coherent spatial frame. It imposes spatial order on phenomena."[65] The practice of cartography is richly developed within the blues tradition in that these musics have created a massive archive of travelogues that capture social relations in an ever expanding number of places. Its global resonance has much to do with the focus of these sung travelogues, the unending African American working-class mission of avoiding social and economic traps, surviving multiple forms of heartache, and the existential search for loved ones and refuge. Every instance of blues music, literature, art, film, and criticism is concerned with mapping places and consciousness. Its very genres are often defined by their regional origins, and this practice has continued in hip hop. In 1926 blues poet Langston Hughes mapped the metaphoric wall that stood between African Americans and their freedom. His poem was resurrected by hip hop artist Scarface in 1993.[66] Both artists explore and compare the psychic destruction visited upon those forced to live behind the walls of racial enclosures, and both conclude that action is needed to tear down these walls:

As I Grew Older

And then the wall rose . . .
Rose until it touched the sky . . .

Shadow.

I am black.

My hands!
My dark hands!
Break through the wall!
Find my dream!
Help me to shatter this darkness,
To smash this night,
To break this shadow
Into a thousand lights of sun,
Into a thousand whirling dreams
Of sun!

– Langston Hughes, 1926

The Wall

I see my future and its coming in plain view
I blame myself, but mommy dear I blame you
Cause the world was fucked from the first
And havin' me only made the matters worse
. . .
Muthafuckin' dealin' after dealin', killin' after killin' . . .
The world's going straight to fuckin' Satan . . .
Damn, suicide is quicker

I try to break the wall, the wall keeps getting thicker . . .
I try to climb the wall, it's higher than a muthafucker
I wondering what that sound is
I'm having major trouble trying to walk around it
There ain't no getting up I'm trapped
I really should've dropped my muthafuckin' strap
Cause when I think about it now
I shouldn't have tried to climb the muthafucker
I should've broke the muthafucker down

– Scarface, 1993

Another central pillar of geographic knowledge is the measure of "space-time." Harvey, like Edward Soja, argues that space cannot be absolutely separated from time and vice versa. This statement emerged to challenge historians and social scientists who discuss periods without exploring the very different meaning of race, class, gender, and power in distinctive places. It also emerged in response to geographers and planners who discussed spaces without a consideration of time: social movements, emerging and fragmenting social structures, shifting social conditions, and competing forms of explanation. Those who attempt to delink time and space produce "dead and immovable structures of thought and understanding."[67] Conversely, "space-time" or "spatio-temporality" provides observers with tools to understand the dynamics of social transformation and the power of places. The social-spatial dynamic in blues geography enables us to understand how marginalized people in marginalized places, such as African Americans in the Mississippi Delta, the South Bronx, South Central Los Angeles, or New Orleans, are central to an understanding of the origins and evolution of neo-liberalism despite their exclusion from the critical literature on this very subject.

Another aspect of the social-spatial dynamic in blues geography is the remarkable practice of naming of periods in U.S. history according to the blues-based intellectual movements: Ragtime, the Jazz Age, the Swing Era, Bebop, post-Bop, the Rock and Roll Era, and the Hip Hop Era. This practice involves capturing shifts in consciousness, political economies, spatialization, and rhythm. In an address to the 1964 Berlin Jazz Festival, Rev. Dr. Martin Luther King Jr. captured the critical, yet unrecognized, relationship between blues aesthetic movements and global social transformation:

> God has wrought many things out of oppression. He has endowed his creatures with the capacity to create – and from this capacity has flowed the sweet songs of sorrow and joy that have allowed man to cope with his environment and many different situations. Jazz speaks for life. The blues tell the story of life's difficulties, and if you think for a moment, you will realize that they take the hardest realities of life and put them into music, only to come out with some new hope or sense of triumph. This is triumphant music.
>
> Modern Jazz has continued in this tradition, singing the songs of a more complicated urban existence. When life itself offers no order and meaning, the musician creates an order and meaning from the sounds of the earth which flow through his instrument.
>
> It is no wonder that so much of the search for identity among American Negroes was championed by Jazz musicians. Long before the modern essayists and scholars wrote of "racial identity" as a problem for a multi-racial world, musicians were returning to their roots to affirm that which was stirring within their souls.
>
> Much of the power of our Freedom Movement in the United States has come from this music. It has strengthened us with its sweet rhythms when courage began to fail. It has calmed us with its rich harmonies when spirits were down. And now, Jazz is exported to the world. For in the particular struggle of the Negro in America there is something akin to the universal struggle of modern man. Everybody has the blues. Everybody longs for meaning. Everybody needs to love and be loved. Everybody needs to clap hands and be happy. Everybody longs for faith. In music, especially this broad category called Jazz, there is a stepping-stone towards all of these.[68]

Another foundation of geographic knowledge is the concept captured by the terms place, territory, region, or locality. Geographers use several approaches to define these socially constructed places: physical attributes, function, administrative boundaries, political boundaries, and cultural attributes. With these approaches comes a strong tendency to naturalize existing boundaries. The relational regional approach demands that we distinguish regions, or places, based on a historical understanding of the processes that create distinctive identities, relations, and characteristics. For Anne Gilbert, distinctive regional identities and relations are constructed, and reproduced, through mobilizations and countermobilizations:

> The existence of a particular region is assumed to depend on the actual domination of certain social groups in the regional structure. If a group within this structure is strong enough to impose standardization in a certain area at a certain time, the regional entity emerges, and its differentiation from other areas is sharpened. . . . The regional whole comes from the power of certain groups to impose their values and norms upon the majority and the cultural solidarity necessary to the specification of an area.[69]

To comprehend this process, we must utilize a dynamic conception of how various regional blocs respond to, and anticipate, the general processes of uneven development. From the "St. Louis Blues" to the hip hop classic "Tennessee" by Arrested Development, tens of thousands of lyrical/musical regional analyses have emerged from schools of organic intellectuals operating within distinctive regional blues blocs. Artists and audiences within this tradition have sought to "impose their values and norms" by specifying the identity of a region. The words and thoughts of a demonized working-class youth were considered abhorrent by proponents of the uplift and assimilation models of social development. Yet the blues tradition works to provide refuge, affirmation, and inspiration. For example, in the 1930 song "Black Mountain Blues," Bessie Smith celebrates the "riffraff " and "rough elements":

> Back in Black Mountain, a child will smack your face. (2x)
> Babies cryin' for liquor, and all the birds sing bass.
> Black Mountain people are as bad as they can be. (2x)
> They use gunpowder just to sweeten their tea.[70]

Other intellectuals operating within the blues tradition have attempted to impose their will upon regions by making local conflicts sacred. For example, many blues songs commemorate local heroes, natural disasters, jewellery, trains, cars, new technologies, and every shack, village, block, field, public housing project, club, and prison within the region. This democratic approach to achieving sacred status allows places such as prisons, Parchman Farm in Mississippi and Sugarland in Texas, to enter into the African American pantheon of sacred sites. From the blues to hip hop, the imprisoned are not discarded as outcasts; rather, they are often considered witnesses to, and students of, a particular stage of regional reproduction and conflict. Also, the expressed desire to escape from the traps of particular places has made the place, the community, and the intellectual sacred. For example, the anthems of Robert Johnson, in 1936, and Tupac Shakur, in 1996, simultaneously analyze the daily reproduction of regional relations in the Mississippi Delta and urban America while imposing their sense of supernatural doom, sacredness, and triumph upon them.[71]

Hellhound on My Trail

I got to keep moving . . .
Blues falling down like hail
Blues falling down like hail . . .
And the day keeps reminding me
there's a hellhound on my trail
Hellhound on my trail . . .

– Robert Johnson

Changes

I see no changes wake up in the morning and I ask myself
Is life worth living should I blast myself?
I'm tired of bein' poor & even worse I'm black
My stomach hurts so I'm lookin' for a purse to snatch
Cops give a damn about a Negro
Pull the trigger kill a nigga he's a hero
Give the crack to the kids who the hell cares, one less hungry mouth on the welfare
First ship 'em dope & let 'em deal the brothers
give 'em guns step back watch 'em kill each other
It's time to fight back that's what Huey said
2 shots in the dark now Huey's dead.

– Tupac Shakur

The process of making communities sacred and significant beyond their value as commodities is a key aspect of what Harvey calls the "fourth pillar" to all forms of geographic knowledge; the question of "how people do and should understand the relationship to environment and nature."[72] During the rise of mercantile capital, nature was conceptualized as natural resources waiting to be discovered and exploited. African lands were resources to be exploited and Africans and their descendants were commodities to be sold and exploited. Harvey cites an ongoing debate within the World Bank over the question "Is geography destiny?" It is still argued in some quarters that black communities and African nations are geographically determined to fail. They are said to be zones of chaos and corruption absent the moral capacity for self-governance. They are said to be governed by either Afro-pessimism or an infectious underclass mentality. Consequently, the creation of stable black communities is viewed as the worst use of land. An external spark or role model must be found to help residents find the road to civilization. This spark is often said to be the dissolution of communities, the external administration of key institutions, and/or colonization.

Blues geography will look at and disclose the creation and preservation of stable and sustainable black working-class communities as one of the highest and best uses of land. The African American environmental ethic has been shaped by the treatment of families and communities as friable. Repeated violent enclosures and family separation also led to a broad definition of community and a desire to become intricately intertwined with sacred communal places. Nature occupies a sacred place in the doctrines of several denominations and religions. Also, historically, African Americans have been among the strongest and most consistent supporters of co-operative rural and urban land reform. In 1971 civil rights champion and blues promoter Fannie Lou Hamer outlined elements of the blues agenda that could have been written in 1871. In an essay, "If the Name of the Game Is Survive, Survive," she argued that the political victories in the South were only the first steps towards sustainability and social justice. Co-operative forms of development would be necessary to reach the "ultimate goal of total freedom":

> The concept of total individual ownership of huge acreages of land by individuals is at the base of our struggle for survival . . . individual ownership of land should not exceed the amount necessary to make a living. . . . Cooperative ownership of land opens the door to many opportunities for group development of economic enterprises which develop the total community rather than create monopolies that monopolize the resources of a community.[73]

The co-operative environmental ethic present among African Americans emerges from their centuries-long conflict with plantation capitalism. The most environmentally, and socially, destructive settlement and development form, plantation capitalism continues to imperil regions, nations, states, and continents in distinct ways. Their opposition to this militaristic model of rapid environmental degradation has fundamentally shaped African American identities. The blues tradition dialectically emerged from the attempt to create sustainable communities and regions within a political economy built upon the non-sustainable pillars of social fragmentation, economic monopoly, and racial, and ethnic, conflict. Scientific and technological advances built upon the sustainability ethic present in the blues environmental critique could limit the constant and competitive "overthrowing" of environmental conditions that Harvey has noted. The neoliberal advocacy of a weakened state and the plantation model of industrial and rural development necessitates the use of the blues and other indigenous, and populist, knowledge systems as foundations for innovative sustainablity theories, methods, and practices, and for new forms of interregional, and global, co-operation.[74]

Finally, in carving out a new role for geography, Harvey views the rise of analogic reasoning as providing an unprecedented opportunity for geography to function as a Rosetta stone between the disciplines:

> Analogic reasoning seeks connections and interrelations, pushes forward metaphors and underlying unities within disparate phenomena, seeks analogies to illuminate phenomena in one area by examination of another. Above all, it seeks translations between different modes of thought (often emanating from quite different institutions). It is profoundly open and avoids all the turf-wars and exclusions that typify a world dominated by purist and essentialist categories. . . . But for geographers to take advantage of this positionality, it is necessary to abandon essentialist attitudes (the negative effects of which are all too plain to see in other spheres of knowledge like multiculturalism, nationalisms, or gender studies.[75]

In many ways, the blues tradition captures several of the elements outlined here. It weaves together the four structural pillars of geographical knowledge into a coherent system of "geographic wisdom."[76] Globally, it is used to investigate disparate social phenomena based on a methodology that requires comparative study. However, the core of this tradition revolves around proceeding from a particular social position. Therefore, those who are marginalized based on their culture, ethnic, race, class, gender, and regional position find this epistemology and its analogic reasoning empowering. It enables them to reach inward to explore new depths while simultaneously allowing them to reach beyond enforced boundaries in order to unite with other demonized communities – the "wretched" of the earth.

While these ethical debates are central to the blues tradition, can we say the same for academic geographers? If they choose analogic reasoning to promote "emancipatory socio-ecological change," how will they avoid the essentialisms of racism, nationalism, and sexism? Harvey suggests that "geographical knowledges can be mobilized to humanistic ends" and away from the purposes of domination for which they are often used.

> The problem . . . is to take these forms of knowledge, appreciate the circumstances of their origin, evaluate them or translate them (with the aid of analogic reason) into different codes where they might perform quite different functions. . . . The construction of geographical knowledges in the spirit of liberty and respect for others, as for example in the remarkable work of Reclus, opens up the possibility for the creation of alternative forms of geographical practice, tied to the principle of mutual respect and advantage rather than to the politics of exploitation. Geographical knowledges can become vehicles to express utopian visions and practical plans for the creation of alternative geographies.[77]

With its focus upon "alternative and multiple definitions of rationality" and geography as a vehicle to "articulate the legitimate and frequently conflictual aspirations of diverse populations and so become embedded in alternative politics," this formulation is admirable. Yet the blues tradition does this and more.

Blues, blues pedagogy, and music-making use several forms of reasoning simultaneously: analogic, symbolic, dialectic, materialist, surrealistic, asymmetric, and utopian. In addition to being intertextual and polyphonal, the blues has a highly developed geographic critique embedded within it. Schools within the blues tradition have been concerned with crossing physical, national, cultural, and intellectual boundaries for over a century. Additionally, the question of translating and coding black experiences has long been a central focal point. A rich tradition of cartography exists to locate historical, actual, metaphorical, and imagined places. The blues method of measuring space-time is widely used to periodize both African American and U.S. history. The relational conception of region present in this tradition necessitates the examination of social hierarchy and social change. Finally, its geographic practices are premised on the need for co-operation, yet its conception of nature is highly politicized due to its focus on the utopian visions of the dispossessed. Is it "profoundly open"? Has it not been the soundtrack of successive waves of globalization for nearly a century?

It is unknown whether Harvey's formulation has space for the blues. It is clear that blues geography can incorporate his formulation. The blues is just one of many indigenous traditions that will reorder the disciplines during the coming century while contributing greatly to the expansion of global social justice. In a 1952 speech, "The Negro Artist Looks Ahead," Paul Robeson argued that an understanding and appreciation of black culture was a prerequisite to political progress. While this comment was directed towards whites within the United States, given the nation's current position in world governance it is equally instructive for the world at large. Robeson was one of the world's first global artists and intellectuals. His father, William, escaped slavery in North Carolina at the age of fifteen and later became a minister of an African Methodist Episcopal Zion church in New Jersey. A famed athlete, singer, actor, and lawyer, Robeson began to ally himself with campaigns for worker and peasant rights throughout the world during the 1930s. He served in the leadership of campaigns designed to defeat fascism, African colonialism, racism, and the waves of terror that defined the South. A student of world music and a historian of African American song, particularly the spirituals and the blues, Robeson was a profound social theorist. In his 1952 speech Robeson stated that attempts by progressives to subsume the blues tradition was a dangerous exercise and that new forms of non-hierarchical co-operation had to be imagined:

> Negroes have carried on an important struggle in the United States throughout the history of this country, even before there was any significant progressive movement in the U.S.: this is a lesson progressives must learn – and accept it as a duty and a privilege to join in the struggle. The progressive movement must understand with crystal clarity that the Negro people have never retreated or compromised in their aspirations, and progressives must follow a dynamic path with them. For if they do otherwise, they will find themselves conscious or unconscious allies of reactionaries and pseudo-liberals. Progressives must re-orient themselves to the qualitative change that has come about in the unalienable and rightful demand of the United States Negro. The Negro men and women of the United States want equality for everybody, in everything, everywhere, now.[78]

Robeson reminds us that all "local" knowledges are not the same, and that many are not even local. Some knowledges may be subject to interpretation while others provide the very rules of grammar. He also insists upon the power of history and upon the power of place as a warning to those who insist upon taking the disastrous road of conflating and juggling objects absent a knowledge of their mass, volume, and gravity. My purpose here is to begin a long-delayed discussion of blues geography. Existing disciplinary boundaries are still firmly arrayed against the advancement of comparative scholarship on knowledge systems, including the blues tradition. In this period of crisis, rather than selecting one approach, we should encourage and study many epistemological innovations. "By their fruits ye shall know them."

Notes

1 Mississippi Sheiks, "Sittin' on Top of the World (Version 3)," *Honey Babe Let the Deal Go Down: The Best of the Mississippi Sheiks*, Sony (1930, 2004).

2 Elijah Anderson, "The Code of the Streets," *Atlantic Monthly*, 273 (May 1994), pp.81–94; Michael Eric Dyson, *Is Bill Cosby Right? Or Has the Black Middle Class Lost Its Mind?* (New York: Basic Civitas Books, 2005); Jon Michael Spencer, *Self-Made and Blues-Rich* (Trenton, N.J.: Africa World Press, 1996).

3 Anwar Shaikh, "The Economic Mythology of Neoliberalism," in *Neoliberalism: A Critical Reader*, ed. Alfredo Saad-Filho and Deborah Johnston (London: Pluto Press 2005), p.41; Michael Hardt and Antonio Negri, *Empire* (Cambridge, Mass.: Harvard University Press, 2001).

4 David Harvey, *Spaces of Capital: Towards a Critical Geography* (New York: Routledge, 2001), p.211.

5 Ibid.

6 Clyde Woods, "Do You Know What It Means to Miss New Orleans? Katrina, Trap Economic, and the Rebirth of the Blues," *American Quarterly*, 57:4 (2005), pp.1005–18.

7 Ruth Wilson Gilmore, "'You Have Dislodged a Boulder': Mothers and Prisoners in the Post-Keynesian California Landscape," *Transforming Anthropology*, 8:1/2 (1999), pp.12–38.

8 No study would be truly complete without examining the intersectionality of demonization involving African Americans and other historically racialized groups: Native Americans, Chicanos, and Asian Americans as well as refugees and immigrants. See Laura Pulido, *Black, Brown, Yellow, and Left: Radical Activism in Los Angeles* (Berkeley: University of California Press, 2006).

9 Hilbourne Watson, *Globalization, Liberalism and the Caribbean: Deciphering the Limits of Nation, Nation-State, and Sovereignty under Global Capitalism* (Río Piedras: University of Puerto Rico, Instituto of Caribbean Studies, 1995).

10 See, for example, Katherine McKittrick, *Demonic Grounds: Black Women and the Cartographies of Struggle* (Minneapolis: University of Minnesota Press, 2006); Alexander Weheliye, *Phonographies: Grooves in Sonic Afro-Modernity* (Durham, N.C.: Duke University Press, 2005); Clyde Woods, *Development Arrested: The Blues and Plantation Power in the Mississippi Delta* (London and New York: Verso, 1998).

11 David Harvey, "Cartographic Identities: Geographical Knowledges under Globalization," paper presented at the 29th International Geographical Congress meeting, Seoul, South Korea, August 2000.

12 Sterling Brown, "The Blues as Folk Poetry," in *Jazz: The Jazz Cadence of American Culture*, ed. Robert G. O'Meally (New York: Columbia University Press, 1998), p.550. See also Benjamin Albert Botkin, *Folk-Say: A Regional Miscellany, 1929–32* (Norman: The University of Oklahoma Press, 1929), pp.324–39.

13 Howard Washington Odum, *Social and Mental Traits of the Negro: Research into the Conditions of the Negro Race in Southern Towns, a Study in Race Traits, Tendencies, and Prospects* (New York: Columbia University, 1910), p.19.

14 Les Blank et al., *The Blues Accordin' to Lightnin' Hopkins with the Sun's Gonna Shine* (El Cerrito, Cal.: Flower Films, 2004), videorecording.

15 John W. Frazier, Florence M. Margai, and Eugene Tettey-Fio, *Race and Place: Equity Issues in Urban America* (Boulder, Col.: Westview Press, 2003); Peter Jackson, "Geography, 'Race' and Racism," in *New Models in Geography*, ed. Nigel Thrift and Richard Peet (London: Unwin Hyman, 1989); John T. Metzger, "Planned Abandonment: The Neighborhood Life-Cycle Theory and National Urban Policy," *Housing Policy Debate*, 11:1 (2000); Jerome G. Miller, *Search and Destroy: African-American Males in the Criminal Justice System* (New York: Cambridge University Press, 1997); Susan Ruddick, "Constructing Difference in Public Space: Race, Class and Gender as Interlocking Sys-

tems," *Urban Geography*, 17:2 (1996); Brett Williams, "Poverty among African Americans in the Urban United States," *Human Organization*, 51:2 (1992).

16 Maxine Bacca Zinn and Bonnie Thornton, "Theorizing Difference from Multiracial Feminism," *Feminist Studies*, 22:2 (1996); Michael Omi and Howard Winant, *Racial Formation in the United States: From the 1960s to the 1990s*, 2nd ed. (New York: Routledge, 1994); Lynn Weber and Heather Dillaway, *Understanding Race, Class, Gender, and Sexuality: Case Studies* (Boston: McGraw-Hill, 2002).

17 Anne Gilbert, "The New Regional Geography in English- and French-Speaking Countries," *Progress in Human Geography*, 12:2 (1988); Edward W. Soja, *Postmodern Geographies: The Reassertion of Space in Critical Social Theory* (London and New York: Verso, 1989).

18 Harvey, *Spaces of Capital*, p.211.

19 Ibid., p.213.

20 Ibid., p.211.

21 Ibid.

22 Ibid., p.182.

23 Richard Wright, "Foreword," in *Blues Fell This Morning: Meaning in Blues*, ed. Paul Oliver (Cambridge: Cambridge University Press, 1960[1990]), pp.xii, xv.

24 Tony Mitchell, *Global Noise: Rap and Hip-Hop Outside the USA* (Middletown, Conn.: Wesleyan University Press, 2001); Michael Urban, "Getting by on the Blues: Music, Culture, and Community in a Transitional Russia," *The Russian Review*, 61 (2002).

25 United Nations, *The World Conference against Racism, Racial Discrimination, Xenophobia, and Related Intolerance*, 2001 <www.un.org/WCAR> (accessed June 20, 2006).

26 Brown, "Blues as Folk Poetry," p.550.

27 Michael W. Fitzgerald, *The Union League Movement in the Deep South: Politics and Agricultural Change during Reconstruction* (Baton Rouge: Louisiana State University Press, 1989).

28 Gerald David Jaynes, *Branches without Roots: Genesis of the Black Working Class in the American South, 1862–1882* (New York: Oxford University Press, 1986), p.295.

29 Fitzgerald, *Union League Movement in the Deep South*, p.170.

30 Ibid., pp.66–70, 216–25. See also Dorothy Sterling, *The Trouble They Seen: Black People Tell the Story of Reconstruction* (Garden City, N.Y.: Doubleday, 1976), p.454.

31 James W. Lowen and Charles Sallis, *Mississippi: Conflict and Change* (New York: Pantheon, 1974); Woods, *Development Arrested*.

32 J. Earl Williams, *Plantation Politics: The Southern Economic Heritage* (Austin, Tex.: Futura Press, 1972); Woods, *Development Arrested*, pp.246–70.

33 George L. Beckford, *Persistent Poverty: Underdevelopment in Plantation Economies in the Third World* (Morant Bay and London: Zed Books, 1983[1971]); Edgar Tristram Thompson, "The Plantation: The Physical Basis of Traditional Race Relations," in *Race Relations and the Race Problem: A Definition and an Analysis*, ed. Edgar Tristram Thompson (New York: Greenwood Press, 1968), pp.192–94.

34 Addison Gayle Jr., "Cultural Hegemony: The Southern White Writer and American Letters," in *Amistad I: Writings on Black History and Culture*, ed. John A. Williams and Charles F. Harris (New York: Vintage, 1970); Woods, *Development Arrested*, pp.51, 54. See also Alexis de Tocqueville, *Democracy in America*, ed. J.P. Mayer, trans. George Lawrence (Garden City, N.Y.: Anchor Books, 1969), pp.360–61. During the 1830s the French observer de Tocqueville described this intellectual transformation, making this conclusion concerning democracy in the plantation states: "They have, if I may put it this way, spiritualized despotism and violence. In antiquity men sought to prevent the slave from breaking his bonds; nowadays the attempt is made to stop him from wishing to do so."

35 David Harvey, *A Brief History of Neoliberalism* (New York: Oxford University Press, 2005).

36 Hazel V. Carby, "It Just Be's That Way Sometime: The Sexual Politics of Women's

Blues," *Radical America*, 20: 4 (1986); Angela Yvonne Davis, *Blues Legacies and Black Feminism: Gertrude 'Ma' Rainey, Bessie Smith, and Billie Holiday* (New York: Vintage Books, 1999).

37 Davis, *Blues Legacies and Black Feminism*, p.46.

38 Richard Wright, *Black Boy: A Record of Childhood and Youth* (New York: Harper and Row, 1969), p.253.

39 Alan Lomax, *The Land Where the Blues Began* (New York: Pantheon Books, 1993), pp.241, 251. According to Walter Brown, levee workers were paid weekly, monthly, semi-annually – or not at all: "All it was, was a privileged penitentiary. When you worked, you wasn't locked up. But other than that, it was just like a penitentiary. They paid you what they wanted you to have. If you didn't do it like they want, somebody's gon' beat you up."

40 Ibid., pp.xii–xiii. Lomax discusses the unifying and expansionary aspects of the blues: "[It] could be argued that the new song styles of the Delta symbolized the dynamic continuance of African social and creative process as a technique of adaption. Moreover, the birth of the blues and the struggle of its progenitors could be seen as a creative deployment of African style in an American setting, the operation of African temperament in new surroundings. In a sense African American singers and dancers made an aesthetic conquest of their environment in the New World. . . . The tales and songs return again and again to a few themes – to the grievous and laughable ironies in the lives of an outcast people who were unfairly denied the rewards of an economy they helped build. One black response to this ironic fact was to create the blues – the first satirical song form in the English language – mounted in cadences that have now seduced the world. It is heartening that both the style and inner content of this new genre are bold symbols of an independent and irrepressible culture."

41 Robert Palmer, *Deep Blues: A Musical and Cultural History of the Mississippi Delta* (New York: Viking Press, 1981), pp.101, 104.

42 Brown, "Blues as Folk Poetry," pp.540, 551, 545.

43 Daphne Duval Harrison, *Black Pearls: Blues Queens of the 1920s* (New Brunswick, N.J.: Rutgers University Press, 1988).

44 William Barlow, *"Looking up at Down": The Emergence of Blues Culture* (Philadelphia: Temple University Press, 1989); Palmer, *Deep Blues*, pp.64–66, 105–11; Charley Patton, "Down the Dirt Road Blues, " in *Charley Patton: King of the Delta Blues* (Yazoo Records, 2000).

45 Robert Fitch, *The Assassination of New York* (London and New York: Verso, 1993), p.viii.

46 Ibid., p.vii.

47 Tricia Rose, *Black Noise: Rap Music and Black Culture in Contemporary America* (Hanover, N.H.: University Press of New England, 1994), pp.33–34.

48 Richard Powell, "The Blues Aesthetic: Black Culture and Modernism," in *The Blues Aesthetic: Black Culture and Modernism*, ed. Richard Powell (Washington, D.C.: Washington Project for the Arts, 1989), pp.21–23.

49 Marvin Gaye, "Inner City Blues (Make Me Wanna Holler)," in *What's Goin' On* (Motown, 1971); Last Poets, "True Blues," in *This Is Madness* (Sunspots Records, 1971).

50 Gil Scott-Heron, "H20 Gate Blues," in *Winter in America* (TVT Records, 1973); Bob Marley, "Talkin' Blues," in *Talkin' Blues* (PolyGram Records, 1991 [1973]).

51 James Brown, "Funky President (People It's Bad)," in *Reality* (Polydor Records, 1974).

52 Williams, *Plantation Politics*, pp.46–56; Woods, *Development Arrested*, pp.183–246. Williams cites a 1962 article in the *Louisville Courier Journal* that heralded the birth of "Racial Republicanism": "The truth is that this Republican upsurge, if that is the word, owes much of its momentum to the very thing that has kept the South in one-party bondage for nearly a century – an unreasoning passion to maintain 'white supremacy' which the Supreme Court sometime ago made an outlawed relic of the past."

53 James C. Cobb, *The Most Southern Place on Earth: The Mississippi Delta and the Roots of Regional Identity* (New York: Oxford University Press, 1992), p.333. According to Cobb, "Many of the human and material extremes that were the keys to the Delta's identity either as the 'South's south,' or 'America's Ethiopia' were shaped not by its isolation but by pervasive global and national influences and consistent with interaction with a federal government whose policies often confirmed the Delta's inequities and reinforced its anachronistic social and political order as well. . . . The social polarization that is synonymous with the Mississippi Delta may be observed wherever and whenever the pursuit of wealth, pleasure, and power overwhelms the ideals of equality, justice and compassion and reduces the American dream to a self-indulgent fantasy. As socioeconomic disparity and indifference to human suffering become increasingly prominent features of American life, it seems reasonable to inquire whether the same economic, political, and emotional forces that helped to forge and sustain the Delta's image as the South writ small may one day transform an entire nation into the Delta writ large." See also Bill Barich, *Big Dreams: Into the Heart of California* (New York: Pantheon Books, 1994). According to California journalist Bill Barich, the Western and Southern alliance led by Nixon and Reagan did not result in the Californization of the South but, rather, in the Mississippification of California.

54 Cheryl Lynette Keyes, *Rap Music and Street Consciousness* (Urbana: University of Illinois Press, 2002), p.49.

55 Dorothy E. Roberts, *Shattered Bonds: The Color of Child Welfare* (New York: Basic Books, 2002); Bruce Western, Becky Pettit, and Paul Guetzkow, "Black Economic Progress in the Era of Mass Imprisonment," in *Invisible Punishment: The Collateral Consequence of Mass Imprisonment*, ed. Marc Mauer and Medea Chesney-Lind (New York: The New Press, 2002).

56 Paul Gilroy, *The Black Atlantic: Modernity and Double Consciousness* (Cambridge, Mass.: Harvard University Press, 1993), p.103.

57 William Ferris, "Folklore and Black Migration from Mississippi," in *Those Who Stayed*, ed. Doris Smith (Jackson, Miss.: Margaret Walker Alexander Research Center for the Study of the 20th Century African American, Jackson State University, 1990), p.18; Schomburg Center for Research in Black Culture, *In Motion: The African American Migration Experience* <http://www.inmotionaame.org/home>; Keyes, *Rap Music and Street Consciousness*, pp.41, 50.

58 Steve Barrow, "The Story of Jamaican Music: Liner Notes," in *Tougher Than Tough: The Story of Jamaican Music – Various Artists* (Mango Records, 1993).

59 Davey D., *Interview with Dj Kool Herc*, May 3, 2003 <www.daveyd.com> (accessed June 20, 2006).

60 Davey D., *Davey D's Hip Hop Corner: Chuck D. Speaks on James Brown*, May 3, 2002 <www.daveyd.com> (accessed June 20, 2006); Cliff White and Harry Weinger, "Are You Ready for Star Time?" liner notes in *James Brown: Star Time – 35th Anniversary Collection* (Polydor, 1991).

61 Universal Zulu Nation, "The Beliefs of the Zulu Nation" <http://www.zulunation.com>.

62 Kurtis Blow, "Kurtis Blow Presents the History of Rap, Volume 1," liner notes in *Kurtis Blow Presents the History of Rap – Various Artists* (Rhino, 1997).

63 Fred L. Hord and Jonathan Scott Lee, *I Am Because We Are: Readings in Black Philosophy* (Amherst: University of Massachusetts Press, 1995).

64 Davis, *Blues Legacies and Black Feminism*, p.297.

65 Harvey, *Spaces of Capital*, p.220.

66 Langston Hughes, *The Weary Blues* (New York: Alfred A. Knopf, 1926). See also Arnold Rampersad, ed., *The Collected Poems of Langston Hughes* (New York: Vintage, 1995); Scarface, "The Wall," in *The World Is Yours* (Rap-A-Lot, 1993).

67 Harvey, *Spaces of Capital*, pp.222–23.

68 Martin Luther King Jr., "Opening Speech at the 1964 Berlin Jazz Festival: Humanity

and the Importance of Jazz," 1964 <www.jazzforpeace.org/mlk1964.htm> (accessed June 20, 2005).

69 Gilbert, "New Regional Geography in English- and French Speaking Countries," p.217.

70 Chris Albertson, *Bessie* (New York: Stein and Day, 1972), p.175.

71 Barlow, *"Looking up at Down"*, p.47; Robert Johnson, "Hell Hound on My Trail," in *The Complete Recordings* (Sony, 1936 [1990]); Tupac Shakur, "Changes," in *Greatest Hits* (Death Row, 1998).

72 Harvey, *Spaces of Capital*, p.227.

73 Fannie Lou Hamer, "If the Name of the Game Is Survive, Survive," in *Fannie Lou Hamer Collection* (Tougaloo College, Ruleville, Miss.: Sept. 27, 1971).

74 Harvey, *Spaces of Capital*, p.229.

75 Ibid., pp.230–31.

76 Ibid., p.231.

77 Ibid., pp.232–33.

78 Paul Robeson, "The Negro Artist Looks Ahead," in *Paul Robeson Speaks: Writings, Speeches, Interviews, 1918–1974*, ed. Philip Sheldon Foner (Larchmont, N.Y.: Brunner/Mazel, 1978), pp.298–305.

Angel David Nieves

4

Memories of Africville

Urban Renewal, Reparations, and the Africadian Diaspora

> Building an awareness of the persons and events that helped shape Canada is critical to Canadian pride, identity, and sense of country. Hence, it is also critical that Canadians are engaged to ensure the commemorative integrity of the National Historic Sites of Canada. If our children's children are to share Canada's historical consciousness, we must take action to recognize and safeguard our collective heritage.
>
> — Parks Canada, *National Historic Sites of Canada: System Plan*, 2000

The history of forced removals across the globe is still being documented, recorded, and debated. In the United States and South Africa, that history has led many marginalized community groups to demand reparations for those acts of racial hatred and violence that destroyed their homes, places of worship, and schools.[1] Unfortunately, the field of historic preservation and conservation in the Americas is ill equipped to deal with the complex history of forced removal. Community-based demands placed on restorative justice through memory-making and commemoration often fall short and fail to respond to the pressures of competing interests. Meanwhile, the kinds of methodological tools now being developed (a methodological "tool box," as it were) to promote social justice through historic preservation increasingly rely on a better understanding of various theoretical and applied fields, including human geography, architectural history, black studies, and heritage studies. This chapter suggests a preliminary approach to the study of forced removal and lays out a means of "restorative social justice" through civic engagement.[2]

Restorative Social Justice and the Reparations Debate

In 2003 human rights activists, liberal educators, and policy-makers witnessed attempts by right-wing U.S. conservatives to create a national campaign for the dismantling of affirmative action by filing "friend of the court" briefs opposing the University of Michigan's use of racial preferences in admissions. By attempting to reverse the landmark U.S. Supreme Court *Regents of the University of California v. Bakke* case of 1978, which held that "race" can be a factor in college admissions, the state's machinery, if used in this way, would continue to deny responsibility for a history of legalized American apartheid (now officially outlawed) that created the conditions of white privilege and black subordination that we see all around us – a legacy particularly apparent when the American cultural landscape is seen as a system of interlocking racial hierarchies.[3] Some advocates of cultural diversity in historic preservation warn that the "multicultural approach to historic preservation must be maintained on the basis of equality," as Dirk H.R. Spennemann, a professor of "Cultural Heritage Management" in Australia, points out: "One can foresee that affirmative action, which established a preference over the Anglo-Saxon heritage, should be executed in order to make up for the losses incurred in the past." Still, he argues, "Despite affirmative action there needs to be a mechanism by which to ensure that the pendulum swings back a degree at a set date in order to avoid the denigration of yet another cultural minority: the Anglo Saxon."[4]

Some preservationists exhibit an inherent fear that the very process of uncovering the ideologies and practices of conquest and domination that have kept the "Other" in its place might somehow compromise the integrity of the U.S. National Register of Historic Places. Yet, despite the many efforts to correct the historical record and to work for further minority inclusion, these efforts rarely lead to economic or political empowerment for the disadvantaged or result in further victories in heritage politics. Hence, new strategies are needed. For example, those categories of historic and cultural resources associated with Africans in the diaspora need to be further expanded if we are to break free from the "standard and narrow definition of what is 'significant.'"[5] Formerly viable black U.S. communities and historic places, such as "Black Wall Street" in Tulsa, Oklahoma, Rosewood in Levy County, Florida, or Seneca Village in New York City's (or Frederick Law Olmstead's) Central Park – all destroyed in part by state terrorism – will remain marginalized as long as we continue to privilege structures built by and for European Americans. Similarly, in Canada, sites such as Hogan's Alley in Vancouver, Toronto's Caribbean Festival (Caribana), or Uncle Tom's Cabin in Buxton, Ontario, reveal similar histories of "benign neglect." Several of those sites share one thing in common: acts of racial hatred and state terrorism left few, if any, of the historic structures extant, and the sites remain unlikely candidates for preservation or historic designation given current policies and professional practice. Of over 76,000 properties listed on the National Register of Historic Places, only 823 are associated with African American heritage. Only 1 per cent of the total number of sites deal directly with diverse communities.[6] The numbers are not dissimilar in other parts of North America, including Canada.

Similarly, the reparations debate over chattel slavery continues to attract increased national and international attention, with conservative economists such as Walter Williams observing, "The problem, of course, is both slaves as well as their owners are all dead. What moral principle justifies forcing a white of today to pay a black of today for what a white of yesteryear did to a black of yesteryear?"[7] Solutions vary widely on either side of the debate. Some suggest the creation of a federal commission to study the era of slavery and the ensuing decades of discrimination and to make recommendations to Congress for repairs – much like Tulsa's Reparations Coalition or the Truth and Reconciliation Commission in post-apartheid South Africa. Others have argued for creating a national "slavery fund" to provide new resources to impoverished black communities. Meanwhile, some cities have attempted to respond to the debate. In 2002 Chicago, for example, passed a new law, the *Slavery Era Disclosure Ordinance*, requiring all corporations seeking business with the city to disclose whether they ever profited from the global slave trade. A similar California law requires insurers that did business during the slave era to examine their records and report the names of slaves they insured and the holders who owned the policies.[8] The debate over reparations is, in part, a struggle over the memory of the Civil War – a memory too often monopolized by "lost cause" advocates – rather than an acknowledgement of the collective amnesia regarding the nation's role in perpetuating human bondage. Meanwhile, the preservation of "place" and other cultural expressions that do not comprise intact historic buildings remains a troublesome concept for many contemporary preservationists, not only in the United States, but also at sites associated with the black diasporic experience throughout North America.

For scholars and activists in the community, the controversy over New York's African Burial Ground was a watershed event that contested traditionally white cultural resource management practices. There, in 1991, workers excavating foundations for new government buildings uncovered a six-acre cemetery and the well-preserved remains of slave and free blacks from the colonial period. However, little of the African Burial Ground controversy seemed to engage preservationists as to the site's possible importance to those African Americans rallying for the reparations movement, or as a means of spotlighting black diaspora history through new preservation strategies. Despite attempts to preserve the entire burial-ground site and to forestall further desecration of the remains, the dual forces of property and profit prevailed, and only a small section of the site was preserved.

Ultimately, we must ask ourselves if historic preservation advocacy, broadly defined, can act as a vehicle for social justice and as a catalyst for community redevelopment as we struggle to understand – perhaps even come to terms with – our historical responsibility vis-à-vis the global slave trade and the resulting African diaspora. Can the field of historic preservation provide viable solutions in a national and international movement for reparations – not only for African Americans but for other marginalized racial and ethnic groups? Ned Kaufman, founder of the Place Matters project in New York City, also questions preservation practice and the assignment of historical significance. Kaufman asks, "Can a non-traditional preservation practice evade or subvert the underlying ideology of heritage and present a more genuinely inclusive, or even oppositional, cultural inheritance? One way to do so might be to oppose historic preservation's celebratory tendencies by focusing attention on some of the deplorable episodes of injustice in our past."[9] Kaufman provides a less than desirable strategy for evading preservation's celebratory tendencies when he argues that by extending celebratory tendencies "to new subjects that expand society's cultural inheritance," a "*quiet means*" can be justified. He continues: "As long as the historical themes in question do not challenge majoritarian views of what deserves celebration, upset the balance of the historical record or threaten important political or economic interests, this sort of progress gains the support of preservationists and the general public."[10] Instead of proceeding quietly, as Kaufman argues, might not proponents of cultural diversity question whether a National Register of African American Historic Places should be established because the National Register, as we know it, does not adequately recognize African American historic places? Lacking such a register, preservationists will continue to overlook sites across the United States and Canada that are critical to our study of the impact of the global slave trade.

Despite a genuine belief that the *National Historic Preservation Act of 1966*, along with its 1980 and 1992 amendments, sets the stage for a greater appreciation of historic resources of state and local significance, African American sites remain marginalized. Projects such as Weeksville in Brooklyn, New York, the Mt. Auburn neighbourhood in Cincinnati, Ohio, or the Maggie Lena Walker Home in Richmond, Virginia, reflect the continued emphasis of the national historic preservation programs on the need for sites that contain what some have labelled "tangible remains of history."

But what happens to sites with "little pure architectural integrity" or with no physical remains whatsoever?[11]

Unfortunately, U.S. architectural history continues to be driven by matters of style and technical analysis of building details instead of considerations that include the shaping of our built environment by the concept of race – which I argue is most significant when considering new ways of protecting and preserving a black past.[12] Dwight T. Pitcaithley, chief historian of the National Park Service (NPS), provides us with a "reminder of how ideas about race have influenced the preservation of places in the past and how [race] can affect, in both positive and negative ways, the interpretation of historic sites today." He suggests: "By understanding how past and present generations have interpreted the past through the lens of race, practitioners of public history can better determine how historic sites should be interpreted to present and future generations."[13]

The National Park Service's *Taking the Train to Freedom: Special Resource Study* has forced many preservationists to begin rethinking the impact of race on historical interpretation. In 1990 the U.S. Congress authorized the NPS to conduct a study of the Underground Railroad, especially its routes and operations, in order to preserve and interpret this important aspect of U.S. history. Researchers explored many alternative routes in an effort to determine the significance of sites spread out over hundreds of miles from Canada to the Caribbean. Some of those involved even suggested the creation of a new national park system unit to commemorate the sites. Luckily, many sites remain that meet established criteria for designation as national historic landmarks. But what of those places that no longer exist but remain significant to African Americans? What about sites that establish important linkages between the United States and Canada and Mexico?[14]

One now vanished "place" that remains controversial, both in the United States and Canada, is a little-used green area called Seaview Park in Halifax, Nova Scotia. It is a place that holds a grand vista of Halifax's Bedford Basin and its surrounding shores. Many tourists come to Seaview Park to view the Basin's western shore, where the Duc d'Anville arrived with the remnants of his French invasion fleet just a few years prior to Halifax's founding. But a sun-dial-styled monument stands in the centre of the Park to commemorate something very different: the names of the original black families of "Africville" who once lived on the site of Seaview Park – family names that live on in Halifax even today.

Africville: Nova Scotia's Forgotten History of Slum Clearance

> There is a little frequented part of the City, overlooking Bedford Basin, which presents an unusual problem for any community to face. In what may be described as an encampment, or shack town, there live some seventy Negro families. . . .
>
> The citizens of Africville live a life apart. On a sunny, summer day, the small children roam at will in a spacious area and swim in what amounts to be their private lagoon. In winter, life is far from idyllic. In terms of the physical condition of buildings and sanitation, the story is deplorable. Shallow wells and cesspools, in close proximity, are scattered about the slopes between the shacks.
>
> There are no accurate records of conditions in Africville. There are only two things to be said. The families will have to be rehoused in the near future. The land which they now occupy will be required for the further development of the City.[15]

The making of place by marginalized or subaltern groups in Canada, and their subsequent erasure due to race-based governmental heritage policy, are significant forces: they allow us to understand how the nation has inscribed its colonial rule in spatial terms. Theorist Katherine McKittrick, in *Demonic Grounds: Black Women and the Cartographies of Struggle*, describes the "absented presence" of blacks in Canada, with their historical lives constantly being rewritten and presented as "new" in varying historical narratives. She writes, "The geographies of black Canada . . . are not simply de-centering colonial and national geographies; rather these black geographies cite a spatial terrain that makes available a place – and places – to produce and/or underscore varied responses to geographic domination."[16] Previous academic scholarship on Africville has not yet moved us beyond the disciplinary confines of social history, or the social sciences, and taken into account the once extant buildings as spaces of self-empowerment. Examining how space and place might complicate, or even question, our understanding of the importance of commemorating Africville may lead us to a more fully realized and social justice–based preservation practice.

Africville was a small settlement established by former American slaves shortly after the War of 1812. Some of Halifax's oldest families descend from men and women who fled slavery in the United States via the Underground Railroad, arriving throughout the region in the late eighteenth and early nineteenth centuries. While many were descendants of blacks who were either British Empire Loyalists or escaped American slaves, the settlement also housed Maroons from Jamaica and refugees from the United States who settled the barren farmlands of Halifax County.

During the American War of Independence, the British, in an attempt to bolster their flagging armies, made a promise to enslaved blacks: they offered the blacks their freedom in exchange for military service. Some 20,000 blacks accepted the British offer. As recruits were joining the British side, the U.S. Congress, reversing a previous decision, responded by allowing free blacks to enlist. The war later turned against the British and, with the 1783 signing of the Treaty of Paris, the United States gained its independence from British rule. That same year, 5,000 U.S. blacks – roughly two-thirds of them free, and one-third who came as property – crossed the border into Canada. For these United Empire Loyalists, freedom meant land and a place to call "home." The promise of a comparatively utopian existence, with a black population large enough to maintain cultural identity and secure enough to raise families, marked the beginnings of Maritime black Loyalist settlements throughout the region.

Unfortunately the 1783 black maritime settlers received inadequate compensation – or none at all – for their service on the side of Britain in the war. A tradition of white European privilege, power, and racism infected the administration and distribution of promised land grants. Quality lands were awarded to prominent whites and war officers. The "lucky" black settlers who did receive land were generally stuck on small, rocky, marginal, and often waterless allotments. A full four years after arrival, most blacks, even the experienced farmers, found themselves landless, fighting bureaucracy, and increasingly dependent on low-paying manual labour jobs. Segregated settlements became the basis of an evolving British ideology that saw "non-white" peoples as belonging to a lower level of civilization.[17] A black underclass was forming, and with racial segregation taking a firm hold, white resentment over the acceptance by blacks of subsubsistence wages (thereby freezing whites out of employment) led to town riots, destruction of black property, and calls for the "removal" of the "migrants."

Facing growing hostility, early Africville founders William Brown and William Arnold purchased Halifax City properties from white merchants in the 1840s. The families that lived in this small, isolated community numbered eighty in the census of 1851. By 1854 nearby congregations formed the African Baptist Association, at the centre of which was their new church. While the majority of Halifax's black population did not live in Africville, it was home to those who wanted to live in privacy, relatively free from the racist attitudes of the predominately white population.[18] The name "Africville" first appears in the 1860s in several petitions to the government and in some land deeds. Railroad documents around 1860 referring to business dealings in the area used the phrase "African village," and the first reference to the settlement as Africville appears in 1867 minutes of the Halifax City Council.[19]

Africville's residents experienced the direct and severe effects of racial discrimination at the hands of city officials who placed little value on their interests and concerns. As a result, essential institutions and facilities that other Halifax neighbourhoods rejected were placed in Africville – Rockhead Prison (1853), the city's night soil disposal pits (1858), an Infectious Disease Hospital (during the 1870s), a Trachoma Hospital (1903), and, finally, an open city dump and incinerator (in the early 1950s). The Nova Scotia Railway Company constructed the Bedford Basin track, which ran parallel to Campbell Road and passed through Africville. The city encouraged industries to locate on the site and habitually failed to install water and sewage services, or streetlights.

With its stigma as a destination for unwanted industry and its lack of public services, Africville gained the reputation of a dirty, lawless slum. The lack of adequate fire or police protection not only reflected the city's serious neglect but also inspired plans for redevelopment. As early as 1915 the City maintained, "The Africville portion of Campbell Road will always be an industrial district and it is desirable that industrial operations should be assisted in any way that is not prejudiced to the interests of the public; in fact, we may be obliged in the future to consider the interests of industry first."[20] Undoubtedly the presence of railway tracks in close proximity to waterfront property increased the importance of Africville's land as a way of expanding the city's tax base and promoting the area to local businesses as an ideal industrial site. The municipality acquired property to the south, east, and west of the black community, putting the city into a favourable bargaining position with industries seeking new land deals.[21]

A 1945 civic planning commission began preparations for postwar renewal projects to further develop Halifax. In 1947 the area was rezoned, and the city council approved the designation of Africville as industrial land.[22] In the aftermath of two major fires – in 1947 and 1957 – city planners made clear their intentions to raze the area where Africville stood; this despite countless petitions filed by residents calling for much-needed improvements.

In hindsight residents agree that many mistakes were made concerning Africville's preservation, long before the bulldozers arrived to destroy the neighbourhood. Community activist and former resident Irvine Carvery recalls, "It started with the building of a railroad which split our community down the middle. After that, there was an infectious disease hospital built. . . . We had fertilizer plants . . . And the last thing to come to Africville was in 1955 with the city dump being located 300 metres from the nearest home."[23]

Ignoring the resistance of the Africville community, Halifax expropriated the townsite, and family after family was forced to accept offers from the city to move out to alternative housing. In the mid-1960s bulldozers were sent in and the community was razed to the ground. Not only the houses, but also the means of livelihoods, including the successful local stores and businesses, and, finally, even the church – the centre of community life – were all destroyed in the dead of night. Residents were shipped off to slums or public housing. Many of them were given less than $500 in compensation; their personal belongings were transported to the new locations in city garbage trucks. By the end of 1967 the neighbourhood had literally disappeared from the map.

The community had been levelled with the understanding that the sort of improved living conditions envisioned by urban and social planners would be offered elsewhere. The *Stephenson Report* (1957), which called for Africville's removal, stated, "Despite the wishes of many of the residents, it would seem desirable on social grounds to offer alternative housing in other locations within the city."[24] And despite decades of continued neglect, government officials promised better model homes, jobs, and economic opportunities.

Canadian legislation of the period attempted to defend the relocation of residents, using the legality of social betterment for the greater good as a kind of moral foundation for "slum clearance."[25] Halifax city officials had consulted with Albert Rose, a prominent urban planner from Toronto, and a mixed group of liberal Nova Scotian volunteers to devise a scheme for Africville's relocation. They recommended, unfortunately, that the city buy out Africville's residents, move them into public housing, and raze the entire community. Officials and urban planning experts thought that relocation and urban development could "cure" housing considered to be "substandard." Sociologist Donald H. Clairmont recalls that period in North America: "The least advantaged and poorest were being moved all over the place – from the Arctic, to the slums of St. Louis and Boston, to Halifax." The issue of resettlement, he says, "was couched in terms of new opportunities for people and a golden era of beautiful cities. The urban planners leading the parade suffered from considerable hubris."[26]

At the time Africville was not seen as laden with "value" – its fate was determined by outsiders who knew little of its importance in the larger history of a U.S. black and Africadian shared past. As scholar Jennifer J. Nelson points out, legal decision-making too often relies entirely on a form of social history that perpetuates racist practices with designations of terms such as "slums" as categories synonymous with blackness and therefore worthy of regulatory measures.[27] The City of Halifax had already predetermined the fate of Africville, and its residents' relocation was inevitable. It was not until the 1970s and early 1980s that national, provincial, and municipal governments would enact legislation to protect buildings considered worthy of historic designation. By the 1970s preservationists began to use a scoring system, based on an established and legally sanctioned value-based judgment model for determining the fate of buildings nominated as historic structures. If a building scored high during its evaluation, it was saved from the wrecking ball. If it scored low, it was not normally saved.

In 1951 the Royal Commission on National Development in the Arts, Letters and Sciences noted a great imbalance in the commemorative program of the Historic Sites and Monuments Board of Canada (HSMBC) and urged that more attention be paid to historic preservation. In 1953 the *Historic Sites and Monuments Act* established the HSMBC by statute, enlarged its heritage mission, and gave it increased resources for public projects. An amendment passed in 1955 specified HSMBC's power to recommend national designation for buildings by reason of their age or architectural design.[28] However, it remained to be determined how those buildings seemingly outside of any national value could yet be deemed worthy of preservation.

As in instances of postwar urban renewal in the United States, it was only after residents had settled elsewhere that they fully realized what they had lost: the heart of their community life, their circle of support, and the place where they had a strong sense of belonging. Inspired by the Black Power movement in the States, community leaders called for immediate action. Community members spoke out against the injustice that had been committed against them – soon realizing that their very survival was in jeopardy, much as Africville's had been. In 1982, frustrated by their isolation, two former residents, Debbie Dixon and Brenda Steed, formed the Africville Genealogical Society.

As part of that Society's work, since 1982 surviving citizens have been gathering annually in July at Seaview Park and continuing their efforts to recover the history of the community. Seaview Park has become the rallying point for Nova Scotia's black community, with activists like Irvine Carvery urging the City of Halifax to settle land claims with the former residents of Africville. Interestingly, Halifax is now considering settling those claims, in part, by rebuilding the Seaview African United Baptist Church, which had long stood as the symbolic centre of the community. Former community leaders, including Carvery, now argue that housing should also be rebuilt on site as a form of reparations to the surviving residents of Africville and their descendants.

Given that mainstream preservationists often consider replicas and reproductions to be an "inferior 'brand' of preservation or not preservation at all," what do communities like Africville – bereft of any surviving artifacts and caught up in the struggle over reparations – decide if offered an opportunity to redevelop their lost communities? (Interestingly, Antoinette Lee of the United States Park Service engages with the "heresy" of the building replica, contending that "replicas are a common way for diverse cultural groups to create environments that are familiar and comfortable."[29]) Indeed, a few former residents want the city to rebuild all eighty of Africville's lost residences as part of its reparations settlement.

The preservation field cannot continue to uphold a set of standards that fails to recognize the unique cultural heritage of minority populations. The struggle over reparations provides us with an opportunity to move beyond the strict standards outlined by government bodies in the United States and Canada and towards a more inclusive dialogue across cultural divides. At the same time, it allows us to propose a more critically engaged interdisciplinary methodology. Developing an alternative methodology adapted to grasp the multiple meanings of "difference" in the North American cultural landscape and concurrently articulating a new model for historic preservation require new modes of interpretation. We must first of all begin to rethink how meaning is inscribed in the landscapes of marginalized groups in North American society, and in particular how black cultures have used their everyday spaces to establish their collective identities in the face of racialized oppression. By examining the embedded history of these cultural landscapes, we can better understand how historical meaning is layered. This approach also suggests the importance of a re-examination and re-analysis of documented sites related to Africans in and across the diaspora; and it should permit us to focus on everyday working-class spaces as sites of intentional place-making. A renewed politics of preservation in the United States and Canada requires such thinking outside the academy and outside long-established government guidelines. Such politics not only underscores local struggles but could also potentially highlight alternative forms of heritage preservation, as witnessed in a film such as Dana Inkster's *Welcome to Africville,* which reimagines and critically repositions the history of this space through queer cultures.[30] How might the "queering" of other sites across Canada, like Africville, lead us to more complex spatial narratives about the Africadian experience across the diaspora? The possibilities for further debate and discussion are limitless, but they are irrelevant if we do not include the voices of former community members and their relatives in our preservation efforts.

Pierre Nora, in *Between Memory and History: Les Lieux de Mémoire*, warns that we are in a critical moment in our own history as sites of memory continue to be destroyed in the wake of industrial growth and expansion. He suggests that "a process of decolonization has affected ethnic minorities . . . that until now have possessed reserves of memory but little or no historical capital."[31] Helping to define what is significant and important to minority populations remains a challenge. For example, Patricia L. Parker, co-author of "Guidelines for Evaluating and Documenting Traditional Cultural Properties," a National Register publication, found that American Indians have long argued that traditional cultural properties might be kept on a "parallel register" rather than on the National Register and held to different standards of evidence.[32] Perhaps turning to American Indian sources might provide additional answers: a comparative ethnographic study of black and Native sites, with local community informants, could suggest guidelines for this "parallel register."

In *The American Mosaic: Preserving a Nation's Heritage*, Antoinette Lee outlines the factors that contribute to what society deems worth preserving. She writes:

> Historical knowledge, interest in architectural styles and construction methods and perceptions about threat to the environment all contribute to what is studied and valued in the built environment. Decisions about significance are also a result of the kinds of individuals participating in the preservation process. Family background, professional training and personal interests influence judgments about what is important. Access to financial resources and to the political process are also important factors in what is ultimately saved.[33]

For both Lee and Kaufman, a major threat to advancing cultural diversity in preservation practice is the divisive effect that heritage politics can have when an emphasis on specific ethnic or racial experiences masks shared historical experiences that could otherwise help to unite disparate groups. Other threats may be found in the casual conceptualizations of heritage by historians such as David Lowenthal, who writes, for example:

> African American physical realms are not ethnically distinctive in recognizably Old World ways; many Chinatowns are little more than Hollywood variants; most Native American villages forget or forgo ancestral forms. . . . It is vital to celebrate local diversity. But for minority impress, we must look to other realms of culture – worship, foods, social traits, the arts. There,

> more than in building or landscape, ethnic America displays a dynamic living heritage.[34]

If Lowenthal's assertions had been fully accepted, the 2002 publication of the National Park Service's *Teaching Cultural Heritage Preservation: A Course Outline* might not have made an important first step.[35] Despite the Park Service's efforts to send out the course outline to hundreds of schools and lay practitioners, minority colleges and universities have yet to respond by initiating such courses in significant numbers.[36] That should alone make us reflect on cultural, academic, and activist work on preservation and history – in particular how this work is relevant to people of colour. Indeed the question of preservation and history is vital to Africans in the diaspora who, as in the case of Africville, continue to lose sites of cultural and social significance through neglect or continued forms of racial violence and state terrorism.

Our responsibility as practitioners and activists is clear – we should ensure that cultural groups articulate what resources are important to them, how resources should be protected, and who should be empowered with the management of those resources.[37] These may appear to be basic issues of heritage culture, but they are issues that will remain marginalized if we persist in ignoring race in preservation practice. A broader methodological framework, one that includes some of the aspects I have outlined as important to cultural preservation in communities of colour across the African diaspora, takes us beyond the basic historical narrative of removal, relocation, and segregationist public policy.

Africville, as a case study, advances new political avenues for thinking about contemporary preservation. In Africville the community buildings, like the Seaview African United Baptist Church, were destroyed, and local history was made "visibly absent." The desires and strategies expressed by local black communities in Halifax, in favour of rebuilding and commemoration, provide an example of a way of reimagining – and therefore respatializing – the racial landscape in and across the African diaspora. We can no longer accept the ways in which the academy, the state (through heritage policy), and preservation practitioners who are "landscaping blackness out of the nation" continue to "put blackness out of sight" and overlook the possible role of a social justice framework in our professional and personal lives.

Notes

1 James L. Gibson, "Truth, Reconciliation, and the Creation of a Human Rights Culture in South Africa," *Law & Society Review*, 38:1 (2004), p.6.

2 Ellen Hirzy, "Mastering Civic Engagement: A Report from the American Association of Museums," *Mastering Civic Engagement: A Challenge to Museums*, ed. Freda Nicholson and W. Richard West (Washington, D.C.: American Association of Museums, 2002), p.9; Nicholas Tavuchis, *Mea Culpa: A Sociology of Apology and Reconciliation* (Palo Alto, Cal.: Stanford University Press, 1991).

3 "Spinning Race," *Newsweek*, Jan. 27, 2003, p.27; Sherene Razack, ed., *Race, Space, and the Law: Unmapping a White Settler Society* (Toronto: Between the Lines, 2002), pp.5, 7, 9.

4 Dirk H.R. Spennemann, "Multicultural Resources Management: A Pacific Perspective," *Historic Preservation Forum*, January/February 1993, p.25.

5 Antoinette Lee, "Cultural Diversity in Historic Preservation," *Historic Preservation Forum*, 7:1 (January/February 1993), pp.28–41.

6 Ned Kaufman, *Cultural Heritage Needs Assessment, Draft Report* (Washington, D.C.: National Park Service, 2004), p.1.

7 Quoted in Manning Marable, "In Defense of Black Reparations," *ZNet Magazine*, Oct. 30, 2002 <www.zmag.org/sustainers/content/2002–10/30marable.cfm> (accessed Oct. 12, 2005).

8 "Slavery Disclosure Time," *Newsweek*, Jan. 27, 2003, p.11.

9 Ned Kaufman, "Speaking of Places: Heritage and the Cultural Politics of Preservation," *Places,* 11:3 (Winter 1998), p.59. See also Kaufman, *Cultural Heritage Needs Assessment*.

10 Kaufman, "Speaking of Places," p.60.

11 Antoinette J. Lee, "Discovering Old Cultures in the New World: The Role of Ethnicity," in *The American Mosaic: Preserving a Nation's Heritage*, ed. Robert E. Stipe and Antoinette J. Lee (Washington, D.C.: US/ICOMOS, 1987), p.202.

12 Ibid., pp.202–03.

13 Pitcaithley quoted in Paul A. Shackel, *Memory in Black and White: Race, Commemoration, and the Post-Bellum Landscape* (New York: Altamira, 2003), p.xiii.

14 Shannon Ricketts, *The Underground Railroad in Canada: Associated Sites* (Ottawa: Historic Sites and Monuments Board of Canada, 1998), p.2.

15 Jennifer Jill Nelson, "The Space of Africville: Creating, Regulating, and Remembering the Urban 'Slum,'" in *Race, Space, and the Law*, ed. Razack, p.212.

16 Katherine McKittrick, *Demonic Grounds: Black Women and the Cartographies of Struggle* (Minneapolis: University of Minnesota Press, 2006), pp.94, 98.

17 Bridglal Pachai, "Before Africville: The Black Presence in Nova Scotia," *Africville: A Spirit That Lives On* (Halifax: Mount Saint Vincent University, 1989), p.22.

18 Africville Genealogy Society, *The Spirit of Africville* (Halifax: Formac Publishing, 1992), p.39.

19 Ibid., p.41.

20 Ibid., p.43.

21 Donald H. Clairmont and Dennis William Magill, *Africville: The Life and Death of a Canadian Black Community* (Toronto: Canadian Scholars' Press, 1999), pp.93–96.

22 Ibid., p.99.

23 "Africville Named Historic Site in Halifax," CBC News <www.cbc.ca/stories/2002/07/05/Africville020705> (accessed Oct. 12, 2005).

24 Gordon Stephenson, *A Redevelopment Study of Halifax, Nova Scotia* (Halifax: Corporation of the City of Halifax, 1957).

25 Nelson, "Space of Africville," pp.224–25.

26 Barbara Stewart, "Long Razed, Settlement Not Forgotten" <www.boston.com/news/world/articles/2005/01/02/long_razed_settlement_not_forgotten> (accessed Oct. 12, 2005).

27 Nelson, "Spirit of Africville," p.232.

28 Historic Sites and Monuments Board of Canada, Parks Canada <www.pc.gc.ca/clmhc-hsmbc/clmhc-hsmbc/clmhc-hsmbc1_E.asp> (accessed July 3, 2006). See also Thomas H.B. Symons, *The Place of History: Commemorating Canada's Past* (Ottawa: The Royal Society of Canada, 1997).

29 Antoinette J. Lee, "Multicultural Dimensions to the Nation's Cultural Heritage," *History News: The Magazine of the American Association for State and Local History*, 59:3 (Summer 2004), p.18.

30 Dana Inkster, *Welcome to Africville* (Canada Video, 1999). See also Rinaldo Walcott's discussion of Inkster's film in "Isaac Julien's Children: Black Queer Cinema after *Looking for Langston*," *Fuse Magazine*, 24:2 (July 2001), pp.10–17.

31 Pierre Nora, "Between Memory and History: *Les Lieux de Mémorie*," in *History and Memory in African American Culture*, ed. Geneviève Fabre and Robert O'Meally (New York: Oxford University Press, 1994), pp.284–85.

32 Patricia L. Parker, "Traditional Cultural Properties: What You Do and How We Think," *CRM: Cultural Resource Management*, 16 (1993), p.5. See also Patricia L. Parker and Thomas F. King, "Guidelines for Evaluating and Documenting Traditional Cultural Properties," *National Register Bulletin,* 38 (National Park Services, 1990).

33 Lee, "Discovering Old Cultures," p.180.

34 Lowenthal quoted in Diane Barthel, *Historic Preservation: Collective Memory and Historical Identity* (New Brunswick, N.J.: Rutgers University Press, 1996), p.24.

35 National Park Service (in co-operation with Coppin State University, Goucher College, and Morgan State University), "Teaching Cultural Heritage Preservation: A Course Outline" <www.cr.nps.gov/crdi/colleges/TCHP.htm> (accessed Oct. 12, 2005).

36 A program in historic preservation was started at Delaware State University (DSU), a historically black college, with a focus on African American Heritage Preservation. Founded in 1890 as the State College for Colored Students, DSU began as a land grant college for agriculture and mechanical arts.

37 Lee, "Cultural Diversity in Historic Preservation," pp.1–2; Ned Kaufman, "Historic Places and the Diversity Deficit in Heritage Conservation," *CRM: The Journal of Heritage Stewardship*, 1:2 (Summer 2004), pp.68–85. I want to thank Katherine McKittrick for her insightful comments in helping me clarify my thoughts on "black Canada" and my reading of Africville.

5

Katherine McKittrick

"Freedom Is a Secret"

The Future Usability of the Underground

> [It] is not just the habitus of death, suffering, and terror, it is also the painful (re)birth of something new and different. — Rinaldo Walcott

In *Harriet's Daughter*, a short novel for young adults by Marlene Nourbese Philip, the protagonist, fourteen-year-old Margaret, promises her "ab-so-lute friend" Zulma that she will help her escape from Toronto, Canada.[1] Zulma has just arrived from the Caribbean. Toronto, for Zulma, is unfamiliar, cold, and violent; her knowledges, of food and transportation, of love and clothing and seasons, seem to be bound up in another place: Tobago. Zulma's different way of knowing is not, Margaret explains, "any good to her in Toronto."[2]

Harriet's Daughter is a story of friendship, youth politics, and differential diasporas. As a recent Caribbean migrant Zulma is unfamiliar with Toronto, but Toronto is also unfamiliar with Zulma. Margaret is Zulma's hopeful and confident Canadian-born friend. She knows the city, she knows the streets. She shows Zulma how to make snow angels and how to use her Toronto Transit Commission transfer for lengthy stopovers. Margaret has never been to her ancestral home, Barbados – even though her father continually threatens to send her "back" to the West Indies, for some proper discipline. The lives of Margaret and Zulma intersect with the lives of their racially diverse classmates and neighbours, as well as with their migratory parents, who are the purveyors of "West Indian Discipline" and family remembrances. All of the central characters are participating in local urban struggles, from questioning school curriculums and resisting violence against women to experiencing the betrayals of friends, racism and sexism, sibling rivalries, and economic constraints.

While her home life in Toronto is frustrating, Margaret is continually dreaming up ways of working through this frustration. One of the many ways in which she does this is to develop and initiate a game, which she calls "The Underground Railroad." In this game, children play slaves, slave-owners, dogs, and conductors. The gaming begins at a school on Winona Street, and slave-owners and dogs chase the slaves around St. Clair Avenue and Christie Street. The school itself is named "slavery"; several homes of the children are designated safe houses; the deserted YMCA at St. Clair Avenue and Robina Street is marked as "Freedom" – a secret location unknown to the gaming slavers and their dogs.

In this chapter I explore the Underground Railroad as it is presented in *Harriet's Daughter* and consider the ways in which Philip imagines "the political currents of transatlantic insurgency"[3] in a post-slave context: Toronto, Canada, in 1989. The history of the Underground Railroad in Canada is central to the nation's legacy of racial tolerance and benevolence. Fugitive escapes, plotted from the United States to the North, positioned Canada as a safe haven for black subjects, a "place called heaven," that construed the United States, particularly the Southern United States, as a violent region whose slaveholding citizens engaged in antiquated inhuman practices such as bondage and racism. In a post-slave context, this history has been extremely significant in the production of Canada's self-image as a white settler nation that welcomes and accepts non-white subjects. The history of the Underground Railroad has been one of the more important narratives bolstering perceptions of Canadian generosity and goodwill – of Canada's and Canadians' friendliness, neutrality, and likeability. It is precisely through this engagement with blackness and enslaved (U.S.) black bodies that the nation is able to position racial matters as being anachronistically elsewhere, only touching "race" or blackness vis-à-vis paternalism. What I mean by this is that many histories begin to disappear within the discursive celebratory confines of the Underground Railroad, and the past, particularly as it is understood within Canada, is written to cast the Southern United States/elsewhere as racist and unprogressive.[4]

Thus, *within and beyond* nineteenth-century black diaspora histories, one region of North America (the United States) is "out of time" while another region (Canada) is simultaneously advanced, socially evolved, and, perhaps most importantly, only engaging with blackness as it escapes to Canada in search of liberation. The history of benevolence, highlighted by ongoing celebrations of the Underground Railroad in Canada and the United States, conceals and/or skews colonial practices, Aboriginal genocides and struggles, and Canada's implication in transatlantic slavery, racism, and racial intolerance. That is, the Underground Railroad continually historicizes a national self-image that obscures racism and colonialism through its ceaseless promotion of Canadian helpfulness, generosity, and adorable impartiality. It is meaningful, then, that Philip chooses to explore the Underground Railroad in *Harriet's Daughter*, not only because this narrative is so central to how Canada is constructed as a benevolent safe haven, but also because her recontextualization of this history, in 1989, refuses a simplistic production of anachronistic space.

Harriet's Daughter is not a forthrightly historic text or slave narrative that draws on archives, primary sources, and remembrances. It is not, furthermore, what I would call a "typical" children's book that retells the story of the legacy of nineteenth-century black fugitive slave journeys. And the novel is not explicitly a neo-slave narrative – a contemporary fiction that writes and revisits the traumas of transatlantic slavery through black political subjectivities.[5] *Harriet's Daughter* is, rather, a text that collapses time-space, and integrates the histories of black diasporic peoples and their attendant ethnically diverse communities, in order to recast the present landscape of Toronto, Canada, and to question the seemingly natural flows of south-to-north emancipatory migrations. Philip's creative decision, to envision a narrative of violence, escape, and bondage in the present, and through the experiences of a fourteen-year-old black Canadian youth, troubles the celebratory spatial workings of the Underground Railroad while also maintaining its historic significance.

Before turning to *Harriet's Daughter* I will briefly discuss how particular historicizations of the Underground Railroad produce three entwining geographic assertions: the claim of black geographic ignorance; the intimate knowledge that black slaves had about their surroundings; and how the Underground Railroad, in the present, gets mapped as a knowable location. My reasoning for visiting these particular historical sources is to reveal that while the Underground Railroad is a geography that is necessarily contested, a location of celebration and pain that is underwritten by the horrors of transatlantic slavery, it is also a geography that both white and non-white communities desire to map and therefore know.

Some versions of the Underground Railroad, therefore, produce what Edouard Glissant calls "a fixed primordial spot."[6] This fixity refuses diasporic continuities while also spatializing the secret railroad as a finished emancipatory location. It is in Toronto, in the urban space inhabited by Margaret, that the railroad is "unfixed," and she opens up a diasporic game in which "anybody can be a slave" regardless of racial background or ethnic ties.[7] Philip presents an urban geography that uses the underground as a way of imagining Toronto from the perspective of struggle. She is not seeking to find and discover blackness, or Canada, or Caribbean-ness. Rather she imagines the underground as a tool that discloses the complexity of urban space where subaltern communities are understood as integral to, rather than outside, common-sense mappings of the city.

Losing Our Way

In 1933 historian E. Delorus Preston Jr. wrote an essay, "The Genesis of the Underground Railroad." In attempting to find what he calls the "origin of the Underground Railroad" he wrote that black slaves "were so completely ignorant of geography and relative distances" that escape was often impossible.[8] Preston Jr. prompts me to ask three questions that can lead us into an exploration of why mapping the Underground Railroad is a difficult exercise that involves unthinking our present geographic organization. What actually constitutes complete geographic ignorance? Are bondage, immanent death, and/or dismemberment really evidence of not knowing the complexities of scale and time-space, of not knowing the meaning of place? Or is it the desire to map and document origins that throws Preston Jr. off, thus not permitting him to think through the ways in which the constitution of spatial knowledge is deeply Eurocentric, exclusionary, and, in this case, bound up with black unfreedoms?

North American history has depicted the Underground Railroad as one of the more familiar and subversive geographic histories that white and black anti-slavery communities developed to assist in the escape of slaves. While this history is often cast as legend and myth, due to the clandestine routes that were maintained by oral, rather than written, documents, the Underground Railroad's impact upon the meaning of slavery, liberation, resistance, and race in the United States and Canada is considerable.[9] Despite the lack of knowledge in the popular imagination regarding the actual fugitives and their travels – Harriet Tubman, Fergus Bordewich rightly notes, often remains the only figure remembered – the Underground Railroad itself was, and continues to be, a renowned story of black men, women, and children "stealing themselves" and secretly subverting a dehumanizing system of bondage.[10] Primarily identified through famous conductors and escapees (Harriet Tubman, Henry "Box" Brown) and secret messages (hidden in constellations, quilts, landmarks, songs, enigmatic newspaper advertisements) the Underground Railroad was considered to be unwritten and unmapped. Disclosure of routes and places would curtail, often violently, black freedoms.[11] This subversion was a radical spatial act, an explicit reconfiguration of the spaces of white supremacy and a socio-spatial resistance that, if discovered, would incite death, bodily violence, and a return to enslavement.

While there has been much debate about the actual secrecy of the

Underground Railroad, as well as the number of slaves who actually used and survived this clandestine route to freedom, it has, without a doubt, become an embedded North American historical narrative.[12] In Canada and the United States, children's books, government pamphlets, Canadian "heritage" commercials, websites, and museums have illustrated how we have spent considerable time documenting and unlocking the secrets of the Underground Railroad. Indeed, the maps that illustrate escape routes and the landmarks identified by the U.S. National Park Service and Parks Canada tell us, unquestionably, that the underground is now above ground. In Canada specifically, markers in Chatham, Dresden, Owen Sound, Amherstburg, Windsor, and several other locations allow us to know and visit Underground Railroad terminuses; in the United States and Canada, safe houses/stations (churches, shops, homes, hidey-holes) are marked, identifying some of the important infrastructures on the escape routes.[13] Furthermore, post-slave scholarship, fictional investigations into the Underground Railroad, and fugitive narratives are upheld by stories and histories that attempt to "break geographic codes," or crack open underground secrets. Titles such as *A Record of Facts*, *Authentic Narratives*, *Letters*, the *Hippocrene Guide to the Underground Railroad*, *Disclosures and an Accurate Account of the Underground Railroad: What It Is and Where It Is Located*, "Retracing the Route to Freedom," and *Hidden in Plain View: A Secret Story of Quilts and the Underground Railroad* reveal that historic and contemporary investigations of this clandestine history are mapped onto "disclosures," "accuracies," and authentic routes to liberation that are right before our very eyes: in plain view, findable, and traceable. A link to EBay reads, "find the Underground Railroad on EBay," while other Internet sites claim, "Find the Underground Railroad – no clutter, just answers: go get it!"[14]

These titles and documents also point to the idea that the process of finding and retracing the Underground Railroad is implicitly or explicitly underwritten by questions of freedom and liberation. That is, narratives of the Underground Railroad couple our accurate "discovery" of it with emancipatory language: *Journey to Freedom*, *Freedom Train*, *A Winding Road to Freedom*, *Five Journeys to Freedom*.[15] This suggests, then, that the historically present railroad, once found, reveals sites of liberation, specifically within Canada, and/or the Northern United States. To put it another way, exploration, discovery, and gathering authentic facts are now, in the present, intimately bound up in the idea that we have mapped a route to freedom, and thus discovered liberation through unearthing spatial secrets, making black geographies purposeful and with clear, concise, seeable direction. But, in terms of geography, this means that liberty is necessarily coupled with seeable territoriality, the fixed primordial spots of finished business.

I do not want to eschew the compulsion to map the Underground Railroad; nor do I want to suggest that the history of bondage, survival, escape, and freedom should go undocumented. Rather I want to point to the ways in which these practices can sometimes mask the painful trade of humans through fixing them in the past and attaching them to freedom. The exploration and discovery of the Underground Railroad celebrate liberation rather than the continuing struggles of being a subaltern subject inhabiting nations and regions that refuse to attend to a different sense of place. These histories often hide the "Northern" implication in slavery and the hurried departures of blacks from Canada after they experience local racisms and alienation.[16] Further, if the alternative forms of geographic thought that black freed, unfreed slaves, and white abolitionists produced are depicted as knowable, is this suggesting that Eurocentric classificatory systems resolve past pain? Does documenting the Underground Railroad, then, render violence a past act and liberation achieved? Or are there other ways of thinking about spatializing the historical present?

In his *Invisible Man*, Ralph Ellison has the protagonist claim that learning to live without direction – outside geographies of normalcy, beneath the city – allows him to embrace "a slightly different sense of time, [where] you're never quite on the beat. Sometimes you're ahead and sometimes behind."[17] This sense of place can perhaps allow us to think about geography in new ways, ways that do not necessarily replicate our present geographic organization that is fraught with claims of desirous ownership, spatial domination, and racial-sexual marginalization. A different sense of time and space, the invisible man claims, is what allows him to come alive, to discover "new analytical ways" of inhabiting place.[18] And this different sense of time and space, the subject underneath the city – who might also be negotiating space in unfamiliar ways, as escaped slaves did, although for different reasons and in different ways – is not perhaps about geographic ignorance but rather about different kinds of maps: song maps, jazz maps, a new way of living to new beats; a new way of inhabiting place in a world that seeks to categorize, and keep in place, black subjects.

I want to suggest that the "underground" is a black geography that reframes spatial knowledges. The lack of direction that Ellison invites us to consider appeals to me because it situates black and other subaltern geographies in opposition to what I elsewhere call seductive and comfortable geographies of domination and ownership.[19] Because mapping occurs *in* the underground, it is a point of seeming frustration and confusion. The ostensible frustration and confusion do not necessarily identify enslaved ignorance but are, rather, evidence of a radically different sense of place. Geographic ignorance is an impossibility in the underground because this strategy of subversively claiming and living unmapped routes demands that black subjects are, in fact, intimately aware of their surroundings – albeit on different terms than we may know. An apt question is, then, under whose terms is geographic ignorance actually produced? It is precisely this loss of direction, *within* white supremacy, rather than ignorance, that allows the invisible man to claim his humanness in a world that refuses his black sense of place. The moment he learns to live without direction is the same moment in which he begins to claim his environment on his own terms.

The work of Marlene Nourbese Philip illustrates how the historically present Underground Railroad might attend to the complexities of urban space and thus illuminate an ongoing, rather than resolved, struggle. This struggle, I suggest, attends to an Ellisonian loss of direction that "leads to a new demand for another concept of freedom."[20] It is the protagonist, Margaret, in *Harriet's Daughter*, attempting to claim Toronto on her own terms, who highlights this struggle. The city acts as both a backdrop and an initiator to the cross-human and intercultural exchanges that capture the ways in which the Underground Railroad discloses what Glissant refers to as the "subterranean convergences of our histories."[21] And it is Margaret's re-historicization of the city space that discloses how a brutal past can also initiate new and different ways of being.[22]

Tough Geographies, Future Geographies

> "I was thinking we could set up a kind of Underground Railroad right here, with other kids, you know: choose slaves, slave-owners, dogs, guides, safe houses, and have a game with slave-owners and dogs trying to find the slaves. We could have a place that would be 'Freedom,' and the slaves would have to try to get from slavery to 'Freedom' . . . well? What d'you guys think?"[23]

The representation and reconfiguration of the Underground Railroad in *Harriet's Daughter* implicitly note the ways in which the work and the lives of historic fugitives and Maroons – Henry Brown, Harriet Tubman, Frederick Douglass, and Nanny, among countless other escapees and abolitionists – respatialize the common-sense geographic contours produced under a system of bondage. The geographies of slavery were fundamentally spaces and places of brutal black captivity; for the most part, black bodies were territorialized and deemed property, while white subjects were positioned as property-owners.[24] The racialization and ownership of space and place under slavery occurred across multiple scales, rendering a black sense of place virtually impossible under Eurocentric geographic arrangements.

Harriet's Daughter suggests, however, that the geographies of terror and slavery cannot simply be understood through white supremacist practices. Philip and her protagonist Margaret remind us that the production of space should also be understood through those who have challenged the seemingly natural racial-sexual hierarchies of black subjection. Harriet Tubman, then, occupies the name-title of this book, and preoccupies the protagonist Margaret, who researches Tubman's dangerous life and claims the fugitive's namesake as her own. Fugitive histories, then, underwrite this narrative, allowing us to consider how the Underground Railroad is now bound up in radical geopolitical challenges to slavery, nation, and racial hierarchies. To challenge socio-spatial bondage as fugitives, as Maroons and abolitionists did, both reaffirms and calls into question the power of slave spaces and the geopolitics of freedom. Imagining a black sense of place through these particular resistances returns us to Ellison's geographic formulation: fugitive geographies radically subverted the question of captivity through mapping a new and different understanding of geographic freedom, an unknown "spatialization of secrecy" that is enacted outside white supremacist cartographic rules precisely because these rules cannot lead the way to ethical sites of being. Within and across the geographies of transatlantic slavery, these fugitive acts map a loss of direction that is also, perhaps, a politics of *redirecting* how to reveal both freedom and unfreedom.

Philip's decision to portray an Underground Railroad game in 1989 thus immediately speaks to the history of escaped slaves finding freedom in Canada and the possibilities that "unknown" maps disclose. References to this history, in addition to Harriet Tubman, range from North Star shoes to Free Papers to the children dressing in what they consider period clothing: cut-offs, long skirts, head-ties. In suggesting that the Underground Railroad can be fun – an elaborate game of hide-and-seek, a newly racialized version of "Cowboys and Indians" – Philip gives us a provocative entrance into black history. In situating the story in Toronto, at the intersection and around St. Clair Avenue and Christie Street, and making clear that this is an urban game produced and played by fourteen-year-old youths, Philip has the key characters in the text illustrating their agency through the innovative reconfiguration of their local streets. Indeed, this reconfiguration is troubling. What is at stake in imagining slavery in Toronto in 1989? Is this kind of play appropriate? How can the Underground Railroad be fun?

The traumatic history being performed in the present as a game, the reclamation of the streets, and concealing this information from adults and teachers excite Margaret and her friends. Still, as the text makes clear, these two themes – the game and the history of the railroad – are disturbing to Margaret. She knows it is troubling, she knows it must be secreted, and she knows that she has perhaps lost her way in terms of how the city and black history are imagined. The youths are not positioning Toronto or Canada as Freedom; they are pretending that slavery is happening right in the middle of the city, home to some of the last safe houses.[25] While a few of the characters know a little about slavery, the only way in which they explicitly address this history is during game time, when they are at play. The unspeakable, then, for these youths becomes articulated as they chase each other through the streets of Toronto, seeking freedom at the YMCA. Yet the whole process speaks to a kind of playful urban creolization – a game that is clearly rooted/routed in African diasporic histories and white supremacy, because of its historical traces, but also has children of Caribbean, Italian, Portuguese, and Irish descent (slaves) being chased by children of Caribbean, Italian, Portuguese, and Irish descent (slave-owners, dogs). After all, in this game *anyone* can be a slave. The game, then, is fun because it is a reclamation that is unknowable to those in power: adults. It is exciting because it is unspeakable: a disturbing reminder of a past that the players are unable to fully recapture yet desire to map in a new context. And this playfulness brings together Toronto youths through mobilizing a difficult black history – a history that, in Canada and Toronto, has been hidden, rendered elsewhere, or wrapped up in paternalistic narratives of liberation.

The game of the Underground Railroad in Toronto, then, sets the stage for a much deeper engagement with the past, the present, and "the where" of freedom. In situating the Underground Railroad in Toronto Margaret discloses a national secret: slavery did happen in Canada, and it happened in Toronto. Slave advertisements were circulated at St. Lawrence Market in downtown Toronto, or York, as it was then known; the confessions of Marie-Joseph Angélique, enslaved in Montreal, New France, is considered to be one of the oldest records of slavery in North America; "Nigger Rock," in the Eastern Townships of Quebec, is the burial ground of hundreds of Canadian slaves.[26] So, Margaret inadvertently implicates Canada in slavery. The game of the Underground Railroad is telling a story that suggests that Canada is not always a site of freedom, a national safe haven. How do we remember and engage with the Underground Railroad if Canada was also a place of enslavement and is a location of continuing racisms?

Philip's decision to recall the history of the Underground Railroad is therefore more than a celebration of freedom in "the North" and of resistances to subjection. *Harriet's Daughter* is also presenting the connections between past and present diasporic activities. The novel plays with and compresses time-space: the history of slavery looms as Margaret pulls it into the present through her research, questions, and social activities.

Margaret's curiosity regarding slaves, Harriet Tubman, and her imaginary "home," the Caribbean/Barbados, allows Philip to suggest that Canadian history might also be explored through our present diasporic condition. The past and present history of slavery is recounted in conjunction with Caribbean migratory narratives, consequently presenting dispersed, and heterogeneous, time-space responses to the legacy of bondage and ongoing racisms. It is *within* the present borders of Toronto, on local urban streets, that the south-to-north underground history is coupled with a much later south-to-north Caribbean migration towards Canada, the United States, and the United Kingdom.

These black narratives and experiences are entangled; they are what Rinaldo Walcott, borrowing from Dionne Brand, describes as a "tough geography": black mappings and poetics that are haunted by a dehumanizing past as it is experienced and imagined, at present, by diasporic subjects in Toronto.[27] The entanglements, the "toughness" of these geographies, are prompted and articulated by city dwellers such as Margaret. Spatially, the black diaspora is simultaneously migratory and settled, evincing what we might call historically present geographies. Within a historically present framework, geographies of the black diaspora are shaped by and shaping grounded local experiences, imaginary homes, itinerant subjects, and geographies beyond the local, including past geographies such as slave sites and slave migrations. The historical present is a way of considering how the past informs and shapes the present, and it is connected to the idea that historical structures (geographic organization, political desires, legal and administrative frameworks) are open to our critical engagement precisely because they are locations that connect time and space. For example, racial-sexual oppressions can be detected through geographies such as plantations, ghettos, or racialized workplaces not as unchanging transhistorical spaces, but as sites that reveal an uncompleted, but differential, socio-spatial process. The historical present provides a framework for thinking about the ways in which the production of space is not only a normalizing system that underscores historic racial-sexual hierarchies, but also evidence of continuing subaltern struggles that destabilize and live these hierarchies.

These past-present connections and migrations, from the Southern United States and Caribbean, might appear to be inappropriately conflated. However, I suggest that *Harriet's Daughter* uses these two very different historic moments to demonstrate that past and present black diasporic geographies are deeply entwined with one another, rather than cohesive and linear. Margaret's narrative and the game of the Underground Railroad emphasize that "learning to live without direction" is one way of disclosing the geographic contours of blackness in a post-slave context. Her present black Canadian identity cannot be understood outside the history of transatlantic slavery, insurgent fugitive lives, and recent migrations from the Caribbean to Canada. These disparate histories, exiles, and travels are folded into one another, setting in motion Margaret's risky segues into a multi-ethnic, and playful, return to bondage. Margaret's story does not make sense within the national and regional codes of historic benevolence and paternalism; she must lose her way, and imagine her identity through and beyond these codes, in order to come to terms with and envision a new meaning of freedom. In *Harriet's Daughter* the historical present discloses the intellectual limits to imagining that the "end" of the Underground Railroad is a double marker of freedom/Canada and the end of slavery. Instead, Philip presents us with a story that leads us to consider how working through, and creatively merging, the subject of slavery, Caribbean migration, and present diasporic matters allow us to encounter our present human condition in new ways. It is within the geographies of the text – the urban streets, the city – that new forms of being entwine and push the legacy of black/white differences beyond the confines of modern classificatory systems and towards what Sylvia Wynter describes as "interhuman exchanges."[28]

Connective histories and experiences, including stories of the unknown and the uncertain – those lives beyond and *outside* "our" particular place, community, nation, shared ethnicities – make this narrative and the Underground Railroad game possible. Margaret is not only unfamiliar with Zulma's life history, but also struggling with displaced memories of the Caribbean/Barbados, a nation-space that does not forthrightly "belong" to her; she is engaging with the various lives of her multi-ethnic and "inter-island" classmates and neighbours, all the while consuming and researching Mata Hari, Angela Davis, Denise Huxtable, Bob Marley, and Harriet Blewchamp, her mother's former Jewish employer, who "had numbers tattooed on her wrist."[29] The secret history of fugitives, migrations, and the urban cannot be told without interhuman places, social actors, and narratives that remake the seemingly undisturbed freed locations ostensibly found at the end of the Underground Railroad.

The novel, then, refuses a unitary, linear, or nationalist celebratory story of black pride and/or white/Canadian paternalism. *Harriet's Daughter* reminds us that these histories, as they are articulated through the present lives of diasporic subjects, are predicated on exchanges within and beyond the African diaspora. That is, the traces of historic bondage, the memory of Harriet Tubman, the planned escape of Zulma, and, perhaps most importantly, the Underground Railroad game that Margaret initiates are not stories of past-violence-South/present-liberation-North. Rather, this novel presents a segue into the interhuman through its creolized landscape that insists that our sense of place, the ground beneath our feet, continues to be predicated on the violence of both the past and the present. The game and Margaret's social activities point to this violence, but also insist that this history be imagined as both a mapping of insurgency that points to the appearance of early black subjects within Canada – nineteenth-century interhuman/multicultural Canadian histories – and a present site of inter-ethnic connections. The fugitive and Caribbean migratory histories, the present story of Margaret and Zulma and their friends and families, are not revised repetitions of black/white classifications and linear histories of liberation; rather they configure place through meeting points, political encounters that reveal an ensemble of racially diverse and interracial subject positions that, together, explore the stakes of imagining more humanly workable geographies.[30]

More specifically, the various geographic scales of this text (the regions, nations, streets, school, homes, bodies) are not simply envisioned as hierarchically mapping biocentric differences – indeed, the geographic distances – between Man and his human others. Rather, the multiscalar geographies of this text insist that the experiences of Zulma and Margaret, and the history of transatlantic slavery, are strikingly *human* geographies wherein three-dimensionality, material locations, and historic routes can only be conceptualized as creolized time-space.

The geographies in *Harriet's Daughter* are more humanly workable precisely because Philip is writing this text from the perspective of struggle: Margaret, as protagonist and game co-ordinator, researcher, and critic, orients us towards a conceptualization of geography that is not biocentrically partial (read: black or Caribbean) or biocentrically hierarchical (read: white supremacist) but rather produced with and alongside human and environmental *connections*. Outside and deeply implicated in the geographies of normalcy and modernity, this particular mapping of the black diaspora *must* be produced through past-present multi-ethnic interhuman subject positions in order to make new sense of the world.

Philip's conceptualization of the Underground Railroad opens up new ways of imagining both the city and this clandestine but increasingly knowable history. The novel's respatialization of Toronto creates a political reworking of public history and how we attend to the tensions between past and present. Blackness, black identities, and black histories, then, are not constructed on the margins, or in the United States, in the past, or at a safe distance from whiteness. Rather, the Underground Railroad game incites a series of historical and contemporary encounters in Toronto that are not peripheral; these urban encounters allow many identities to converge without erasing pain and cloaking it in liberation. There are several ways in which we can unravel this respatialization of Toronto – ways in which the historically present Underground Railroad demonstrates a different sense of place and therefore a Canadian urban geography that is haunted by slavery and difference, but refuses to remember this past as fixed and/or presently emancipatory.

Importantly, the Underground Railroad in Toronto is not a black narrative that immediately defines this urban space. The Underground Railroad game, at first, appears to be a complete loss of direction, the wrong black geography in the wrong place. Although historical investigations identify Toronto safe houses and the residences of former slaves, the Underground Railroad is primarily imagined beyond Toronto, in small cities and towns such as Buxton, Sandwich, Amherstburg, and Chatham.[31] Popular and mainstream narratives of black Toronto are, for the most part, developed around the government's Caribbean Domestic Scheme, Caribana, black masculinity, and the activities of recent migrants from the continent of Africa.[32] Imagining the Underground Railroad in Toronto situates blackness in Canada as long-standing and urban, an idea that writer and critic George Elliot Clarke has refused to accept.[33] The positing of the Underground Railroad in Toronto reconfigures the assumption that the urban black community is relatively recent and primarily Caribbean. While the protagonist of the novel does not explicitly attend to this long-standing history, Philip's decision to name the Underground Railroad as an urban geography complicates settlement patterns and popular narratives about "the where" of black Toronto.

In pushing this history of bondage and escape into the present Philip also gestures to more contemporary socio-spatial patterns. It has been argued that the black geographic experience in downtown Toronto, while certainly arranged vis-à-vis racialized community connections and population density, also intersects with other ethnic communities. As Joseph Mensah notes, while diverse black communities appear to be highly concentrated outside the city, in the downtown core blacks are less spatially concentrated.[34] The game of the Underground Railroad is creolized: it is not simply about a black youth seeking black roots within an enclosed black community; rather it is about multiple encounters, inter-island and multicultural histories. This approach suggests that identifiable black, African Canadian, or Caribbean areas in the downtown, such as Bathurst Street and St. Clair Avenue, or Eglinton and Oakwood avenues, only tell part of the story; and that they are necessarily coupled with other, non-black experiences.

The game thus speaks to disparate cultures, all of which are all residing in and around Margaret's neighbourhood. Diversity allows the youths to claim that anyone can be a slave, and to move forward the game needs multi-ethnic players. The black history of the Underground Railroad is not just about playing with the past, but also about allowing this past to seep into multi-ethnic areas. The streets and the neighbourhood where the Underground Railroad game takes place are also where McDonald's is preferred over Albert's Jamaican Foods, where Harriet Tubman's dark complexion is preferred over Denise Huxtable's light complexion, where the Jewish diaspora is bound up in the Caribbean Domestic Scheme, a government work program that led to south-to-north migrations, economic possibilities, and very difficult working conditions for "single" black women. Taking place in the late-1980s, *Harriet's Daughter* does not presume racial and therefore geographic segregations; instead, it works the Underground Railroad into an urban setting that is necessarily bound up in encounters with "the Other." That is, the Underground Railroad is figured into a complex urban culture in which interrelated differences, rather than sameness or exclusion, advance the flows of life and youth politics.

Underwriting the Underground Railroad game, the disparate lives of the community, and the histories of escape and bondage is Margaret's concern for her best friend, Zulma. In her Toronto home, Zulma faces the violence of her stepfather, who abuses her mother, and longs for Tobago, where her grandmother resides. In positioning Zulma's diasporic narrative and her exposure to violence against women alongside the Underground Railroad game, Philip further complicates the geographic patterns in the novel. The questions of liberation, violence, and safety are, on one hand, strikingly localized, as Zulma and Margaret, as well as their mothers, seek refuge in the home of Mrs. B, an African American woman who escaped poverty and indentured labour in the United States decades earlier. The intellectual and strategic work of these women takes place in Mrs. B's kitchen while she prepares food and the women gather both funds and ideas that will assist in Zulma's return to Tobago.

Philip orients us, then, to a new and different kind of safe house, one that is not only woman-centred but also signifies the locality of violence: the body, the home, the community. Concurrently, as we know, the violence experienced by Zulma and her mother is not limited to their local and ethnic particularities – violence against women and other groups crosses all sorts of borders, communities, sexualities, ethnicities, and genders.[35] Multiple local-to-global violences suggest, further, that the safe house of Mrs. B is not a unitary site of refuge but perhaps that, underneath and across our biocentric social arrangements, there are many intellectual, material, and geographic strategies subverting, and "re-housing," struggling communities. Under our current hierarchical system, Philip reminds us, there is no such thing as a "last safe house," for this linear progression towards liberatory finality refuses to attend to ongoing post-slave intercultural inequalities.

Insurgency, then, is not only about "losing our way" and refusing or subverting the cartographies of white supremacy, but also about imagining the ways in which Philip's merging of time, place, geography, region, and inter-ethnic communities demonstrate that the critical history of the Underground Railroad is, in fact, "usable in the future."[36] Additionally, Margaret's role is not to find a safe haven in Canada – in the past or the present – but rather to help Zulma escape to the south, to Tobago, to the Caribbean. This particular return "home" – a southern safe haven – radically reverses the myth that Canada and freedom are synonymous with one another. More than this, Margaret's story suggests that the diaspora is not a one-way process in which non-white communities are rushing north in search of liberty – her story refuses to claim that travels from the south to the north are emancipatory. This opens up the possibility that escapes and dispersals are also initiated by everyday violences as they occur in global contexts – rather than economically driven migrations towards northern "freedoms."

In situating the historically present Underground Railroad in the middle of Toronto, Marlene Nourbese Philip opens up a place in which encounters are not axiomatically hostile. Instead, Philip envisions how a different sense of place operates in a white settler society. Toronto, then, does not mask pain or liberate the subaltern; rather, it inspires innovative narratives that are continually articulating possibilities that cut across the city. As Margaret notes before the Underground Railroad game begins, "Freedom" – the place – is a secret. Philip suggests that freedom is unmappable, perhaps gesturing to the ontological and psychic work we need to attend to in order to reimagine the livability of Toronto and urban futures. The unmappability of freedom also brings to light, Glissant writes, the "subterranean convergences of our histories" and alternative philosophical demands that engage with place in radically different ways than we are familiar with: not demarcating the material landscape through racial-sexual ideologies and keeping blackness "in place," but noting spatial convergences that recapture unrecorded histories, their dimensions "unexplorable, at the edge of which we wander, our eyes wide open."[37]

Notes

1 Marlene Nourbese Philip, *Harriet's Daughter* (Toronto: Women's Press, 1988), p.5.
2 Ibid., p.7.
3 Suzette Spencer, "An International Fugitive: Henry Box Brown, Anti-Imperialism, Resistance and Slavery," *Social Identities*, 12: 2 (2006), p.229. See also chapter 6 here.
4 Anne McClintock, *Imperial Leather: Race, Gender, and Sexuality in the Colonial Context* (New York: Routledge, 1995), pp.40–42.
5 Historic texts include Frederick Bancroft, *Slave Trading in the Old South* (New York: Frederick Ungar Publishing, 1959); Fergus M. Bordewich, *Bound for Canaan: The Triumph of the Underground Railroad* (New York: Harper Perennial, 2005); Benjamin Albert Botkin, *Lay My Burden Down: A Folk History of Slavery* (Chicago: University of Chicago Press, 1957); Afua Cooper, *The Hanging of Angélique: Canada, Slavery and the Burning of Montréal* (Toronto: HarperCollins, 2006); Henry Louis Gates, *The Classic Slave Narratives* (New York: New American Library, 1987); Glenelg and Peter Meyler, *Broken Shackles: Old Man Henson from Slavery to Freedom* (Toronto: Natural Heritage Books, 2001); Walter Johnson, *Soul by Soul: Life inside the Antebellum Slave Market* (Cambridge, Mass.: Harvard University Press, 1999); Marcus Wood, *Blind Memory: Visual Representations of Slavery in England and America* (New York: Routledge, 2000). Children's books include Dennis Brindell Fradin, *Bound for the North Star: True Stories of Fugitive Slaves* (New York: Clarion Books, 2000); Barbara Greenwood, *The Last Safe House: A Story of the Underground Railroad* (Toronto: Kids Can Press, 1998); Deborah Hopkinson, *Sweet Clara and the Freedom Quilt* (New York: Random House 1993); William Kashatus, *In Pursuit of Freedom: Teaching the Underground Railroad* (Portsmouth, N.H.: Heinemann, 2005); Faith Ringgold, *Aunt Harriet's Underground Railroad in the Sky* (New York: Crown Publishers 1992); Jeanette Winterson, *Follow the Drinking Gourd* (New York: Alfred A. Knopf, 1988). Neo-slave narratives include Octavia E. Butler, *Kindred* (Boston: Beacon Press, 1988); Toni Morrison, *Beloved* (New York: Random House, 1987); Sherley Anne Williams, *Dessa Rose* (New York: Berkley Books, 1987). For a discussion of neo-slave narratives, or slave narratives, see Angelyn Mitchell, *The Freedom to Remember: Narrative, Slavery, and Gender in Contemporary Black Women's Fiction* (New Brunswick, N.J.: Rutgers University Press, 2002); Ashraf H.A. Rushdy, *Neo-Slave Narratives: Studies in the Social Logic of a Literary Form*, *Race and American Culture* (New York: Oxford University Press, 1999); Jenny Sharpe, *Ghosts of Slavery: A Literary Archaeology of Black Women's Lives* (Minneapolis: University of Minnesota Press, 2003); Rinaldo Walcott, "Pedagogy and Trauma: The Middle Passage, Slavery, and the Problem of Creolization," in *Between Hope and Despair: Pedagogy and the Remembrance of Historical Trauma*, ed. Roger I. Simon, Sharon Rosenberg, and Claudia Eppert (Lanham, Md.: Rowman and Littlefield 2000).
6 Edouard Glissant, *Caribbean Discourse: Selected Essays*, trans. J. Michael Dash (Charlottesville: University Press of Virginia, 1989), p.67.
7 Philip, *Harriet's Daughter*, p.64.
8 E. Delorus Preston Jr., "The Genesis of the Underground Railroad," *The Journal of Negro History*, 18:2 (1933), p.167.
9 Bordewich, *Bound for Canaan*; Larry Gara, "The Underground Railroad: Legend or Reality?" *Proceedings of the American Philosophical Society*, 105:3 (1961).
10 Bordewich, *Bound for Canaan*, p.4.
11 Cf. Frederick Douglass, *Narrative of the Life of Frederick Douglass, an American Slave*, ed. Houston A. Baker Jr. (New York: Penguin, 1982 [1845]), p.138.
12 Jean M. Humaz, *Harriet Tubman: The Life and the Life Stories* (Madison: University of Wisconsin Press, 2003).
13 See, for example, the pamphlet *A Visitor's Guide to Ontario's Underground Railroad*, developed by the Central Ontario Network for Black History, African Canadian Heritage Tour, and the provincial and federal governments of Ontario and Canada. The

pamphlet includes detailed maps with over thirty Underground Railroad sites (churches, stations, plaques, museums, archives) identified.

14 Charles Blockson, *Hippocrene Guide to the Underground Railroad* (New York: Hippocrene Books, 1994); Anthony Cohen, *Retracing the Route to Freedom*, National Parks Conservation Association, 1996 <www.npca.org/walk> (accessed Dec. 1, 2005); William Still, *The Underground Railroad: A Record of Facts, Authentic Narratives, Letters, Etc.* (Philadelphia: Porter and Coates, 1872); Jacqueline L. Tobin and Raymond G. Dobord, *Hidden in Plain View: A Secret Story of Quilts and the Underground Railroad* (New York: Anchor Books, 2000); Franklin A. Wilmot, *Confessions of Frank A. Wilmot, the Slave, Thief and Negro Runner with an Accurate Account of the Underground Railroad: What It Is and Where It Is Located* (Philadelphia: Barclay and Company, 1860).

15 Doreen Rappaport, *Escape from Slavery: Five Journeys to Freedom* (New York: HarperCollins, 1992); Dorothy Sterling, *Freedom Train: The Story of Harriet Tubman* (New York: Scholastic Press, 1987); Randall Wisehart, *A Winding Road to Freedom* (Philadelphia: Friends United Press, 1999); Courtni Court Wright, *Journey to Freedom: A Story of the Underground Railroad* (New York: Holiday House, 1994).

16 Jane Rhodes, "The Contestation over National Identity: Nineteenth-Century Black Americans in Canada," *Canadian Review of American Studies*, 30:2 (2000).

17 Ralph Ellison, *Invisible Man* (New York: Random House, 1952), p.8.

18 Ibid., pp.7, 8.

19 Katherine McKittrick, *Demonic Grounds: Black Women and the Cartographies of Struggle* (Minneapolis: University of Minnesota Press, 2006), p.145.

20 Sylvia Wynter, "On Disenchanting Discourse: Minority Literary Criticism and Beyond," in *The Nature and Context of Minority Discourse*, ed. Abdul Jan Mohamed and David Lloyd (New York: Oxford University Press, 1990), p.452. See also Alexander Weheliye's discussion of Ellisonian time-space: Alexander Weheliye, *Phonographies: Grooves in Sonic Afro-Modernity* (Durham, N.C.: Duke University Press, 2005), pp.46–72.

21 Glissant, *Caribbean Discourse*, pp.66–67; Nevzat Soguk, "Incarcerating Travels: Travel Stories, Tourist Orders, and the Politics of the 'Hawai'ian Paradise,'" *Tourism and Cultural Change*, 1:1 (2003), p.30; Sylvia Wynter, "Beyond the Word of Man: Glissant and the New Discourse of the Antilles," *World Literature Today*, 63 (1989), p.638.

22 Walcott, "Pedagogy and Trauma," p.149.

23 Philip, *Harriet's Daughter*, p.63.

24 While whites were the primary subjects who owned slaves, the question of ownership during transatlantic slavery was also differentially distributed. Depending on the time and place, for example, some black slaves were given the opportunity to purchase themselves, freed blacks owned slaves and/or had the opportunity to purchase and therefore free their relatives, and Aboriginal communities in North America were enslaved and owned slaves.

25 Adrienne Shadd, Afua Cooper, and Karolyn Smartz, *The Underground Railroad: Next Stop, Toronto!* (Toronto: National Heritage Books, 2004).

26 The publication of *Harriet's Daughter* in 1989 preceded many current engagements with Canadian slavery; and publishers, scholars, and activists are still struggling to put slavery on the Canadian map. While the work of Robin Winks, Marcel Trudel, and Daniel G. Hill in the 1960s, 1970s, and 1980s began to unravel the history of slavery in Canada, recent work by scholars such as Afua Cooper and George Elliot Clarke from the late 1990s to the present has positioned slavery as integral to the popular understanding of the nation. In the 1990s Canada saw a little more of black Canada included in some public school curriculums, especially the lives of Mary Anne Shadd Carey, Marie-Joseph Angélique, Harriet Tubman, and Jim Henson, the history of Africville, and the black presence in Nova Scotia. Claude Arpin, "The Desecration of a Slave Cemetery," *The Ottawa Citizen*, Jan. 20, 1997; Claude Arpin, "Slave Cemetery Stirs Controversy," *The Gazette* (Montreal), Jan. 19, 1997; George Elliot Clarke, "Raising

Raced and Erased Executions in African-Canadian Literature: Or, Unearthing Angélique," *Essays on Canadian Writing*, 7 (Winter 2002); Cooper, *Hanging of Angélique*; Glenelg and Meyler, *Broken Shackles*; Daniel G. Hill, *The Freedom-Seekers: Blacks in Early Canada* (Agincourt, Ont.: Book Society of Canada, 1981); McKittrick, *Demonic Grounds*, pp.91–119; Marcel Trudel, *L'esclavage au Canada Francais: Histoire et conditions de l'esclavage* (Quebec: Presses Universitaires Laval, 1960); Robin W. Winks, *The Blacks in Canada: A History*, 2nd ed. (Montreal and Kingston: McGill-Queen's University Press, 1997).

27 Dionne Brand, *No Language Is Neutral* (Toronto: McClelland and Stewart, 1998), p.40; Rinaldo Walcott, *Black Like Who? Writing Black Canada*, 2nd ed. (Toronto: Insomniac Press, 2003), pp.43–55.

28 Sylvia Wynter, "1492: A New World View," in *Race, Discourse, and the Origin of the Americas: A New World View*, ed. Vera Lawrence and Rex Nettleford (Washington and London: Smithsonian Institution Press, 1995), p.8.

29 Philip, *Harriet's Daughter*, p.23.

30 McKittrick, *Demonic Grounds*.

31 Bordewich, *Bound for Canaan*; Shadd, Cooper, and Smartz, *Underground Railroad*; Winks, *Blacks in Canada*.

32 The Caribbean Domestic Schemes (1911–12; 1955) were labour initiatives to recruit Caribbean women to Canada as domestic labourers. The second scheme (1955) recruited Caribbean women aged eighteen to forty with no dependants and at least a Grade 8 education – they were allowed entry into Canada if they agreed to work as domestics for one year. There were attempts to ensure that the women stayed as domestic workers beyond one year, and that they remained "single" (that is, did not sponsor their Caribbean-born children, partners, husbands, did not marry). See, for example, Agnes Calliste, "Canada's Immigration Policy and Domestics from the Caribbean: The Second Domestic Scheme," in *Race, Class, Gender: Bonds and Barriers*, ed. Jesse Vorst et al. (Toronto: Socialist Studies and Garamond Press, 1989); Linda Carty, "African Canadian Women and the State: 'Labour Only Please,'" in *'We're Rooted Here and They Can't Pull Us Up': Essays in African Canadian Women's History*, ed. Peggy Bristow et al. (Toronto: University of Toronto Press, 1994); Audrey Macklin, "Foreign Domestic Worker: Surrogate Housewife or Mail Order Servant?" *McGill Law Journal/Revue de Droit de McGill*, 37 (1992); Makeda Silvera, *Silenced: Talks with Working Class Caribbean Women about Their Lives and Struggles as Domestic Workers in Canada*, 2nd ed. (Toronto: Sister Vision Press, 1989).

33 George Elliot Clarke, "Honouring African Canadian Geography: Mapping Black Presence in Atlantic Canada," *Border/Lines*, 45 (1997).

34 Joseph Mensah, *Black Canadians: History, Experiences, Social Conditions* (Halifax: Fernwood, 2002), p.82.

35 Too many to list, sadly, but the following are some overviews and discussions of violence. Clare Beckett and Marie Macey, "Race, Gender and Sexuality: The Oppression of Multiculturalism," *Women's Studies International Forum*, 24:3 (2001); Tess Chakkalakal, "Reckless Eyeballing: Being Reena in Canada," in *Rude: Contemporary Black Canadian Cultural Criticism*, ed. Rinaldo Walcott (Toronto: Insomniac, 2000); Leslie Moran et al., "Property, Boundary, Exclusion: Making Sense of Hetero-Violence in Safer Spaces," *Social & Cultural Geography*, 2 (2001); Joni Seager, *The State of Women in the World Atlas*, 2nd ed. (London and New York: Penguin, 1997), pp.26–29.

36 Weheliye, *Phonographies*, p.101. Gayl Jones also raises the future usability of the Underground Railroad in her discussion of illegal U.S./Mexico border crossings. See Gayl Jones, *Mosquito* (Boston: Beacon Press, 1999).

37 Glissant, *Caribbean Discourse*, pp.66–67.

6

Suzette A. Spencer

Henry Box Brown, an International Fugitive

Slavery, Resistance, and Imperialism

On March 23, 1849, in Richmond, Virginia – the same year that Harriet Tubman escaped from slavery to become a legendary convoy to fugitives – the slave Henry Brown, with the help of a white shoe-dealer, Samuel A. Smith, and a black freedman, James Cesar Anthony Smith, camouflaged himself as "dry goods" by crawling into a wooden shipping box one-and-a-half-foot deep, two feet wide, and three feet long. He had asked his co-conspirators to nail up the box and mail him via overland express to the anti-slavery office of James Johnson at 131 Arch Street in Philadelphia. Wrapped with five sturdy lengths of hickory wood, the box was marked "THIS SIDE UP WITH CARE."

Henry Brown spent roughly twenty-seven hours entombed in his escape apparatus before emerging in Philadelphia, and his extraordinary venture earned him the appellation Henry Box Brown and gave fresh meaning to the nineteenth-century legend of the "underground railroad." In the years after his escape Brown memorialized his efforts by touring on an abolitionist circuit, restaging his escape for curious nineteenth-century North American and British anti-slavery audiences, but he would significantly revise anti-slavery scripts.

Many commentators have long been fascinated with Brown's story as a truly great escape and marvelled over his inventive ruse as a testament to his dauntless determination to break the bonds of American slavery. The 2002 republication of Brown's 1851 slave narrative, which includes contributions by Henry Louis Gates and Richard Newman, Jeffrey Ruggles's groundbreaking biography *The Unboxing of Henry Brown*, a Richmond, Virginia, monument of Brown's box on Canal Walk, and Baltimore's Great Blacks in Wax Museum exhibit of Brown in his escape box are all restoring attention to Brown's life.[1] In 2000 art critic Marcus Wood wrote about the assumptions implicit within anti-slavery portraits that replicate Brown's escape, astutely critiquing nineteenth-century paternalist appropriations of Brown's images that reduce the fugitive to racialized stereotypes. In 1997 Samira Kawash dedicated a portion of her study about the problematics of race and freedom to Henry Brown's condition of captivity in his box.[2]

The spectacular nature of Brown's own imagery is one of the most fascinating and perplexing issues surrounding his subsequent travels on the abolitionist circuit; his escape makes him perhaps the most memorable and symbolic fugitive in American history. Still, as we study Brown's story as a means of reconsidering the problematics of freedom and resistance, our analyses need to extend beyond the fascinating details of his escape, beyond considering him as an American phenomenon of the Underground Railroad, and move towards repositioning him as part of a broader geopolitical circuit of New World Maroon resistances to both American and British dominative regimes.[3]

A rich geopolitical discourse, an anti-colonial and anti-imperial discourse, remains camouflaged beneath Brown's escape story and his nineteenth-century performances dramatizing his escape, eclipsed in many respects by seductive images of Brown rebounding from (or entrapped in) his escape apparatus. But if North American and British anti-slavery activists were fascinated with Brown as a paradoxical living corpse – a "resurrected" "new" (hu)man who rose up from the "tomb of slavery" and from his box as metaphorical coffin and prison – it is worth inquiring into how Brown correspondingly engaged with a transnational political activism and discourse of diaspora resistance through a range of activities that can be considered an insurgent and insurrectionary Maroon corps. I designate the complex of Brown's activities as a Maroon corps to link this man to the larger trajectory of Maroons who fled plantation slavery yet remained interested in contesting its authority, and to suggest moreover that Brown was not merely or exclusively preoccupied with escaping American slavery but with marshalling his *oeuvre* to critique global modes of industrialization and colonial expansion rooted in the subjugation of Africans through enslavement and institutions like law, religion, and world capitalism.

Brown's Maroon corps consisted of several public performances in North America and Britain; two slave narratives, one published in 1849 in the United States with the aid of an amanuensis, Charles Stearns, and another independently in 1851 in England; several songs and broadsides chronicling his feat; a self-copyrighted lithograph of his emergence from his escape box; painted panoramas of slavery exhibited in the United States and Britain;[4] and a host of mutating anonymously authored illustrations of his escape that proliferated in various media from book advertisements (for

Figure 1: "Resurrection of Henry Box Brown," 1850 (Library of Congress, LC-USZC4–4659)

example, William Still's *Underground Railroad*) to almanacs to children's books. In this light, it seems prudent to re-evaluate Brown's complex corps here, if only briefly, in order to take notice of how this body of work mobilized an anti-coloniality of power that enabled him to construct visual and political currents of transatlantic insurgency.[5]

Brown strategically launched his body and illustrations of his escape, both nationally and internationally, as coded allegorical signifiers, indeed metonymic and synecdochic figurations of strategically allied interracial transnational uprising and Maroonage. His practice of movement, his live (that is to say moving) body, and roving illustrations of his uprising functioned as the raw seductive capital in which he invested the symbolic value of anti-coloniality and upon and from which he built an ensnaring transatlantic spectacle that spoke publicly against global colonialism and extended to energize white and black resistances to the 1850 U.S. *Fugitive Slave Act*. To unmoor or unbox Brown from a decidedly American geography and historical context, then, is to discern at once the implications of reading him as a transatlantic Maroon subject (idea and figure) whose elliptic movements within and beyond the U.S. nation-state and its laws correlate in many respects with the elliptic currents of resistance employed by African diaspora Maroon groups. Brown's elliptical currents – traces of his circulating fugitive body as well as the political currency of sensational tales of his escape and mutating illustrations of his escape – all defied the American laws of slavery and circumscribed the transatlantic routes (or pathways) that bound North America and Britain in slave-trading and colonialism, haunting both imperial sites with si(gh)tes of resistance from blacks marooned by New World slavery's diaspora, and others, namely East Indians and the Poles, exploited by the ravages of "modern" industrialization.

By reading Brown's North American activities alongside his efforts in Britain, this approach works through his emphasis on spectacularity and showmanship, but it seeks as well to establish some measure of political and international significance to this nineteenth-century fugitive who has long been considered ingenious, theatrical, comical even, but seldom political and certainly not a transatlantic Maroon. Uncovering the interlocking political and ideological links between Brown and his American, British, and Caribbean contexts enables us to reconsider his contributions to a discourse of diaspora and to larger currents of nineteenth-century black resistance. What follows is an examination of how Brown strategically manipulated the concept of his "rising" from the box, the extent to which his panorama productions in Britain between 1851 and 1875 sustained a dialectic with Britain's Great Exhibition of the Industry of all Nations, and the manner in which his images functioned as mutinous mutations.

Figure 2: Closing Image, Brown's 1849 narrative, published in the United States (used with permission of Documenting the American South, The University of North Carolina at Chapel Hill Libraries)

Uprising, Resurrection, and Insurrection

Brown's slave narratives have not garnered much scholarly attention, perhaps because at least one of them was authored by an amanuensis, and literacy/authorship has become an important scholarly focus of slave narratives. James Olney observes that Brown's preface is "a most poetic, most high-flown, most grandiloquent peroration that, once cranked up, carries right over into and through the narrative." Thus, Olney continues, once the "facts have been dressed up in the exotic rhetorical garments provided by . . . Stearns, there is precious little of Box Brown (other than the representation of the box itself) that remains in the narrative."[6]

Indeed, the 1849 edition evinced heavy-handed editorship, emphasizing the box's cramped dimensions in its title, opening conventionally with authenticating prefatory elements, and closing prescriptively with an image of a tightly sealed box, as if both to seal the image of emboxed horror into the mind, presumably leaving readers haunted with the fantasy of what lay enclosed therein, and to underscore the anti-slavery proscriptions placed on slave narrators.[7] In fact, to discern the box's injunction – this time reading "Right side up with care" – readers had to literally engage in a simulation of Brown's topsy-turvy travels by turning the page on its side.

Figure 3: Opening Image, Brown's 1851 narrative, published in Manchester, England (courtesy of James E. Shepard Memorial Library, North Carolina Central University)

Brown's 1851 narrative differs significantly, however, not so much because he claimed singular authorship, but because, unlike the first, it opened with a bang – an image of Brown rising from his box – and closed with a strike: an appendix of laws addressing various slave strikes against the master class. Through these two innovations, Brown capitalized upon the ideological affiliations between resurrection and uprising to conjure visions of his and other fugitives' uprisings. Where the first narrative sentimentalized him as trapped corpse and gloried over the numerical dimensions of his closed box, in the second narrative Brown ruptured the wooden ties constraining the box and jettisoned descriptions of it as his introduction, opting instead for a figure of himself as an allegorical rising subject and giving readers another view of the box's ironically enabling dimensions. Perched upright and poised for exit with the help of Frederick Douglass, James Miller McKim, Charles Dexter Cleveland, and Lewis Thompson, all of whom might be considered as strategically allied in Brown's uprising, Brown obstructs a plainly sentimental view by initiating a twin-sided camouflaged discourse that gestures to more than his rise from "the grave of slavery." On a literal level the image does depict his physical rise from the box, but interpreted together, Brown's copyright, sale,[8] and circulation of his "rising image," and his editorial changes to this second narrative (the inclusion of Douglass and the random enumeration of law as a new signature ending) are engaging in increased political resistance work and include a vision of interracial alliance that confounds race as the singular basis for the slave uprising. Brown achieves this, moreover, by working in and through the popular death-resurrection teleology that was so familiar and palatable in anti-slavery circles – certainly more acceptable than forthright endorsements of a literal slave uprising would have been.[9] His narrative "appeal to free white audiences on both sides of the Atlantic was fundamentally rooted in the language of Christological resurrection and apotheosis."[10]

But if "Brown's image resonated easily, familiarly, and unambiguously on the evangelical eye, ear, and . . . imagination," as Richard Newman reasons, one wonders, still, whether Brown's transatlantic anti-slavery audiences gleaned the riotous undercurrents of this multilayered opening vision.[11] Wood argues:

> Brown's suffering and resurrection, his mythic appeal, can be established only through the minute observation of the facts of his escape, and at the heart of these facts is the box itself, womb and tomb, object of torture and vessel of liberation. The box is a paradox, a holy abolition relic.[12]

Yet Brown's box also serves as a seductive decoy, deflecting attention from his opening image's more politically insurgent valences. The incorporation of Douglass, who had escaped from slavery in 1839 and become a major anti-slavery force, is a telling point of departure in a rethinking of Brown's political and allegorical strategies and the insurrectionary intonations encoded in the notion of resurrection as rise. Evidence indicates that it was William Still and not Douglass who helped Brown unbox in Philadelphia in 1849. Why, then, use Douglass? Perhaps Brown desired to confound authorities with the switch, because implicating Still would have jeopardized other fugitives; besides, Douglass was more politically and internationally renowned. Even so, however, Brown's manoeuvre also draws upon the explosive energies of Douglass's fiery rhetorical style to punctuate this image's import as political allegory of fugitive uprising. In this sense, one both hears and sees the image. Douglass adds a level of eminence and militancy to Brown's opening, politicizing and animating it in a way that neither Still nor others could, for Douglass bore national and international distinction as a revered rhetorician and reviled Negro activist. Figured in complicity with Brown, Douglass recalls his own famous uprising with the slave-breaker Covey, popularized in his 1845 narrative, which was translated into French and published in Ireland and England. Similar to Brown's idea that his box equipped him for the "battle of liberty," Douglass described a literal boxing match with Covey and deployed a set of terms – "battle," "rise," "resurrection," and "turning point" – which Brown used strategically. Revisiting Douglass reveals this interconnected coded signification and helps us to view Brown's introduction of himself in a new light:

> From whence came the spirit I don't know – I resolved to fight; and suiting my action to the resolution, I seized Covey hard by throat; *and as I did so I rose*. . . . My resistance was so entirely unexpected, that Covey seemed taken all aback. He trembled like a leaf. This gave me assurance and I held him uneasy, causing the blood to run where I touched with him with the ends of my fingers. . . . We were at it for nearly two hours. Covey at length let me go, puffing and blowing at a great rate, saying that if I had not resisted, he would not have whipped me half as much. The truth was, that he had not whipped me at all. I considered him as getting entirely the worst end of the bargain; for he had drawn no blood from me, but I had from him.
>
> This battle with Mr. Covey was the turning-point in my career as a slave. . . . He only can understand the deep satisfaction I experienced, who has himself repelled by force the bloody arm of slavery. I felt as I never felt before. *It was a glorious resurrection, from the tomb of slavery, to the heaven of freedom. My long-crushed spirit rose, cowardice departed, bold defiance took its place*; and I now resolved that however long I might remain a slave in form, the day passed forever when I could be a slave in fact. I did not hesitate to let it be known of me, that the white man who expected to succeed in whipping, must also succeed in killing me.[13]

Surely, Brown had not confronted his own master in the manner in which Douglass had, but he was now doing this through the force that he rallied to his side in citing Douglass. Through political portrait, public performance, and narrative, Brown was confronting an international audience, introducing them to his own "unexpected resistance," which yielded profound "turning points" in repelling the "bloody arm of slavery" and made him in a sense uncontrollable.

Viewed in this light, Brown's introductory image to the 1851 narrative adds more importance to his gloss on Nat Turner's 1831 insurrection in Brown's own home state, Virginia, while also recalling Gabriel Prosser's uprising in 1800 (nearer still, in Richmond), neither of which Brown endorsed outright but both of which can be related to his rhetorical gestures, use of imagery, and citation of law, which he derisively designated "the trash which is called justice by slave-holders and quasi-legal authorities."[14] What I am suggesting, then, is that Brown's opening and ending to his 1851 narrative might be read as a conversation with events outside of his narrative that represent emancipatory fugitive strikes and anti-legal maroonist resistance. While his introduction used the visual to inscribe a rhetoric of uprising, his appendix deployed the written to conjure visions of Maroon insurgency in Virginia and North Carolina's Great Dismal Swamp – used as a hideout by runaway slaves – and public thoroughfares.

Brown's citation of law was certainly not a unique gesture, but it performs important work in the structure of his narrative when we read it in relation to his introductory image and to Turner's insurrection: we can discern a logic of progression, an escalation really, that slides from indexing the marooned disposition of the enslaved – their disfranchised sociopolitical condition – to furnishing visions of runaway slaves committing manifold infractions, from striking their masters, to meeting secretly, to travelling by foot, horseback, and boat without written permission and passes. Examining the laws in the order in which Brown enumerates them exemplifies how they escalate from start to finish. A seeming enigma, Brown's last citations under the heading "Miscellaneous" specify the penalties for those who let loose boats and those determined on "going about without permission," who are consequently branded on the cheek with an "E." This curious hodgepodge, meant to enlighten the British and shame Americans, opens the conceptual gateway to a revaluation of Brown's preoccupation with maroonage and slave uprising – especially if we read the appendix against his introductory image as a figuration of insurrectionary uprising.

Brown's legal citations transport us into the mind of the Maroon, for beneath the legal prohibitions he cites lie the very resistive escape impulses that the law fears and cannot completely prohibit. Writing from an elsewhere beyond the law, Brown himself as "escapee" is evidence of this, despite the law's injunction that escapees be branded, an act that merely recirculated and brandished the possibility of escape and emancipation.

Brown's miscellany is menacing precisely because it recalls Turner's uprising and the white paranoia that tended to arise each time slaves gathered together, got close to a horse or boat – things miscellaneous in themselves that presaged the possibility of uprisings everywhere and nowhere. Just as Turner and his accomplices plotted and met secretly, slaves conspire in Brown's concluding vision, roaming without passes, mobilizing horses, boats, and feet as escape apparatuses, while his final invocation of "E" sears the impression of his own express escape in the imagination.

Of course, while Brown's introductory image depicted no Turner or Prosser, both of his narratives include a description of Turner's uprising, and Brown notes in both cases that he was located but a few miles from where the 1831 insurrection took place. He appears to carefully distance himself from this event, assuring his readers: "I did not then know precisely what was the cause of this excitement, for I could got [sic] no satisfactory information from my master, only that some slaves had plotted to kill their owners. I have since learned that it was the famous Nat Turner's insurrection." He recalls the mass hysteria, anti-black violence, and legal restrictions on black mobility: "Whites seemed terrified beyond measure, so true it is that the wicked flee when no man pursueth. . . . Many slaves were whipped, hung, and cut down with swords in the street; and some that were found away from their quarters after dark were shot."[15]

While Brown's connection to Turner may appear tangential in the sense that he felt the consequences of the revolt as opposed to directly participating, and while Brown uses physical geography to distance himself from Turner's uprising, the signature irony of Brown's retelling and use of his image of uprising is that he closes this distance through citation and his own physical escape/uprising. It is his very body, the thing restricted and spatially dislocated after Turner's revolt, that moves through time and space to articulate a connection via a citation of Turner's insurrection, through allegories of uprising and the stolen self.

Throwing Stones through a Glass House: Spectacular Insights, Great Exhibitions, and Scenes in a Panoramic Mirror

Attempts to capture Brown in 1850 in Providence, Rhode Island, led him to embark on another visionary escape journey that took on international and anti-colonial dimensions. This time Brown fled across the Atlantic. He arrived in England in November 1850 during a time when lavish plans were underway for Queen Victoria and Prince Albert's Great Exhibition of the Industry of all Nations, scheduled to convene in the magnificent

110-foot-high Crystal Palace, designed expressly for the event. Having toured the U.S. anti-slavery circuit showing his panorama, lecturing, and selling his 1849 narrative, illustrations of his escape, and leaflets with his imagery and his resurrection song, Brown hit the ground running in Liverpool, so to speak, and immediately began "lecturing" and touring.[16] A savvy showman with an eye for seductive visual production, Brown wasted no time in reconstructing his panorama, "Mirror of Slavery," first exhibited in Boston along with "himself " in and out of his famous box. The *Liverpool Mercury* reported that Brown and J.C. Smith, who helped him escape from Virginia, found their niche quickly amongst the city's anti-slavery audiences, who were both intrigued to learn about slavery in America and fascinated by the panorama's novelty. Besides, just two months earlier prominent fugitive-lecturer William Wells Brown had anticipated Box Brown by exhibiting his twenty-four-scene panorama of "Scenes in the Life of an American Slave," in a sense preparing the way for Box Brown's reception.[17]

In the years leading up to the arrivals of both of the Browns in London, the British nurtured an extensive exhibition tradition that found its apotheosis in the Great Exhibition of 1851. Panoramas of all kinds took off in Europe and were a favourite of the lower classes, who could afford their modest prices and did not have the luxury of travelling to the distant geographical scapes that panoramas often depicted. In other cases, gaudy display shows dazzled common folk and gentry alike, focusing on so-called freakish humans and racial and ethnic exotica – all presented as curious specimens of alterity, fantasy, and ethnological and anthropological intrigue. The Great Exhibition would not extend these imperatives forthrightly, but it sprang from Britain's long-standing impulse to gather, display, and imperialize through classificatory master narratives and colonization of space. Extending invasive sea/see imperatives of British colonial programs, the Exhibition leveraged the ocular as power and matched this with narratives that staked out national achievements as indicative of power, moral calibre, and the international and financial value of its expansive colonial project. In fact, one reason why Prince Albert's idea for a Great Exhibition was so well received is that by the late 1840s the escalation of spectacle had gotten so out of hand that it was evident that nothing short of massive collective effort could possibly come close to satisfying the well-nigh universal public craving for monster displays of special effects.[18]

Yet it was not merely a craving for spectacle that catalyzed the British. Looking back over England's imperial histories, a viewer might find it difficult to separate the Crystal Palace's sprawling collection of raw materials and inventions, bodies and objects, from imperialist and capitalist-colonialist impulses. Prince Albert conceded as much in his opening-day Exhibition speech when he announced, "The products of all quarters of the globe are placed at our disposal, and we have only to choose which is the best and cheapest." Indeed, as Thomas Richards observes, "The exhibition layout essentially balkanized the rest of the world, projecting a kind of geopolitical map of a world half occupied by England, half occupied by a collection of principalities vying for leftover space."[19]

The Exhibition's many maps and diagrams charting originary roots, geographical trade routes, and prospective imperial routings guided British audiences on vicarious journeys to distant territories, inspiring feelings of nationalist pride during a period when distant scapes were identified as British "possessions."[20] The entire affair camouflaged the means and modes of production that became representations of grandeur and industrial progression in the Crystal Palace. What the Exhibition displayed, thus, was what subaltern theorist Anibal Quijano calls the "coloniality of power" – "a planetary system of classification and continental division that works in tandem with capitalism and was consolidated in Europe from the sixteenth to the eighteenth centuries." Walter Mignolo adds that when the coloniality of power is enforced, "European local knowledges and histories [are] projected as global designs."[21]

Quijano's and Mignolo's observations are insightful not only because they shed light on the political trajectory informing the Exhibition, but because they allow us to re-evaluate the "work" that Brown's panoramas performed in the British sphere when exhibited alongside the Exhibition. Peace, international co-operation, worldly camaraderie, commercial and industrial progress, and free trade were all key terms characterizing the Exhibition's benefit to "mankind," another term that found prominence. If these were well-worn key words, however, imperialism and colonialism were pivotal concepts brandished beneath the propitious banner of "free trade." Economic competition and trade between nations, the organizers believed, "would, over the long term, eliminate the need for war."[22] One British newspaper held that "free trade would bind all nations in amity," and writer James Ward claimed that "in lieu of fabricating weapons for mutual destruction . . . mankind seemed tacitly agreed to rival each other in manufacture of commodities. . . . It was simply a transfer of skill and industry from bullets of lead to bales of cotton."[23]

This was but the circular, cross-dressed articulation of British imperialism, for who would pick the cotton to supplant the bullets that were necessary in the first place to subdue the cotton territory and pickers? In a manner similar to Hegel's dialectical overcoming, Ward offered cotton and commerce as ostensible substitutes for violent confrontation, such that a "whole commercial world" would be "bound together as the people of any one nation."[24] Henry Brown would crack open the underside of this bounded vision and discourse of progress with a supplemental vision of bondage, world capitalism, and subaltern resistances. It was against the Crystal Palace's backdrop that Brown exhibited his "Mirror of Slavery," a forty-nine-scene production that problematized and critiqued the Great Exhibition whilst drawing energy, indeed benefiting, from its spectacularity.

Brown's tours, though, began before the Exhibition was opened. By December 1850 Brown had exhibited in Manchester, a factory town considered the seat of the Industrial Revolution – one major turning point in capitalist and global colonial relations. In considering Brown within an anti-colonial, transatlantic context, I want to suggest that many of the terms used to critique and celebrate the Exhibition's achievements are applicable to Brown's panorama as an anti-colonial dialectic in tension not only with the wealth and industry of North America and imperial nations such as Britain and Spain, but also implicitly with Africa, for the African slave trade is the inaugural scene, the primal event, that opens Brown's "Mirror of Slavery."

If Britain colonized geopolitical space with this Exhibition, which marked out nationalized boundaries even as it collapsed them by distilling the globe into one mass exhibit in its "glass house," in a similar yet dialectical fashion Brown's exhibition of his panorama and indeed his very body vaulted across time and space, national boundaries and laws, to articulate the connections between violence and democracy, violence and capitalism – to articulate the way that violence is exercised to create imperial freedoms; to create the racialized apartheid/white state – a global state in which the "darker people of the world" are living sacrifices for capitalist industrialization. Brown's criss-crossed canvas disclosed a number of sites, from the African slave coast – the Cape of Good Hope – to the interior of slave ships; from Havana and the "West India Islands" to the auction blocks and treadmills of Charleston, South Carolina; from Richmond, Virginia's cotton and sugar plantations and its Dismal Swamp, where fugitive slaves mounted resistances, to Washington, D.C.'s slave prisons and Philadelphia's famous Fairmount Waterworks. It went back to the tarring and feathering of fugitives in South Carolina and ranged further still to West Indian emancipation in Britain's slave colonies, and forward to the Grand Industrial Palace. It was a dizzying yet sobering portrait of imperial expansion and industrialization as violence.

Jeffrey Ruggles argues that Brown's forty-eighth scene, "Grand Industrial Palace," was a "view of a township, according to the plans" of French utopian socialist Charles Fourier, whose work influenced the U.S.

painter of Brown's panorama, Josiah Walcott.[25] Fourier believed that society could be transformed into co-operative phalanges – socialist agrarian communities – in which the distribution of wealth would be more equitable than it was in raw capitalism.[26] It was indeed fitting that Brown juxtaposed Fourier's vision of the phalange as a riposte to American slavery and capitalism. Once Brown exhibited his panorama in Great Britain in the context of the Exhibition, however, his "Grand Industrial Palace" assumed another valence: it interrogated the capitalist and imperialist promises of the Great Exhibition and Crystal Palace. While his predecessor in England, William Wells Brown, had exhibited a panorama focused on American slavery, Box Brown's first panorama was, as its title stated, meant to be a "mirror" of slavery. Box Brown did not confine his vision to the U.S. nation-state. Neither his content nor title suggests a specifically American context, although once in England he certainly capitalized upon his U.S. affiliation and his precarious status as marooned fugitive.[27] That precarious status was nonetheless the condition that expanded his physical orbit and related him to a larger circuit of fugitive resistances inside and beyond the U.S. nation-state.

By throwing into visual and ideological crisis the modes and violent means of production, oppression, subaltern resistance, and bodily pain entangled with and constitutive of the political power of Europe and the United States, Brown's "Mirror" highlighted the undersides of capitalism as a burgeoning world system. Such undersides were largely purged from visibility at the Great Exhibition, or if they were there at all they were dressed up in its smooth-sounding if ambivalent rhetoric of peace, progress, and international co-operation. Brown's panorama was a mass allegory of the paradox of New World development, as a reviewer in the *Wolverhampton and Staffordshire Herald* noted rather ironically but tellingly. Daunted by Brown's panorama, the writer assayed the work as "a jumbled mass of contradictions and absurdities, assertions without proof, geography without boundary, and horrors without parallel."[28]

Brown's panoramic "geography without boundaries" implicated Britain, America, Spain, and Africa (at least), and it articulated ideas in tension with the Great Exhibition's own seemingly boundless geography and coloniality of power – perhaps too expansively and too intimately for the Wolverhampton and Staffordshire reviewer to appreciate. In this mass allegory were serial portraits at once frozen and mobilized, augmented by scenes from New and Old World stories: of distressed African families violently marooned by the slave trade; bodies rent from the stress of slave ships, sugar mills, and subjugating scourges; and small knots of resistances mounted by those like himself, William and Ellen Craft, and Henry Bibb, who were caught within and trying to escape from imperilling imperial designs. In his "Mirror," Brown presented a vision of the New World that disturbed the visions set forth by the Great Exhibition. He did not simply tell an alternate story. Rather, he refracted the Great Exhibition's scenes, exemplifying "the need to tell stories not only from inside the 'modern' world but from its borders . . . forgotten stories that bring forward *at the same time* a new epistemological dimension, an epistemology from the borders of the modern colonial world system."[29]

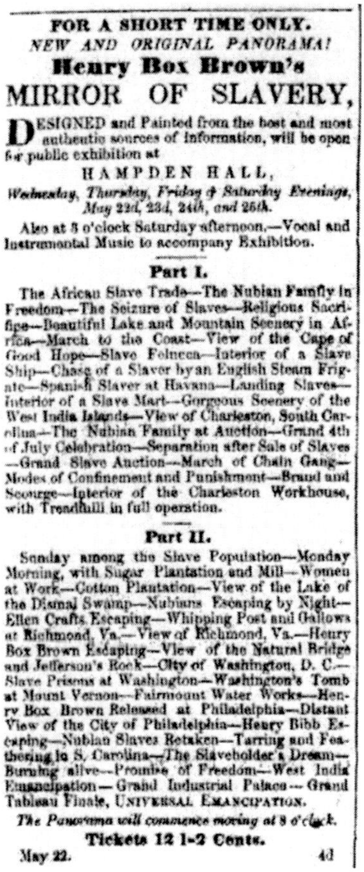

FOR A SHORT TIME ONLY.
NEW AND ORIGINAL PANORAMA!
Henry Box Brown's
MIRROR OF SLAVERY,

DESIGNED and Painted from the best and most authentic sources of information, will be open for public exhibition at

HAMPDEN HALL,
Wednesday, Thursday, Friday & Saturday Evenings, May 22d, 23d, 24th, and 25th.

Also at 3 o'clock Saturday afternoon.—Vocal and Instrumental Music to accompany Exhibition.

Part I.

The African Slave Trade—The Nubian Family in Freedom—The Seizure of Slaves—Religious Sacrifice—Beautiful Lake and Mountain Scenery in Africa—March to the Coast—View of the Cape of Good Hope—Slave Felucca—Interior of a Slave Ship—Chase of a Slaver by an English Steam Frigate—Spanish Slaver at Havana—Landing Slaves—Interior of a Slave Mart—Gorgeous Scenery of the West India Islands—View of Charleston, South Carolina—The Nubian Family at Auction—Grand 4th of July Celebration—Separation after Sale of Slaves—Grand Slave Auction—March of Chain Gang—Modes of Confinement and Punishment—Brand and Scourge—Interior of the Charleston Workhouse, with Treadmill in full operation.

Part II.

Sunday among the Slave Population—Monday Morning, with Sugar Plantation and Mill—Women at Work—Cotton Plantation—View of the Lake of the Dismal Swamp—Nubians Escaping by Night—Ellen Crafts Escaping—Whipping Post and Gallows at Richmond, Va.—View of Richmond, Va.—Henry Box Brown Escaping—View of the Natural Bridge and Jefferson's Rock—City of Washington, D. C.—Slave Prisons at Washington—Washington's Tomb at Mount Vernon—Fairmount Water Works—Henry Box Brown Released at Philadelphia—Distant View of the City of Philadelphia—Henry Bibb Escaping—Nubian Slaves Retaken—Tarring and Feathering in S. Carolina—The Slaveholder's Dream—Burning alive—Promise of Freedom—West India Emancipation—Grand Industrial Palace—Grand Tableau Finale, UNIVERSAL EMANCIPATION.

The Panorama will commence moving at 8 o'clock.

Tickets 12 1-2 Cents.

May 22. 4d

Figure 4: Brown's panorama scenes (*Springfield Republican*, May 22, 1850)

Chased out of America, dubbed fugitive and criminal in the land of his birth, and existing on the borders on British society, Brown occupied a unique vantage point from which he could critique the Old and New Worlds and share his distinct vision with his audiences. On March 24, 1851, only a few weeks after the Great Exhibition officially opened its doors to spectators, the *Mercury Leeds* reported that Brown dramatized his visions in a most theatrical fashion, paralleling the visual impulses driving the Great Exhibition. Brown "arrived in Leeds from Bradford packed in the identical box in which he first made his escape from slavery."[30] Although Bradford is but a few miles from Leeds, Brown spent two hours and forty-five minutes in his box, "parading through the principal streets of the town . . . preceded by a band of music and banners representing the stars and stripes of America." Roughly a few hundred miles from the Crystal Palace, he arrived to a "procession attended by an immense concourse of spectators," showcasing his marooned self and panorama as African America's contribution and supplement to the Great Exhibition's displays. Even more exciting, Brown's former owner, William Barrett, was rumoured to be in London at the time attending the Great Exhibition, while his criminally liberated property was but a few miles away flouting the box technology he had used to outwit the slaver.[31] One imagines Barrett pondering Brown's innovation (if indeed he happened to hear of Brown's performances) as a formidable if crude parallel to the Crystal Palace's exhibits of machinery, specifically its locomotives, because, after all, Brown had first escaped by box and rail.

If British spectators were astute at discerning America's hypocrisy – so adeptly had Brown juxtaposed the "Fourth of July Celebration" and the "Separation after Sale of Slaves" – what seemed perhaps less apparent then but has become clearer from our present distance is how the structural logic of Brown's panorama program complicated Britain's celebration of the Crystal Palace and all that it stood for. In Brown's visual economy it was the "African Slave Trade" and, by implication, Europe's involvement in it, that constituted a founding violence. The slave trade was, in other words, the constitutive limb that undergirded the vision, feeling, and project of modernity represented by the Crystal Palace. The seriality of the images in Brown's "Mirror" and the tales he interspersed from his personal narrative may have in a sense camouflaged this effect, but the very titles of Brown's scenes, taken in sequence, reveal the "African Slave Trade" building slowly up to the "Promise of Freedom" and "West India Emancipation" only to return to the "Grand Industrial Palace." Viewed from a subaltern perspective, the "Palace" scene represents the impossibility of freedom, the entanglements of democracy and violence made real in and through Brown's performing body and his status as international fugitive. The ontological predicament of who could be free, and why, when, where, and under what conditions, was yoked to Brown's body and inseparable from his portraits.

The titles of Brown's panorama scenes indicate a phenomenology of commodity production in the New World, the inverse of the phenomenology of consumption that the Crystal Palace promoted. Thomas Richards asserts that "the Crystal Palace did not isolate production from consumption." Rather, "It successfully integrated the paraphernalia of production into the immediate consumption."[32] Indeed, the Exhibition blurred consumption insofar as the bodies of the Bengalis who carved ivory, or of the Africans who picked cotton, or of the East Indians who produced textiles were all rendered exotic invisible footnotes at the Exhibition, while the fruits of their labour were staged for imperial consumption. These very individuals who were commodity producers (and commodities) were simultaneously alienated from, and consumed and objectified by, the objects they produced.

Where the Crystal Palace used space and layout to alienate and annex commodities from their means of production and to occlude the bodies that produced the commodities it celebrated, Brown historicized this selective ahistoricization by representing slave bodies at work, in pain and in resistance. We need only recall James Ward's heady hope of the peaceful promise of cotton or the *Illustrated London News*' depiction of impressive cotton machines, roped off from spectators at the Exhibition, to understand the import of Brown's contrasting scenes of women slaves at work on a cotton plantation. The Great Exhibition's fine cigars, its enamels, its possession of India's *Koh I noor* diamond, exalted amongst Queen Victoria's Crown jewels; these items find their riposte in Brown's interior view of the "Charleston Workhouse," the slave trade in the Caribbean, the "March of Chain Gang," "Modes of Confinement and Punishment," and sugar plantations and mills, to say nothing of cotton fields.

Although the United States produced more than 80 per cent of the world's cotton in 1850, England was one of the highest consumers of cotton as well as of the sugar produced in its recently "emancipated" West Indian colonies. Thus, while on the one hand Brown's exposition of slavery's evils stroked British egos and gave Britons a sense of remove from the institution, on the other hand the serial portraits that Brown dovetailed, and indeed his tour schedule itself, revealed how Britain indirectly reinforced slavery by supporting the U.S. economy. As an international fugitive, Brown functioned in many respects as a shadow of Britain's own history of slavery. He recalled its violent struggles with the resistant Maroons in Jamaica, with whom Britain signed treaties in 1738 and 1739, partially in recognition of the Maroons' determination to live "free."[33]

That Brown chose to present his "Mirror" in Manchester (1850) and in Bolton (1851) is a telling example of the kind of anti-colonial work that his panorama performed as he moved throughout England, for Bolton was a "manufacturing town with more than sixty cotton factories," and Manchester was a factory town where the English working class endured exploitative labour conditions. Brown's audiences in such cities, then, may well have been receptive to the exploitations he critiqued, or the work may well have sparked an awareness of the connections between their own conditions and that of the slaves who also produced cotton.[34] Brown's tours through manufacturing towns may have had everything to do with the working-class audiences he sought – audiences that may not have been able to attend the Great Exhibition but who would have been intrigued to attend a show that promised to transport them to distant landscapes. Nevertheless, from Liverpool (mercantile exchange) to Manchester (cotton mills and factories), Blackburn (mill town), Bolton (cotton), Preston (cotton), Bradford and Leeds (wool production), Brown's panorama performances covered a circuit of national and international commercial production that implicated England and the United States in the ravages of capitalism and its consequences for Africans in the Americas and Africa as well as for the white working classes in England. If the Britons largely viewed Brown as a jack-in-the-box Lazarus, as Wood observes, once both the presenter and his panorama were unveiled in these shifting British contexts, Brown's entertainment value warrants a re-evaluation alongside the parallel messages encoded in his panorama and articulated in his physical travels as fugitive.

While the Crystal Palace "conjured up visions of commodities and banished from sight the realities of exchange," such that items were displayed "mute and solid," Brown conjured up precisely the opposite by injecting his live fugitive body and images of resisting runways like William and Ellen Craft and Henry Bibb, as well as the enslaved and the dead, into the Great Exhibition's lopsided "free trade" equation.[35] The second half of his panorama depicted his escape in his box, his unboxing in Philadelphia, Henry Bibb's escape, and the escapes of William and Ellen Craft, a fugitive couple who stole freedom when light-skinned Ellen camouflaged herself as a white master, with William pretending to be her slave.[36] The Crafts, like Brown, executed their ruse by rail. Henry Bibb, known in the United States as an incorrigible runaway, was famous for having gone Maroon numerous times in what seemed a dizzying cycle of escape and recapture. By incorporating into his "Mirror" the Crafts and Bibb with Nubians who insisted on escape, and by situating these escapes adjacent to his own escape, the "Dismal Swamp," the "Promise of Freedom," and "West India Emancipation," Brown negotiated both a visual and ideological space for understanding the centrality of fugitive resistance to modern colonial New World projects.[37] Although the "Mirror" was designed to engender sympathy for the enslaved, Brown also put issues of black resistance, maroonage, and agency forthright in his panorama. And though he depicted "Nubian Slaves Retaken" and their "Tarring and Feathering" in South Carolina, Brown did not feature the kneeling broken slave, a familiar anti-slavery trope, as the climax in his presentation: uprising and escaping fugitives constituted his primal scenes of instruction. It was these escapes and Brown's own stature as fugitive that formed the centrepiece of his panorama and thrilled his audiences. In one of the few African American descriptions of the Great Exhibition, William Wells Brown wrote that it was like a "theatre" or "matchless panorama" that allowed observers to see "all the kingdoms of the world and the glory of them."[38] If the Exhibition was like a matchless panorama, Brown's panorama leveraged a challenge of its own without parallel in the event. His significance, however, loomed even beyond this, for a report in *Frederick Douglass' Paper*, "Mr. Box Brown and the Hungarians," reveals that Brown endeavoured through his shows to forge strategic political alliances with Polish refugees, who, like him, had been disfranchised in the land of their birth. On at least one occasion Brown exhibited his panorama "for the Benefit of the Polish and Hungarian refugees . . . residing in Rochdale, who served under Kossuth and his generals in the late Hungarian struggles."[39]

Just as Brown had shrewdly capitalized upon the theme of resurrection and adeptly intimated its affiliation with political uprising, so too in this context he used his imagination creatively and "explained the several scenes presented on [his] canvas, and made appropriate allusions to the case of the Hungarians."[40] Here was a metamorphic, international, and geopolitical dimension to Brown, demonstrating how extensive and important he and his panorama were to transatlantic conversations as opposed to being merely an American phenomenon. Douglass's paper captured the ironies of Brown's situation when it related:

> But the thought of a fugitive from American slavery, who cannot stay in this country, making such an exhibition for the purpose of aiding fugitives from Austrian tyranny, whom the people of this country are doing so much to honour, is an impressive commentary on the strange mixtures that exist in human affairs.[41]

Figure 5: Frontispiece from Brown's 1849 slave narrative as cover page for *The Boston Slave Riot, and Trial of Anthony Burns*, 1854 (Rare Book and Special Collections Reading Room, Library of Congress)

The case was no aberration in Brown's career. By 1859 he had constructed a second panorama chronicling the 1857 Indian Mutiny against British colonialism and domination, an event that resulted in "the Massacre at Cawnpore." A newspaper reported that "since the sad Revolt in our Eastern Empire has occurred . . . Mr. Brown has a panorama of the Great Indian Mutiny, which he now exhibits alternately with his great American panorama, either of which affords excellent entertainment."[42]

Henry Brown's Maroon corps was successful precisely because it pivoted on "strange mixtures," on a slippery but purposive "jumbled mass," unpredictable, unarrestable, and uncontainable. Indeed, in the following years images of his escape quickly proliferated in different contexts, working to motivate various audiences. Like mutations of his original copyrighted escape image, a fitting quip on his political defiance as fugitive, multiple derivative versions of Brown's escape image crept into various venues: from anti-slavery texts to children's books to popular magazines. If we read beyond Brown's box and its symbolism of the repressions of the U.S. republic, when his imagistic "revolutions" are considered within a maroonist frame that holds law in view, their agility (their metamorphic and permutational propensity) opens up a rich allegorical field urging retheorization of their circulation as rapidly shifting insurgent subjects that refuse arrest and seduce precisely because in some seemingly benign contexts they are camouflaged by narratives of black containment and suffering while working towards the opposite.

The rapid proliferation of Brown's escape image thus may not be as thorough a distortion or reductionist appropriation as Marcus Wood has suggested.[43] Years after Brown's escape and his flight to England, it was to his image that white and black Boston anti-slavery activists turned when, after the capture of another Virginia fugitive, Anthony Burns, they rioted and destroyed a Boston courthouse where Burns was confined. In the process they killed a law enforcement official and mounted an extensive community campaign, to which the president responded by dispatching federal troops. On the front page of the circular that these Boston activists produced in support of Burns's case, it was Brown's image that was used to introduce their arguments against the *Fugitive Slave Act* and the policies of the U.S. government. We may never know why these activists turned specifically to Brown's image, but the usage of it is perhaps some measure of just how incendiary Brown's resistance had become in the political imagination – so much so that it was not the image of his box that these activists used to support their anti-legal insurrectionary uprising, but rather the likeness of Brown from his 1849 narrative's frontispiece.

No other example more aptly illustrates how Brown's image travelled above and beyond law, beyond the sentimental politics of containment and into dangerously insurgent ground where interracial uprising could and did happen. Perhaps the Bostonians merely substituted one Virginian for another; but it bears considering that Brown himself had become a telling point of political citation, circulating everywhere and yet remaining beyond physical reach, like the elliptical Maroons.

Though Brown's "Dismal Swamp" figured America's geography in his panorama as a base of fugitive resistance, he clearly extended his resistance geography in and through his movements and strategic alliances, and the circulations of his image. Almost as if to purposely signify on this point, in an interesting reply to a British audience member who inquired as to where in America the Dismal Swamp was located, Brown replied that he did not know exactly. The reviewer would attack Brown for his lack of specificity, caricaturing him as one who "daint asotly know; taint somewhere in the middle of de state."[44] Brown's refusal to answer amounted to a specification of a non-location nonetheless, a rather ironic emblematization of the perilous existence of the fugitive and the strength produced through strategic levels of invisibility from the margins of the colonial world.

In November 1850, shortly after Brown's first set of panorama performances in Britain, a reviewer noted that if any of Brown's viewers "have thought lightly of the injustice done by America to three millions and a half of our fellow-creatures, we feel assured they will leave the exhibition in another frame of mind."[45] Still, we are left wondering whether the English audiences and former slave-holders turned colonizers truly did look into Henry Box Brown's mirror.

Notes

1 Henry Brown, *Narrative of the Life of Henry Box Brown*, ed. Richard Newman (New York: Oxford University Press, 2002 [1851]); Jeffry Ruggles, *The Unboxing of Henry Brown* (Richmond, Va.: Library of Virginia, 2003). The National Great Blacks in Wax Museum, located in Baltimore, Maryland, was founded by Joanne M. Martin and Elmer P. Martin. Ruggles's biography is the most extensive work focusing on Brown's activities in England after his escape in 1849 and Brown's return to the United States in 1875 after the Civil War.

2 Marcus Wood, *Blind Memory: Visual Representations of Slavery in England and America, 1780–1865* (Manchester, Eng.: Manchester University Press, 2000), p.113; Samira Kawash, *Dislocating the Color Line: Identity, Hybridity, and Singularity in African-American Narrative* (Stanford, Cal.: Stanford University Press, 1997).

3 Wood, *Blind Memory*, and Ruggles, *Unboxing of Henry Brown*, have provided groundbreaking research on Brown's activities in Britain, and I have written more extensively about this elsewhere and in a forthcoming project on maroonage, resistance, and black New World existentiality: see Suzette Spencer, "Stealing a Way: African Diaspora Maroon Poetics," unpublished dissertation, University of California, Berkeley, 2002. The point here is to extend the arguments of Wood, Ruggles, and Kawash by situating Brown within a context of maroonist resistance.

4 Invented in 1788 by Robert Barker, panoramas became a popular mode of presentation in Europe and the United States. In the most basic sense they were scenes painted on canvas and stitched together to tell a visual story or multiple stories. The panorama would therefore scroll across the stage from one side to another, allowing viewers to take in its scenes. Panoramas were especially attractive for their ability to give viewers bold views of landscapes. Several offshoots developed, so that in some instances viewing areas were circularly constructed with a viewing platform in the middle of the room; hence the name "cyclorama."

5 I am using the concepts "coloniality of power" and "anti-coloniality of power" in the manner used by theorists Walter Mignolo and Anibal Quijano. See Walter Mignolo, *Local Histories Global Designs: Coloniality, Subaltern Knowledges, and Border Thinking*, Princeton Studies in Culture/Power/History (Princeton, N.J.: Princeton University Press, 2000).

6 James Olney, "I Was Born: Slave Narratives, Their Status as Autobiography and Literature," in *The Slave's Narrative*, ed. Charles T. Davis and Henry Louis Gates Jr. (New York: Oxford University Press, 1985), p.161.

7 The full title of the first narrative is *Narrative of Henry Box Brown, Who Escaped from Slavery Enclosed in a Box 3 Feet Long and 2 Feet Wide*. The second edition is more simply entitled *Narrative of the Life of Henry Box Brown, Written By Himself.*

8 The version of the image that Brown sold (Figure 1 in this chapter), was entered into copyright either by Brown or for Brown in 1850 in the Library of Congress. The LOC does not name an artist responsible for creating the image, nor is the image signed, but it credits the copyright to Brown. Brown most likely had someone else complete the drawing. However, he did sell copies of this image at anti-slavery bazaars. The image in his second narrative is a derivative of the one Brown copyrighted in 1850.

9 In an 1849 review of the Douglass slave narrative, for example, Ephraim Peabody, a Unitarian minister, delivered a scathing review of Douglass's rhetoric and writing style, arguing, "While our sympathies go with him, and because they go with him, we are disposed to make criticism on a mode of address in which he sometimes indulges himself, which we believe is likely to diminish, not only his usefulness, but his real influence." Douglass's style, Peabody claimed, "was a mistaken one if the speaker wishes to sway the judgment of his hearers and to accomplish any practical end . . . flippant, extravagant speaker, especially if he be gifted with the power of sarcasm, will probably be listened to and applauded, but nothing comes of it. Those who applaud the most understand very well that this is not the kind of person to be relied on as a guide in actions. . . . Nothing is less effective, for any practical end, than the 'withering and scorching' eloquence with which American speeches seem to abound. It conciliates momentary passion, and though it may light up momentary passions, it gives no new strength of conviction to friends of the cause. . . . We by no means think these remarks apply peculiarly to Douglass. . . . We think that more often than he is probably aware, he suffers himself to fall into this mode of speech." Frederick Douglass, *Narrative of the Life of Frederick Douglass, an American Slave: With Related Documents*, ed. David W. Blight (Boston: Bedford/St. Martin's, 2003 [1845]), p.137.

10 Wood, *Blind Memory*, p.110.

11 Newman, in Brown, *Narrative of the Life of Henry Box Brown*.

12 Marcus Wood, "All Right: The Narrative of Henry Box Brown as a Test Case for the Racial Prescription of Rhetoric and Semiotics," *American Antiquarian Society: A Journal of American History and Culture*, 107:1 (1998), p.91.

13 Douglass, *Narrative of the Life*, p.88; emphasis in original.

14 Henry Brown and Charles Stearns, *Narrative of Henry Box Brown Who Escaped from Slavery Enclosed in a Box 3 Feet Long and 2 Wide* (Boston: Brown & Stearns, 1849), p.v.

15 Brown, *Narrative of the Life of Henry Box Brown*, p.19.

16 C. Peter Ripley, *The Black Abolitionist Papers: The British Isles, 1830–1865*, vol.1 (Chapel Hill: University of North Carolina Press, 1985), p.298.

17 William Wells Brown, *The Travels of William Wells Brown, Including the Narrative of William Wells Brown, a Fugitive Slave, and the American Fugitive in Europe, Sketches of Places and People Abroad, 1848*, ed. Paul Jefferson (New York: Markus Wiener Publishers, 1991 [1848]), p.190.

18 Thomas Richards, *The Commodity Culture of Victorian England: Advertising and Spectacle, 1851–1914* (Stanford, Cal.: Stanford University Press, 1990), p.57.

19 Ibid., p.28.

20 Jeffrey A. Auerbach, *The Great Exhibition of 1851: A Nation on Display* (New Haven, Conn.: Yale University Press, 1999), has written eloquently on this point.
21 Mignolo, *Local Histories Global Designs*, p.17. The Quijano quote is from this same source.
22 Auerbach, *Great Exhibition of 1851*, p.162.
23 Quoted in Auerbach, *Great Exhibition of 1851*, p.162.
24 Ibid., p. 161.
25 Ruggles, *Unboxing of Henry Brown*, p.103.
26 For more on Fourier, see Jonathan Beecher, *Charles Fourier: The Visionary and His World* (Berkeley: University of California Press, 1986).
27 Some advertisements listed his panorama as one about African and American slavery. See Ruggles, *Unboxing of Henry Brown*, p.155. No portraits of Brown's panorama exist, although the titles of his scenes can be found in several newspaper advertisements. Ruggles has conducted excellent research, suggesting some sources from which Brown may have derived his depictions.
28 *Wolverhampton and Staffordshire Herald*, March 17, 1852; Summer Assizes, Midland Court, *London Times*, July 28, 1852.
29 Mignolo, *Local Histories Global Designs*, p. 52; emphasis in original.
30 "The Mirror of American Slavery," *The Leeds Mercury*, May 25, 1851, p.5.
31 See Ruggles, *Unboxing of Henry Brown*, p.128.
32 Richards, *Commodity Culture of Victorian England*, p.30.
33 I qualify "free" here because the British-Maroon treaties are paradoxical documents, which I explore elsewhere as a process on the part of the British of dialectically overcoming the Maroons: that is, of supplanting the violent fights to the death that Hegel described with more bureaucratic forms of dominance meant to preserve the body in order to exploit it.
34 Ruggles, *Unboxing of Henry Brown*, p.125.
35 Richards, *Commodity Culture of Victorian England*, p.30.
36 The Crafts actually attended the Great Exhibition with William Wells Brown, in addition to lecturing in Britain against American slavery. They too, like Brown, left America on the heels of the passing of the *Fugitive Slave Act* after almost being captured in Boston. For more on the Crafts, see William Craft and Ellen Craft, *Running a Thousand Miles for Freedom: The Escape of William and Ellen Craft from Slavery*, ed. Barbara McCaskill (Athens: University of Georgia Press, 1999 [1860]).
37 On Henry Bibb, see H. Bibb, *The Life and Adventures of Henry Bibb, An American Slave, 1849 (Narrative of the Life and Adventures of Henry Bibb)*, ed. Charles J. Hegler (Madison: University of Wisconsin Press, 2001 [1849]).
38 Brown, *Travels of William Wells Brown*, p.171.
39 "Mr Box Brown and the Hungarians," *Frederick Douglass' Paper* (Rochester, N.Y.), Nov. 27, 1851.
40 Ibid.
41 Ibid.
42 Quoted in Ruggles, *Unboxing of Henry Brown*, p.152.
43 Wood, *Blind Memory*, p.113.
44 Summer Assizes, Midland Court.

7

Kimberly N. Ruffin

"A Realm of Monuments and Water"

Lorde-ian Erotics and Shange's African Diaspora Cosmopolitanism

> shall I tell you how my country looks
> my soil & rains . . .
> it's my space
> a land lovin you gives me . . .
> my space is a realm of monuments & water
> language & the ambiance of senegalese cafes
>
> — Ntozake Shange, "where the mississippi meets the amazon"

> Our erotic knowledge empowers us, becomes a lens through which we scrutinize all aspects of our existence, forcing meaning within our lives. . . . It is never easy to demand the most from ourselves, from our lives, from our work. To encourage excellence is to go beyond the encouraged mediocrity of our society. . . . But giving in to the fear of feeling and working to capacity is a luxury only the unintentional can afford, and the unintentional are those who do not wish to guide their own destinies.
>
> — Audre Lorde, "Uses of the Erotic: The Erotic as Power"

Marcus Garvey, Nancy Prince, Martin Delany, Zora Neale Hurston, C.L.R James, Nicolás Guillén, Pearl Primus, Abdias do Nascimento, Katherine Dunham, Aimé Césaire, Maud Cuney-Hare, Alexander

Crummell, Paule Marshall, W.E.B. Du Bois, George Lamming, Erna Brodber, Buchi Emecheta, and Kwame Nkrumah: these are just some of the impressive range of activists, artists, and scholars who have tried to strike a balance between geographic realities and cosmopolitan desires. Their balancing acts have been as diverse as ex-patriotism, pan-Africanism, the Negritude movement, and the Harlem Renaissance, with purposes as wide as artistic expression and socio-political empowerment. In addressing the cosmopolitan tendencies of African and African-descended people, Michael Hanchard writes:

> Afro-Modern politics are characterized by (a) a supranational formulation of people of African descent as an "imagined community" that is not territorially demarcated but based on the shared belief in the commonalities of Western oppression experienced by African and African-derived peoples; (b) the development of alternative political and cultural networks across national-state boundaries; and (c) an explicit critique of the uneven application of the discourses of the Enlightenment and processes of modernization by the West, along with those discourses' attendant notions of sovereignty and citizenship.[1]

The experience of various societies' racialized oppression inclines many blacks throughout the African diaspora to identify with the ever-changing boundaries of diaspora rather than the more stable boundaries of nation. Taking a disassociation with the nation in a different direction, contemporary philosopher Jason Hill, in his book *Becoming a Cosmopolitan: What It Means to Be a Human Being in the New Millennium*, characterizes cosmopolitanism as a moral evolution and ethical virtue as he berates "tribalists" for organizing "much civic and social life around racial, ethnic, and national tribal lines."[2] In contrast, the activists, authors, and artists that I have named here feel comfort in acknowledging that they are somehow "rooted" in both the historic mistreatment of people of African descent and a multicultural legacy that celebrates Africanity. These roots are based on positive associations with the cultures of Africa and its diaspora and the celebration of resistance to oppressive forces that support what is called the "stigmatization of blackness." This significant tradition of artistic and political responses creates several versions of what I call "African Diaspora Cosmopolitanism" and are the subject of numerous scholarly studies. Ifeoma Kiddoe Nwankwo's *Black Cosmopolitanism: Racial Consciousness and Transnational Identity in the Nineteenth-Century Americas* and Wendy W. Walters's *At Home in Diaspora: Black International Writing* are just two of such studies that identify the early and consistent culturally rooted transnationalism of African-descended peoples.[3]

What are the benefits of this approach to geographic experience and cultural identity? First, African Diaspora Cosmopolitanism acknowledges the complicated geographies of contemporary life in an age of "information" and increased globalism. Given the large-scale and persistent experience of the "stigmatization of blackness," the approach also shows how history informs contemporary societies and cultural life. Stuart Hall comments:

> Far from being eternally fixed in some essential past, [diaspora identities] are subject to the continuous "play" of history, culture and power. Far from being grounded in a mere "recovery" of our past, which is waiting to be found . . . identities are the names we give to the different ways we are positioned by, and position ourselves within, the narratives of the past.[4]

The continued influence of oppressive "narratives of the past" sheds light on another benefit of African Diaspora Cosmopolitanism: it offers ways of defining concepts such as "freedom," "family," or the "erotic" that are alternatives to dominant modes of thinking, especially when these alternatives can tap into groups typically marginalized as intellectually unimportant. Gay Wilentz, in *Binding Cultures: Black Women Writers in Africa and the Diaspora*, highlights the necessity of seeing women as a resource in African diaspora traditions of thought. She writes:

> Until recently, there was little focus on women's role in the creation of a diaspora culture and on the commonalities that exist in female modes of cultural production throughout the African diaspora . . . a diaspora perspective opens up relationships and connections not easily addressed even in continental studies. Without this broader exploration of the works by women of African descent on both sides of the Atlantic, many of the signs and meanings of the discourse are lost.[5]

As a creative writer and theorist who situates herself against "European-American male tradition" as a self-identified "Black lesbian feminist," Audre Lorde redefines dominant modes of thinking about the "erotic" in her essay "Uses of the Erotic: The Erotic as Power." In this essay Lorde reconfigures the erotic because she feels it has been used against black women to limit their potential to enter or alter the status quo. Her definition of the erotic also results in a reconceptualization of "work." A Lorde-ian vision of the erotic suggests that people "evaluate individual worth" and go outside the "encouraged mediocrity of our society" and work "to capacity," giving themselves an alternative to societal definitions of excellence.[6] Suggesting that the erotic can be understood through the lens of work and personal definitions of excellence is an alternative to the idea that the erotic has romantic and/or sexual union as its foundation. This manner of reconceptualizing the erotic addresses the history of African diaspora women whose sexual and non-sexual labour was exploited by institutions and individuals for centuries.

An alternative vision of the erotic has pertinence for contemporary African diaspora woman as well. Patricia Hill-Collins explains, "Work is a contested construct and . . . evaluating individual worth by the type of work performed is a questionable practice in systems based on race and gender inequality within segmented labor markets."[7] Lorde addresses the impact of work in a capitalist society, noting:

> The principal horror of any system which defines the good in terms of profit rather than in terms of human need, or which defines human need to the exclusion of the psychic and emotional components of that need . . . is that it robs our work of its erotic value, its erotic power and life appeal and fulfillment.[8]

Lorde takes the contested construct of "work" and places it within her definition of the erotic as an "assertion of the lifeforce of women, of that creative energy empowered, the knowledge and use of which we are now reclaiming in our language, our history, our dancing, our loving, our work, our lives."[9] As a theoretical offering, this notion of the erotic stands as an intellectual alternative to those willing to think beyond what Lorde calls the "European-American male tradition."[10]

The Shange Geographies

An author of numerous plays, poems, and essays, Ntozake Shange is another feminist voice that gives consistent consideration to the interplay of work and the erotic, especially in the lives of her black female characters. Her attention to the role that geography plays in how her characters understand work and/or the erotic registers a unique contribution to the longstanding tradition of African diaspora artists, activists, and thinkers who articulated a transnational sense of placement in the world long before the mainstream currency of "globalization" developed. The potential of a Lorde-ian sense of the erotic, which reconfigures work, looms large in the various geographies of Shange's multigenre corpus. As her characters grapple with the elements of this philosophy, the erotic and work, they forge an African Diaspora Cosmopolitanism that does not obscure the importance of locally rooted histories.

A vignette from her most well-renowned work, *for colored girls who have considered suicide/when the rainbow is enuf*, reveals how two locales in the African diaspora, St. Louis, Missouri, and Haiti, come together under the umbrella of a Lorde-ian notion of the erotic. The "lady in brown" tells a childhood story about how her intellectual work, as a summer reading-contest winner, is negated because she "raved abt TOUSSAINT L'OUVERTURE." The story of the Haitian revolutionary does not appear to be the only reason why the lady in brown was disqualified from the competition; in addition, the fact that she "ran inta" the "ADULT READING ROOM" to get the book is another unacceptable act. She has her award taken away because she transgresses the age boundaries in the library to find alternatives to the nation-centred stories of "pioneer girls & magic rabbits & big city white boys" in the children's reading room. This transgression positions her sense of self within the African diaspora rather than in the nation. After being disqualified from the contest, the lady in brown recounts:

> Toussaint/waz layin in bed wit me next to raggedy ann/ the night I decided to run away from my integrated home/integrated street/integrated school/ 1955 was not a good year for lil blk girls/ Toussaint said "lets go to haiti"/ I said "awright"/ & packed some very important things in a brown paper bag/ so I wdnt haveta come back/ then Toussaint & I took the hodimont streetcar/ to the river/ last stop/ only 15¢/ cuz there waznt nobody cd see Toussaint cept me.[11]

As she strolls around North St. Louis in the imagined accompaniment of her revolutionary hero-friend, the lady in brown encounters a young boy whose name is Toussaint Jones. She is in disbelief at first, but, curious about any connection that may exist between the boy and the revolutionary, she inquires, "Are ya any kin to him/ he don't take no stuff from no white folks & they gotta country all they own/ & there aint no slaves." He responds, "I am TOUSSAINT JONES/ & i'm right heah lookin at ya/ & I don't take no stuff from no white folks/ ya don't see none round heah do ya?/ . . . come on lets go on down to the docks & look at the boats."[12] She responds:

> I felt TOUSSAINT L'OUVERTURE sorta leave me/ & I waz sad/ til I realized TOUSSAINT JONES waszn't too different from TOUSSAINT L'OUVERTURE/ cept the ol one waz in haiti/ & this one wid me speakin english & eatin apples/ yeah./ toussaint jones waz awright wit me/ no tellin what all spirits we cd move down by the river/ st. louis 1955.[13]

In the conclusion of this brief story, the eight-year-old girl fuses her imagined companionship with the Haitian liberator with friendship with a living peer who shares the Haitian leader's first name. In both the real and imagined friendship, Shange presents an African American female who must find a refuge from the integrated spaces (home, street, school) of 1955 St. Louis. Once she accepts the friendship of Toussaint Jones, she does not return to these integrated spaces, but, rather, they go "down by the river," to commune with the spirit world. The discovery of L'Ouverture's story in the adult section of the library is a bittersweet rite of passage for the eight-year-old: she expands her reading experience by venturing into a new territory, wins a reading contest, and has her accomplishment of reading "15 books in three weeks" invalidated because of her curiosity to see beyond the nation-driven narratives offered to her in a children's section of a library. These narratives of "pioneer girls & magic rabbits & big city white boys" ignore the lives of African-descended people who are both part of the integrated surrounding neighbourhood and the African diaspora. Yet she carries her books to the docks with her newfound friend, the African American Toussaint, and the vision of the two youngsters "moving spirits" down by the river suggests the possibility that connections within the African diaspora, reflected in her new playmate's first name, will continue and mature.

"Toussaint" encapsulates the primary element of Shange's treatment of spatial desire: a balance between local experience and the potential to be realized in understanding oneself as part of the African diaspora. In "Toussaint," reading is the way in which the eight-year-old lady in brown connects her local experiences with life in the African diaspora – the library connects her to both the life of an African diaspora hero and a neighbourhood peer. Her initial disappointment over Toussaint Jones not being biologically related to Toussaint L'Ouverture is diminished by her recognition of some unidentified similarity between the two and the youngsters' intent to move spirits "down by the river." Reading a library book develops the lady in brown's knowledge of the African diaspora as it also solidifies her appreciation of home. Because the lady in brown is able to use the diaspora to reconfigure the value of her intellectual work, she transforms the library's disqualification, giving her the individual power that Lorde's idea of the erotic presumes. She can value her work on her own, and being connected to the idea of diaspora assists this accomplishment.

Shange's 1982 novel *Sassafrass, Cypress, and Indigo* also balances the benefits of local identity enhanced by cosmopolitan connections. Shange's novel includes song, poetry, journal entries, conjuring spells, and letters. In addition, several recipes, either for physical or emotional nourishment, are part of this "verbal mosaic" that celebrates "womanhood, life, and art" in the lives of three sisters (Sassafrass, Cypress, and Indigo) and their mother (Hilda Effania).[14] While Sassafrass and Cypress venture far away from their Charleston, South Carolina, home, by the novel's end they are returning there to reunite with their mother and youngest sister, Indigo. Carol Marsh-Lockett writes:

> Each woman's journey necessitates a return to the place which, for good or for ill, whether she will stay there or not, she must call home. Each returns to Charleston – Sassafrass to give birth, the symbol of a new life, assisted in the act by her sisters; Indigo to carry out last rites for Aunt Haydee; and Cypress to begin a new life with Leroy. Facilitated by the arts motif, the return or circular plot structure is complete as each sister finds herself back in her Charleston origins, having explored her womanhood in distinctly African American terms through the medium of art.[15]

What Marsh-Lockett describes as the "arts motif" shapes the experience of work for the characters. As they move through geographic space, they also search to find a work life with a promise akin to the Lorde-ian erotic. The novel's various forms of "experimental living" (including a separatist lesbian community and "The New World Found Collective" artistic commune in Louisiana) show characters willing to take an adventurous, cosmopolitan direction in their experiences; the ending suggests that "provincial" identity remains crucial in navigating cosmopolitan geographies and approaching a Lorde-ian erotic.

Hilda Effania and Indigo are the clearest representations of provincial characters in *Sassafrass, Cypress, and Indigo.* Even as she tries to ensure the transmission of Southern U.S. culture in the lives of each of her daughters, Hilda is aware that both generational and spatial change will alter the expression of these traditions. When she learns that Sassafrass, living in Los Angeles, will celebrate Kwanza and not Christmas, Hilda does not shun her daughter. Instead she tries to infuse Sassafrass's celebration of Kwanza with food from family Christmas celebrations. Hilda writes in a letter to Sassafrass:

> Maybe this holiday, Kwanza, is not as bad as I thought. When you said you weren't having Christmas, I kept wondering where I had failed. Still, as long as it's a religious ceremony with feasts and gifts like Christmas, I guess it'll be okay. Why does it go on for so many days? You haven't explained all of it to me yet. . . . I was attempting to tell the Bowdry sisters about your goings on, but I just don't have enough information. Is the Maulana the same as the

> Savior, or is like a minister, for you all, I mean? Here is a recipe [Mama's Kwanza Recipe: Duck with Mixed Oyster Stuffing] I want you to have, so there won't be too much heathen in your Christmas this year. . . . Now, that seems like a dish packed full of love and history to me.[16]

Hilda's provincial mind does not understand "all of" Kwanza. She thinks it is a religious rather than a cultural holiday and misunderstands Maulana Karenga's role as the creator of Kwanza as that of a religious leader. The recipe serves as a way of using culinary work to transmit cultural continuity, in this case rooted in a Christian celebration. It is Hilda's hope that the recipe will counteract the "heathen" elements of Sassafrass's holiday celebration, just as the recipe serves to relocate a culinary part of Charleston, South Carolina, in Los Angeles. If successful, Hilda has given Sassafrass a way of coping with the "cultural attenuation" of her migration to Los Angeles and a way of fusing old holiday traditions with new ones through the labour of culinary arts. Hilda is a woman both open to her daughters' experimentations and persistent in her efforts to forward any strength to be had from her provincial world. Arlene Elder describes Hilda as "embodying both the restricting, conservative elements of stereotypical 'mothers' and, simultaneously, a liberating wisdom, inspiration, and love."[17] The balance of these two aspects of Hilda's personality allows Shange to depict a relatively conservative black mother with a provincial identity who acknowledges the power of culinary work to foment cultural continuity amidst the geographic movement of the daughters' lives. Culinary work, valued through Hilda's conceptual lens, provides an opportunity for her provincial influence on new geography. Free from stereotypical and debased understandings of cooking as the job of the "black Mammy," it also symbolizes a necessary and redemptive provincialism from which her daughters draw their strength.

Sassafrass needs this strength to conceive of the erotic outside of her dysfunctional relationship with Mitch. Mitch advocates the abandonment of the work traditions that Hilda instils in Sassafrass. His effort to control her labour is dependent on his debasement of the "domestic arts" that Hilda uses to educate her girls. The conflict over Mitch's vision of Sassafrass's work life and her own represents the distorted experience of work that emerges from a traditional notion of the erotic, one based in romance/sexual relationship. Mitch feels that Sassafrass should "write and create new images for black folks," and while he initially says that "there's nothing wrong with" the handcrafts that Sassafrass prefers to do instead of writing, their exchange escalates with Mitch "forcefully [holding] her face close to his" and verbally abusing Sassafrass. Shange continues the scene by representing Sassafrass's struggle to value her creative preferences and herself. Shange writes:

> Sassafrass was weak from Mitch's torment. . . . Mitch didn't have to say all that even if it was true; it was ridiculous for some man to come tell her she had to create. . . . Sassafrass caught herself focusing in on Mitch again instead of herself, because she did want to be perfected for him, like he was perfected and creating all the time. Sassafrass was running all through herself looking for some way to get into her secrets and share, like Richard Wright had done and Zora Neale Hurston had done.[18]

Sassafrass's "focusing in on Mitch . . . instead of herself" keeps her from embracing an erotic outlook that privileges her own self-perception. This space is made worse when she encounters Otis and Henry, Mitch's friends. They too verbally assault Sassafrass with an excerpt of Otis's book *Ebony Cunt*. Sassafrass withdraws from the men's misogynist diatribe to continue weaving, in a turn to Hilda's legacies. Within the dysfunctional relationship with Mitch, cooking and weaving stand as opportunities for Sassafrass to connect to the power represented by her mother's traditions. Yet ultimately she must move physically to ensure her personal growth. Her first move is with Mitch to The New World Found Collective in "the lush backwoods of Louisiana."[19] This artists' commune "offered spiritual redemption" from the abuse that Sassafrass was experiencing in Los Angeles. But this relief is temporary. "Reinforced by the Afrocentric ethos of the commune and the growth Sassafrass experiences there," she receives "the strength she needs to shake the bonds of male dependency by ridding herself of Mitch" and returns "to Charleston to have a baby."[20] The wide geographic expanse of Sassafrass's life, which culminates in her journey from the West Coast back to the East Coast to start a new life for herself and her baby, indicates a shift in the spatial dynamics of African American literary tradition. Comparing Shange's work with slave narratives that chart a person's internal or external movement, Elder writes:

> In Shange's "novel," the geographic movement is from South to West to East (North), and back to the South again. Whereas in an earlier period the North promised a political liberty which was to carry with it personal liberty, at this later date, roughly the 1960s, largely due to gender-based conflicts, Shange's runaways must first arrive at a different shore – the nurturing home of African and African-American concepts of artistry, healing, and community – before feeling their own vitality and becoming living forces in the world.[21]

The return to Charleston does not negate the importance of Sassafrass's life in California, but it does reiterate that a provincial perspective can help her to refocus her efforts. Hilda's invitation for Sassafrass to "come back to Charleston and find the rest of [her]self" leaves Sassafrass with the chance to recover the strength she finds at home for a journey that may lead her away from home again.

Indigo best represents a daughter who has mastered the strength to be had from her home environment. The continuous refrain in Shange's description of Indigo is that she has "the South in her," sometimes in excessive amounts. Shange writes, "The South in her, the land and salt-winds, moved her through Charleston's streets as if she were a mobile sapling with the gait of a well-loved colored woman whose lover was the horizon in any direction. . . . She made herself, her world, from all that she came from."[22] This fantastical and sensual merging of human being and environment in the description of Indigo, Hilda's youngest child, reveals Shange's association of the South with magical properties that Sassafrass and Cypress need to recoup. In contrast to the lives of her older sisters, Indigo's experiences serve to root her further and further into Southern folk culture, whether they be her adventures with homemade dolls, companionship with Spats and Crunch (the "Junior Geechee Captains") or apprenticeship with Aunt Haydee. Elder writes, "The precocious Indigo neither marries nor leaves the South, choosing, instead, to burrow deeply into it, to apprentice herself, priest-like, to the conjure woman and midwife Aunt Haydee."[23]

Free from a notion of the erotic bound in a romantic/sexual relationship, Indigo flourishes as she gains mastery as a musician, healer, and midwife. Marsh-Lockett comments, "As [Indigo] matures she remains steeped in the folk tradition and so defines her personhood. . . . Armed with her talents and her spiritual and psychic connection with her folk past, Indigo assumes an easy and natural place among the folk and later inherits a position of responsibility when Aunt Haydee dies."[24] Explaining Indigo's fusion of self and place, Shange writes, "Her sisters were artists. Would they understand [Indigo] just wanted where they came from to stay alive? Hilda Effania knew Indigo had an interest in folklore. Hilda Effania had no idea that Indigo was the folks."[25]

Cookbooks, Recipes, Food Practices: Roots of Social Geography

Rather than recipes that revolve around the food practices of this folk culture, the recipes in Indigo's portions of the novel concentrate on ways of addressing emotional wounds and dreams. Recipes such as "If Your

Beloved Has Eyes for Another," "Marvelous Menstruating Moments," "To Rid Oneself of the Scent of Evil," "Realizing Spirits' Hints/ What Your Dreams Can Do for You," and "Emergency Care of Wounds That Cannot Be Seen" give a broad representation of the food practices and rituals, while they underscore Shange's "use of the arts metaphor in the exploration of African American female selfhood."[26] Indigo embodies the psychological strength of rootedness in geography hospitable to "women's arts" as part of "African American female selfhood." Her provincialism promises to value music, healing, and midwifery as aspects of Southern folk culture.

Indigo and Hilda's creative acts stress the benefits of provincialism. Just as in the return of Zora Neale Hurston's Janie to Eatonville, the return of Sassafrass and Cypress to Charleston emphasizes the privilege that Shange gives to provincialism even as she creates characters with remarkably cosmopolitan lives. Yet the novel problematizes a full-scale embrace of provincialism by contrasting the lives of the solidly provincial characters, Hilda and Indigo, with cosmopolitan characters, Sassafrass and Cypress, who return to the South or adopt provincial behaviours or attitudes. In *Sassafrass, Cypress, and Indigo* Shange tells the stories of characters who personify many aspects of an African Diaspora Cosmopolitan approach to spatial desire. No matter how cosmopolitan their experience, it is a cultural or geographic province that saves them. The combination of cosmopolitan experience and provincial rooting offers the main characters the power to value their work within a Lorde-ian sense of the erotic.

In the cookbook and combined personal-collective memoir *If I Can Cook/You Know God Can*, Shange expands on food practices as another way in which people can maintain a sense of self amidst multiple spatial experiences, a sense of self that accommodates both a need to be provincial and a need to be cosmopolitan.[27] As Sarah Sceats explains, "Food and eating are at the core of lives, inscribed in psyches, embedded in culture, vehicle and substance of social interaction, enmeshed with the relationship of the self to the world." Examining how food is "enmeshed with the relationship of the self to the world" identifies "the symbolic nature of food practices" as "a way of understanding" our commonplace attempts to negotiate any gap between provincial and cosmopolitan longings.[28] Here, food practices enable Shange to articulate a distinctly cosmopolitan trajectory, unlike the favoured provincialism of *Sassafrass, Cypress, and Indigo*. Her cookbook does not discount the importance of provincialism; yet it places a marked emphasis on the African diaspora. Shange suggests that African Americans can use food practices to express an African Diaspora Cosmopolitanism.

Using the cookbook to advance that idea puts Shange in the tradition of African American women who have written cookbooks reflective of

African American culinary history. Rafia Zafar points out the magnitude of such an undertaking. In her essay, "The Signifying Dish: Autobiography and History in Two Black Women's Cookbooks," which examines Vertamae Smart-Grosvenor's *Vibration Cooking: Or the Travel Notes of a Geechee Girl*, and Norma Jean and Carole Darden's *Spoonbread and Strawberry Wine: Recipes and Reminiscences of a Family*, she writes:

> For a twentieth-century African-American female publicly to announce herself as a cook means that she must engage with the reigning ghosts of American racism; she must tackle literally visceral ideas with metaphor, individual agency, and historical memory. . . . Each recalled or recreated dish in a community's cuisine signifies mightily, and multiple readings of a simple dish of rice, greens, and meat reveal past and present worlds in which race and culture define our very taste buds. . . . When negotiating the intersections of memory, history, food, and creativity, well might the Black woman author ask: In writing a recipe, can one also write history? . . . Black culinary traditions can be imagined or inscribed – by the author, by her readers – as a way of enacting the cultural, expressive, and historical agenda of the African-American female.[29]

As with the recipe-filled *Sassafrass, Cypress, and Indigo*, the cookbooks that Zafar describes hold the potential of putting African American women in charge of defining culinary work. By taking charge, these women have the power to defeat the "reigning ghosts of American racism" by reconfiguring this work in a vision originating with African American women. At the same time, the focuses of Smart-Grosvenor, the Darden sisters, and Shange are distinct. Immediate differences can be found in the titles of the three cookbooks. Smart-Grosvenor's personal travel notes include "a global roster of recipes enhancing her picaresque adventures in the rural South, inner-city Philadelphia, France, and Cuba." The Darden family "recipes and reminiscences" serve to "deliver a gastronomic social history of African Americans, emphasizing nineteenth- and early-twentieth century ideals of racial uplift in the face of adversity."[30] Shange's title, *If I Can Cook/You Know God Can*, is evocative of her poetry and her famous adage "I found god in myself and loved her fiercely."[31] Her focus is determined by feminist reflections on food and the African diaspora. The book's cover art reiterates this agenda. The title appears in a handwritten script at the top, with the word "God" peeking over a drawing of Shange. Against a green background, three geographical masses are pictured: the African continent, Brazil, and the contiguous United States. Sprinkled around these land masses are a fish, an ear of corn, a garlic bulb, a pod of okra, and a pig. This visual display is a prelude to a cookbook that stresses the relationship of food, self, and place. The collection of images helps the author define African Americans, whom she describes as "a concept of sorts without the substratum of soil." She goes on to explain:

> We've had to circumvent the realities of place and language to re-create a "where" for our people. I am referring here to the tens of thousands of African-Americans who are committed to an "other" way of life besides the American way. Rather than being imprisoned as the perceived other, we have embraced this as an opportunity that turns inward on itself and grows with the density and influences of a black hole in space.[32]

Since the nation has not provided the kind of geographic attachments that she feels African Americans need, Shange gives her cookbook the scope of the diaspora, here described as a "black hole in space." The transatlantic slave trade gives some definition to this black hole. Shange's meditative look at food practices makes stops in the places connected to the trade. The recipe includes those provincial to U.S. blacks such as "Daddy's Barbecue Sauce," "Uncle Eric's Gumbo," "Collard Greens to Bring You Money," and "French-Fried Chitlins" and non-U.S. diasporic offerings such as "Apporreado de Tasajo" (salt-fried beef stew), "Turtle Eggs and Spices," "Brazilian Rice," and "Dominican Bread Pudding." In this collection of recipes, she reflects merits in both cosmopolitanism and provincialism, but her project seeks to advance an African Diaspora Cosmopolitanism that allows African Americans the virtue of their specificity as she encourages them to become or remain connected to the rest of the African diaspora. She notes that African Americans have "had a terrible time taking freely from the table of bounty freedom [has] afforded to other Americans," but adds: "We are blessed, since we can find our ovens and stoves and make up for some of what we long for."[33]

Reflections on a wide array of food practices and food history work to fill this longing for psychic and physical sustenance. Shange identifies food as "the ultimate implication of who we are," able to "commemorate [black] humanity" in numerous ways. In pondering what Haitian revolutionaries Toussaint L'Ouverture and Jean-Jacques Dessalines shared at their victory dinner after realizing that "they were the first African nation, slave-free, in the New World," she identifies food's ability to "consecrate newfound liberty."[34] The refusal to eat during the slave trade, which Portuguese slavers described as "banzo" (a "mortal melancholy" that was said to have attacked Africans), sets a stage for Shange's discussion of drug addiction in black communities. Harvest-time get-togethers are described as giving communal inspiration to coupling. And arguments between Trinidadians and Barbadians over flying fish point to cultural differences and disagreements within the African diaspora. Shange also uses the pages of her cookbook to disclose how negative associations with African foods such as okra have been part of the machinery of racism. She comments:

> The restitution of okra's reputation is one of my projects. I love okra and . . . I refuse to allow our own people to reject an Africanism that is not inanimate or residual. Okra is one of our living ties to the motherland. In celebration I might make me a parade or an Okra Day. . . . It's virtually treason not to enjoy . . . the little bit of Africa that's actually cultivated in this country. . . . I think we should free the okra, the way we freed the watermelon.[35]

Food is linked to liberty, protest, romance, dispute, and cultural pride, giving readers a grand sense of the depth of human interaction involving food. It also activates the power of Lorde's erotic definition by suggesting that people of African descent have agency in making meaning for food itself and culinary work. Clearly, Shange identifies food as an integral part of the liberation of people of African descent. The end results of her symbolic employment of food frame provincial experiences within an African Diaspora Cosmopolitan vision of the world.

Finding, and Clearing, Disaporic Spaces

Contemporary feminist geographer Geraldine Pratt reflects on the current fascination with globalism and mobility, saying, "If we have no sense of placement, we have no stake in places – both locally and globally – and we have no reason to either preserve or change them."[36] The work of Shange that we've considered here, covering three different decades, represents her stake in preserving and changing both local and diasporic spaces, particularly the issues of work and the erotic. The psychological benefits of envisioning oneself outside the nation are perhaps the most promising aspect of Shange's art, infused as it is with African Diaspora Cosmopolitanism and in keeping with a Lorde-ian erotic. The difficulty of preserving and changing the new space created by this outlook is the persistence of a dominant ideology that prevents her characters from escaping the pitfalls of the erotic scripts that work against men and women alike. Yet, claiming space is crucial in moving towards ideological shifts that better serve individuals and groups. Her essay "How I Moved Anna Fierling to the Southwest Territories or My Personal Victory over the Armies of Western Civilization" clearly documents Shange's development as a geographically empowered artist. She writes:

> i had & still grapple with the idea of classics in the lives & arts of third world people. we have so much to do, so much to unearth abt our varied realities/ on what grounds do we spend our talents, hundreds of thousands of dollars, unknown quantities of time, to recreate experiences that are not our own? does a colonial relationship to a culture/ in this case Anglo-Saxon imperialism/produce a symbiotic relationship or a parasitic one? . . . why aren't the talents & perspectives of contemporary third world artists touted in the same grand fashion successful revivals of dead white artists are? . . . i have resolved the conflicts for myself. i owe not one more moment of thought to the status of European masters . . . the battle is over. i am settling my lands with my characters, my language, my sense of right & wrong, my sense of time & rhythm.[37]

While Shange shows she is keen on her own perspective and aesthetic goals in this passage, she considers herself as part of a community of oppressed peoples who deserve the textual space to tell their stories. Her ability to unite her personal struggles, those of other blacks, and non-black oppressed people in same project without denying anyone's specificity is another hallmark of her African Diaspora Cosmopolitanism. She includes Mexican, Palestinian, Algerian, European American, indigenous American, and African American voices in her "A Weekend in Austin: a Poet, the People, and the KKK" poem. In this poem she outlines the specificity of their particular struggles alongside chants such as "Damn the Klan & the Capitalist Hand Behind It" and "Black Brown Yellow White Oppressed People Must Unite." Her poetry collection, *A Daughter's Geography*, results in the geography of a woman concerned with many localities in Africa and its diaspora: Brazil, Haiti, El Salvador, the United States of America, and South Africa. Yet her conclusion is best summarized in her words from the poem "New World Coro":

> we have a daughter/ mozambique
> we have a son/ angola
> our twins
> salvador & johannesburg/ cannot speak
> the same language
> but we fight the same old men/ in the new world.[38]

Ntozake Shange recognizes the varied linguistic realities of the African diaspora as she calls for solidarity. Through her African Diaspora Cosmopolitanism, she clears a space for ideological shifts in concepts such as the erotic. This reconfiguration helps people of African descent be better equipped to see their cultures as valuable and their struggles as interrelated on the continent, in the diaspora, and in the world.

Notes

1 Michael Hanchard, "Afro-Modernity: Temporality, Politics, and the African Diaspora," in *Alternative Modernities*, ed. Parameshwar Gaonkar (Durham, N.C. and London: Duke University Press, 2001), p.275.
2 Jason Hill, *Becoming a Cosmopolitan: What It Means to Be a Human Being in the New Millennium* (Lanham, Md.: Rowman and Littlefield, 2000), p.160.
3 Wendy Walters, *At Home in Diaspora* (Minneapolis: University of Minnesota Press, 2005); Ifeoma Kiddoe Nwankwo, *Black Cosmopolitanism: Racial Consciousness and Transnational Identity in the Nineteenth Century Americas* (Philadelphia: University of Pennsylvania Press, 2005).
4 Stuart Hall, "Cultural Identity and Diaspora," in *Identity: Community, Culture, Difference*, ed. Jonathan Rutherford (London: Lawrence and Wishart, 1990), p.225.
5 Gay Wilentz, *Binding Cultures: Black Women Writers in Africa and the Diaspora* (Bloomington: Indiana University Press, 1992), p.xv.
6 Audre Lorde, "Uses of the Erotic: The Erotic as Power," in *Erotique Noir, Black Erotica*, ed. Miriam DeCosta-Willis, Reginald Martin, and Roseann P. Bell (New York: Doubleday, 1992), pp.78–83.
7 Patricia Hill Collins, *Black Feminist Thought: Knowledge, Consciousness, and the Politics of Empowerment* (New York and London: Routledge, 1991), p.48.
8 Lorde, "Uses of the Erotic," p.80.
9 Ibid.
10 Ibid., p.83.
11 Ntozake Shange, *for colored girls who have considered suicide/when the rainbow is enuf* (New York: Scribners, 1975), p.28.
12 Ibid., pp.30, 75.
13 Ibid., p.28.
14 Carol Marsh-Lockett, "A Woman's Art; a Woman's Craft: The Self in Ntozake Shange's *Sassafrass, Cypress and Indigo*," in *Arms Akimbo: Africana Women in Contemporary Literature*, ed. Janice Lee Liddell and Yakani Belinda Kemp (Gainsville: University Press of Florida, 1999), p.46.
15 Ibid., p.56.
16 Ntozake Shange, *Sassafrass, Cypress and Indigo* (New York: St. Martin's Press, 1982), pp.132–33.
17 Arlene Elder, "Sassafrass, Cypress, & Indigo: Ntozake Shange's Neo-Slave/Blues Narrative," *African American Review*, 26 (1992), p.105.
18 Shange, *Sassafrass, Cypress and Indigo*, p.80.
19 Ibid., p.214.
20 Marsh-Lockett, "Woman's Art; a Woman's Craft," p.51.
21 Elder, "Sassafrass, Cypress, & Indigo," p.102.
22 Shange, *Sassafrass, Cypress and Indigo*, p.4.
23 Elder, "Sassafrass, Cypress, & Indigo," p.102.
24 Marsh-Lockett, "Woman's Art; a Woman's Craft," pp.52–53.
25 Shange, *Sassafrass, Cypress and Indigo*.
26 Marsh-Lockett, "Woman's Art; a Woman's Craft," p.48.
27 Ntozake Shange, *If I Can Cook/You Know God Can* (Boston: Beacon Press, 1998).

28 Sarah Sceats, *Food, Consumption, and the Body in Contemporary Women's Fiction* (Cambridge: Cambridge University Press, 2000), p.186.
29 Rafia Zafar, "The Signifying Dish: Autobiography and History in Two Black Women's Cookbooks," *Feminist Studies*, 25 (Summer 1999), pp.450–51.
30 Ibid., p.453.
31 Shange, *for colored girls who have considered suicide*, p.63.
32 Shange, *If I Can Cook/You Know God Can*, pp.87–88.
33 Ibid., pp.5–40.
34 Ibid., pp.103, 112, 12.
35 Ibid., pp.74–77.
36 Geraldine Pratt, "Geographic Metaphors in Feminist Theory," in *Making Worlds: Gender, Metaphor, Materiality*, ed. Susan Hardy Aiken (Tucson: University of Arizona Press, 1998), p.20.
37 Ntozake Shange, *See No Evil: Prefaces, Essays and Accounts, 1974–1983* (San Francisco: Momo's Press, 1984), pp.34–38.
38 Ntozake Shange, *A Daughter's Geography* (New York: St. Martin's Press, 1983), p.52.

8

Peter James Hudson

"The Lost Tribe of a Lost Tribe"

Black British Columbia and the Poetics of Space

Unless you find yourself in one of those far-flung places and actually encounter those elusive, ashy, burr-headed creatures, the black folk maxim asserting that "no matter where you go, no matter how far, no matter to what unlikely extreme, no matter what country, continent, ice floe, or island you land on you will find someone else black already there," as the African American poet C.S. Giscombe has breathlessly rendered it, has less of the poignancy of vernacular wisdom than the impassive soundings of cliché.[1] Dany Laferrière recounts perhaps the most acute instance of this assertion in his *Down Among the Dead Men*. During Laferrière's first trip back to Haiti after years in exile, a Port-au-Prince neighbour tells him that when Neil Armstrong landed on the moon, the U.S. astronaut was met there by a Haitian desperate for a cigarette. The Haitian, in turn, had been preceded by "a certain Occlève Siméon" – a peasant from the village of Dondon.[2]

Canada's Western province of British Columbia is not Dondon. Nor is it the moon. But within the African diaspora it may as well be the latter. Black people live there, so I am told, and the proliferation (if not deluge) of black writing from the province over the past decade seems to both prove this basic residential contention while simultaneously demonstrating the insistent value of folk knowledge.[3] Moreover, the fact of blackness in British Columbia – marked as it is by both geographic isolation and demographic deficit (black people make up but 0.6 per cent of the population of the province)[4] – also intimates a troubling supplement to Giscombe's versioning of the black folk wisdom. Identified by Frantz Fanon, the supplement suggests that the spatial experience of diaspora is not only in the quantitative detail of the universal diffusion of black people – it contains a qualitative element as well. Not only are black people everywhere, but everywhere there are black people they are also, indeed, *black*. Or, as Fanon wrote, "*Wherever he goes, the Negro remains a Negro*."[5]

For Fanon, the Negro was less an anachronistic racial designation than a discursive object produced by racism. It was the sum total of racial perceptions about black people, the congealed ball of stereotype that, much like the Jew of anti-Semitism, persists across time and space creating a shadow or, to borrow from Sam Greenlee, *spook* diaspora existing in uneasy relation to diaspora as such.[6] Part of the problem of black consciousness for Fanon was the encounter with the dysmorphic blackness of the Negro experienced as an abstraction of the black self; part of the fact of blackness was being known through a black racial "Other," a fictive entity whose presence always precedes oneself. Fanon's description parallels W.E.B Du Bois's celebrated evocation of double consciousness as a way of explaining the vexed condition of African American identity.[7] But in the case of British Columbia this doubling comes as a distant, delayed echo, filtered and distorted by a social world in which there are more black representations than real black people.

If for Du Bois the African American was "a sort of seventh son," the black British Columbian is the seventh son of a seventh son, or what local poet Wayde Compton has called "the lost tribe of a lost tribe."[8] The historical narratives of blacks on the West Coast consist of picayune episodes and decidedly un-epic, un-heroic, sometimes barely historical figures – characters of a decidedly provincial nature, individuals often fleeing unspecified personal demons – often blackness itself – and lone black souls whose great mission seems to be the angelic task of pleasing whites.[9] In this sense, the mildly messianic impulse suggested by the title of Crawford Kilian's classic history of blacks in the province – *Go Do Some Great Thing: The Black Pioneers of British Columbia* – is a little overblown. Mifflin Wistar Gibbs, the African American who led a group of settlers to Vancouver Island in 1858 and the primary figure in Kilian's history, abandoned British Columbia and returned to the United States soon after the Civil War. What was a footnote in Gibbs's life has become a minor epic for everyone else: in his autobiography, *Shadow and Light,* Gibbs, who would go on to become, among other things, the U.S. ambassador to Madagascar, barely mentions his stay in the province.[10] Sir James Douglas, the first governor of Vancouver Island and British Columbia and the Hudson's Bay Company's chief factor, a mixed-race Creole born in British Guiana, was able to – and did – pass for white for his entire life. Mother Divine, the Vancouver-born Edna Rose Ritchings and "spotless virgin bride" betrothed to Father Divine, one of the black gods of early-twentieth-century Harlem, was white.[11]

In *Into and Out of Dislocation*, a travelogue and meditation on genealogy, race, and place that largely takes place in British Columbia, Giscombe recalls asking a woman in the interior town of Fort George why anyone would want to travel to the northern reaches of a province so remote that one historian described it as "on the edge of empire."[12] "She'd looked at me knowingly," Giscombe writes, "and said, 'to be alone.'"[13] But if what Fanon says is true, a black in British Columbia is never alone. Instead, like the repeated return to the site of a primal trauma, akin to Freud's observations of the uncanny, the encounter with the Negro provides the racial unconscious for blacks in the province. Freud's patient found himself continually returning to the red light district of Vienna. Giscombe confesses to a similar impulse in his encounters with British Columbia in particular and Canada in general. "I've always, all my life," he writes, "been going on into Canada, going up to Canada, over into Canada."[14] Adding to this sense of compulsion, *Into and Out of Dislocation* contains three different chapters called "Winter in Fort George."

But the sense of isolation and alienation that Compton's evocation of a lost tribe of a lost tribe implies has not necessarily led to stasis. Instead, this articulation of blackness, in its anxiety, self-consciousness, and doubt, has resisted – or actively denied – any received wisdom on the nature of blackness. This spatial configuration of the province has fought any sense of blackness as a known shape, an a priori entity, whose main goal is to police its own limits and the terms of its membership. It has disrupted the reconstruction of black culture on an anthropological axis stressing racial and cultural continuity, preferring instead ideas of rupture, difference, dissimilitude and, in some cases, straight up disavowal, while at the same time embracing cross-cultural and cross-racial lines of alliance and solidarity.[15]

At the same time, black history in the province has been indelibly linked to the history of colonial settlement and the political economy of the British Empire. Figures such as Sir James Douglas and Mifflin Wistar Gibbs, as well as John Robert Giscome, the Jamaican prospector whose history inspired C.S. Giscombe's *Into and Out of Dislocation* and *Giscome Road*, were critical to the emergence of capitalism in the province. They helped prime the land for development and taxation while aiding the transformation of the province's enormous natural resources into commodities for the world market.[16] Compton describes Gibbs as an "arch-capitalist" and Douglas as a "rampaging colonizer," noting that the governor "used gunboats to blast local First Nations people into compliance on occasion."[17] In the poem "Douglas's Covenant," from *49th Parallel Psalm*, Compton captures the transition from settler to citizen to subject in British Columbia through the exchange of land title and the expansion of taxation:

I land can be purchased for I pound per acre.
II a minimum XXV percent down payment on land is required.
III the balance on the down payment must be settled in IV yearly installments.
IV the down payment will run at V percent interest.
V land will not be taxed until MDCCCLX.
VI holding land for IX months earns one the right to vote and sit on juries.
VII after residing in the colony for VII years, one may take an oath to the Crown
and become subject.[18]

The final line of "Douglas's Covenant" – "and become subject" – ambiguously marks the terms of citizenship in the province: subject *of* the Crown or subjected *to* the Crown? And what happens to the black B.C. subject, and black space in the province, when it is so visibly stained by colonial power?

The claims to black space in British Columbia were rarely, if at all, tied to the radical projects of place elsewhere in the Americas: the Maroon communities in Jamaica or the *quilombos* in Brazil, for instance, or even the black communities in Southern Ontario, such as those at Dawn, Buxton, and Chatham, created by African Americans fleeing slavery via the Underground Railroad. Furthermore, what began as black immigrants aiding the Crown's development of land only recently dispossessed from its Aboriginal owners has, over time, given way to the uses of local black history by contemporary writers to create a discourse of blackness informally working in the service of capital.[19] There is no direct, causal, determining link between local black cultural production and global capital accumulation, but I am continually struck by the overlap of the burgeoning interest in British Columbia's black history and geography with the radical increase of property values and real estate development, especially in the greater Vancouver area.

The clearest confluence of these two seemingly incommensurable phenomena is in the recent historical interest in Hogan's Alley, a mid-twentieth-century black community that stood for a time in Vancouver's rapidly gentrifying, inner-city Strathcona neighbourhood. Hogan's Alley, destroyed by urban renewal schemes in the 1970s, has become poetic and historical fodder for Compton and others whose attempts to recover the neighbourhood's lost black history precariously skirt the line between critical memory and multicultural nostalgia.[20] Furthermore, by overemphasizing the very blackness of black history in the province, we face a danger of complicity in the social and spatial erasures accompanying the policing and repeated displacements of the region's multicultural poor and working-class residents.[21] And by overprivileging the black experience at the expense, especially, of the racial conflicts over space fought by the Aboriginal and Asian communities of the province, we come up against the danger of misrecognizing and misrepresenting the very meaning of black British Columbia.[22]

Ethel Wilson and the Conditions of Blackness

The very notion of a "black B.C.," then, if not entirely oxymoronic, is always marked by a profound ambivalence in its imagination and production. Perhaps more than anywhere, this is demonstrated in one of the signal texts of the black experience in the province, white B.C. writer Ethel Wilson's 1949 novel *The Innocent Traveller*. Born in Port Elizabeth, South Africa, in 1888 to Methodist missionary parents, Wilson moved to England as an infant and, as an orphan adopted by maternal relatives, to Vancouver in 1898. She lived in the city until her death in 1980. Considered the doyenne of B.C. letters, Wilson was a defiant regionalist, even as many of her peers were participating in royal commissions advocating the development of an explicitly nationalist Canadian literature. Her publications are among the earliest examples of literature narrated against the B.C. landscape.[23]

Wilson also inaugurated the epistemological conditions of blackness that subsequent black writers have had to write against in attempting to claim local place. She created a specifically West Coast relationship between blackness and place, capturing the experience of marginality and alienation engendered, in part, through the production of and response to the replication of the Negro within the region. While there has been a black presence in the province dating from the mid-nineteenth century, Wilson, if only suggestively and inadvertently, first codified its existence in the fourteenth chapter – a chapter with obvious numerological significance – of *The Innocent Traveller*. "Once upon a time," Wilson writes, apparently sensing both the concoction of fact and fantasy in the imagination and production of black place in the province, and Fanon's insight into the deep structures of black space, "there was a negro who lived in Vancouver and his name was Joe Fortes."[24]

English Bay Joe. Black Joe. Nigger Joe. "The kindly old darkey."[25] Joe Fortes, whose given name, Seraphim, was deemed too pretty for rough-and-tumble frontier Vancouver, is the patron saint of British Columbia's blacks and Negroes, the unofficial mascot of Vancouver's whites.[26] Local accounts say he was born in Barbados, Trinidad, or Jamaica during the 1850s, and, though he was visibly of African descent, the descriptions by local writers of his parentage suggest that if they did not want to cast doubt on his origins they apparently wanted to separate him as much as possible from his blackness. Fortes was the "son of a Spanish woman from Barcelona and a well-to-do West Indian farmer," one writer noted.[27] "Incidentally," recalled Vancouver journalist Noel Robinson, "it may be mentioned that [Fortes] was not a coal-black negro – in fact, he was not a negro. He was a Bardadoan [sic] from Trinidad and was of very dark brown, tending to black complexion and he may have had some Portuguese blood in his veins."[28]

At some point in his teens, Fortes left the Caribbean for England. He worked as a swimming instructor and lifeguard in Liverpool, winning medals in swimming exhibitions. In 1884 Fortes joined the crew of the *Robert Kerr* and left England for a journey from Liverpool to Panama and then around Cape Horn and north to what would be incorporated as the City of Vancouver in 1886, the year after the *Robert Kerr*'s arrival. The only notable moment in the journey came when one of the crew, for unspecified reasons, "stuck a cotton hook" into Fortes's cheek.[29] Fortes took up a number of jobs in the young city, working as a bootblack, clearing stumps from the townsite, and, although he was a teetotaller who often preached moderation in alcohol consumption, bartending in the Sunrise, Alhambra, and Bodega hotels.

Near the turn of the nineteenth century Fortes settled on the shores of English Bay. He built, within view of the ocean, a small cottage that was among the first permanent residences there. He was soon followed in his endeavours. The Canadian Pacific Railroad began developing an upscale neighbourhood in the area, called the West End, for the city's financial and business elites. Meanwhile, English Bay's beaches were becoming a spot for campers who swam, picnicked, and otherwise socialized on the beach during the summer. Fortes appointed himself as the caretaker of the beach. He acted as its unofficial lifeguard and constable, the latter position eventually formalized by the City. Fortes became an affable and steady presence on English Bay, trawling the waters in his rowboat, leaving the beach only to attend Sunday mass at Holy Rosary Cathedral. He taught three generations of Vancouverites to swim (Ethel Wilson included),[30] reportedly saving a life a year, and tried to keep the beach free of vice and blasphemous language. "Modest and eager to please," one writer wrote, "his personality soon shone as a sort of institution, approved in every household in Vancouver."[31] Fortes apparently derived a simple joy from serving Vancouver's citizens, especially its children, for whom his instinctive understanding made him a favourite. By his bedside he kept a copy of Thomas à Kempis's *The Imitation of Christ* – placed next to a tea canister containing candies for the children who frequently visited him.

On February 4, 1922, Fortes died following a bout of pneumonia. Vancouver's children were granted a half-day's respite from school to attend the funeral; those who couldn't go were asked to observe a moment of silence in class. Vancouverites of all persuasions packed Holy Rosary Cathedral for what was the largest public funeral in the city's young history. Those in attendance included, according to Robinson, "not a few of his own color . . . as well as some Chinamen."[32]

"Old Joe was the living example of broadminded, Christian brotherly love," Father O'Boyle, the presiding minister, noted during the eulogy. "He gave his best and was indeed God's image carved in ebony."[33] As a tribute, the Parks Board filled his rowboat with pine boughs and flowers from Stanley Park. The boat followed the hearse on its journey from Holy Rosary to Mountain View Cemetery, passing hundreds of people lining Granville and Hastings streets who had come to pay their respects. But before his body left Holy Rosary and the mourners spilled out into a typically rainy Vancouver afternoon, the cathedral's organist played the opening chords of American tunesmith Stephen Foster's well-known "Ethiopian" jingle, "Old Black Joe" (1860). The entire congregation broke into song:

> Gone are the days when my heart was young and gay;
> Gone are my friends from the cotton fields away;
> Gone from the earth to a better land I know,
> I hear their gentle voices calling, "Old Black Joe."
>
> Chorus
> I'm coming, I'm coming, for my head is bending low;
> I hear their gentle voices calling, "Old Black Joe."
>
> Where are the hearts once so happy and so free?
> The children so dear that I held upon my knee?
> Gone to the shore where my soul has longed to go,
> I hear their gentle voices calling, "Old Black Joe."
>
> Why do I weep when my heart should feel no pain?
> Why do I sigh that my friends not come again,
> Grieving for forms now departed long ago?
> I hear their gentle voices calling, "Old Black Joe."[34]

Some five years after Fortes's death, the Kiwanis Club erected a fountain to his memory in Alexandra Park near the site of his old cabin. It was inlaid with a bronze bas-relief of his face and inscribed with the words "little children loved him."[35] Years later, a West End branch of the Vancouver Public

Library system was named after him, as was a high-end steak house frequented by stockbrokers and gangsters. During Vancouver's centennial celebrations in 1986, Fortes was named "citizen of the century."

The Imagining of Joe Fortes

Today, of course, a black man living isolated in a cottage with a bottomless jar of sweets by his bedside, a predilection for Christ, and a fondness for children would immediately be suspected as a sexual predator. Regardless, the facts of Fortes's life appear radically disproportionate to the extent of his memorialization by Vancouver's white citizens. Fortes was loved by white Vancouver, and that love was sincere, if not saturated with racial paternalism. Yet if Fortes had been white he would likely not have received such extensive commemoration. And Fortes was not only memorialized *because* he was black, but because of *how* he was black – because of how his blackness allowed him to fit so snugly into an image of white Vancouver's sense of its own self at the beginning of the century. A living, outsized lawn jockey, Fortes was an exception and an anomaly, a non-threatening and passive black man – unlike, for instance, boxer Jack Johnson, who was barred from Vancouver's hotels during a visit in 1909.[36] He was just as easily divorced from the political history of black people within the British Empire as he was from his own personal history, of which no local historians have sought to uncover anything beyond the basic, known facts.[37]

Fortes was imagined and remembered through the kind of racist and universal idea of blackness suggested in Fanon's conception of the Negro. It was this displaced knowledge of blackness that made it possible for Vancouver's citizens to find their grief salved and Fortes's memory honoured by Stephen Foster's "Old Black Joe." Foster's song was inspired by an African American servant whom the songwriter knew in Pittsburgh. But it drew on a well-known stock character within the nineteenth-century minstrel shows that circulated through the United States, and the rest of the anglophone world, after the U.S. Civil War. It drew on an archetypal figure – a "shambling and shambolic icon of explicit racism"[38] – from the minstrel routine, a figure who appeared, variously, as the Old Darkey, Uncle Rufus, Uncle Eph, or Old Black Joe. He was an older, kindly, large-hearted, if somewhat slow-witted former slave, now lost without life on the plantation and the paternal bonds of slavery. He was consumed by an indelible nostalgia for pre-Emancipation life, and possessed of an unbreakable sentimental bond with the master and mistress who once cared for him. According to this narrative, emancipation had destroyed the perfect world of slavery, leaving the Old Darkey abandoned, alone, his life utterly meaningless, with nothing but his nostalgia for the past and the inevitability of his soon-coming death. Often he was granted a redemptive reprieve before death when the white child whom the Old Darkey used to bounce on his knee returned, providing a respite from his suffering and loneliness.[39] White audiences of minstrel shows loved him, just as white Vancouver loved Joe Fortes.

As a black man from the British West Indies, Fortes would have had no first-hand experience of the "cotton fields" of the U.S. South. But because there was no indigenous experience of blackness that white people could draw on to understand black people, Fortes was grafted onto a racist geography of blackness, a diaspora of white racial imagery. In this sense, the transnational circulation of white racism through the dispersal of white cultural forms like the minstrel show and Foster's plantation lullabies offers both a supplement to and a critique of the futile discussions of the nature of black Canadian identity and its possible sources by denaturalizing white Canadian identity through an inquiry into the sources of race thinking that made *white Canadian identity* possible.[40]

At the same time, as Compton argues, "a tradition of strategic utterance in the service of a black experience indigenous to BC" emerged in reaction to the circulation of white racial knowledges and the production of the Negro within the province.[41] For Compton, these strategic utterances were first deployed in the nineteenth-century writings of Mifflin Wistar Gibbs, the African American pioneer, and Isaac Dickson, a barber who lived in the gold-rush town of Barkerville. Both Gibbs's and Dickson's experience of white racism occurred, in part, through what Compton refers to as the "regulation of Black British Columbians through language": attempts by white British Columbians to keep the province's black residents in their place by criticizing them for "speaking and affecting mannerisms above their class and station."[42] But Compton also recounts a story by local writer Bruce Ramsey involving Joe Fortes, first published in *The Province* in 1964, through which Fortes is subjected to a similar form of regulation:

> One of the legends which has grown up around Joe Fortes' memory is that he persuaded the police commission to issue him a uniform, complete with brass buttons. A month later, Joe made his first arrest.
>
> He had warned a couple that their behavior down on the beach was, well, a trifle indiscreet, and when they failed to pay attention to Constable Fortes he hauled them off to jail.
>
> Joe liked to use big words although quite often he didn't know what they meant. He made some up as he went along as well. When the magistrate

demanded to know the details of the charge laid against the young couple, he blurted out they had been acting with "agglutinated auspiciousness."

"Case dismissed!" declared the magistrate.

After that, Joe never made another arrest.[43]

Compton notes that Fortes's unfortunate use of malapropisms replicates a typical trope of the minstrel show. Here, though, Fortes plays the minstrel while the judge plays the white interlocutor. Compton also points out that Ramsey does not provide a source for the story, explaining it instead as "one of the legends which has grown up around Joe Fortes's memory."[44] "One wonders," muses Compton, "if [such] stories had any truth to them at all, or were merely scripts rehearsed over top of real-life figures."[45]

The "Different Worlds" of the "Innocent Traveller"

In this light, the opening sentence of Wilson's "Down at English Bay" and her introduction to Fortes make sense. The "once-upon-a-time" phrasing is less a sign of lazy or mediocre writing than the deliberate invocation of a historical narrative based on cliché, fantasy, disbelief, and truth – the placement, as Compton suggests regarding Bruce Ramsey's story of Fortes, of a racist script over a real-life figure. In some ways, all of *The Innocent Traveller* is built upon a similar premise – though not always so overburdened with the text of race: Wilson prefaces *The Innocent Traveller* by claiming that it is "part truth and part invention." Largely based on the experiences of a circle of matriarchs dominating Wilson's own family, the novel centres on Topaz Edgeworth, the "innocent traveller" of the book's title and a figure modelled after Wilson's maternal aunt Eliza Malkin. The Edgeworth clan, like Wilson's own family, arrived in Vancouver at the end of the nineteenth century, when "it was a very comfortable little place to live in," and witnessed "the growth of a young frontier town into a real city."[46] Topaz Edgeworth, however, has little to say about these transitions. She is depicted as a slightly batty British spinster, vapid, naïve, imbued with a child-like curiosity about the world, passive, non-judgmental to a fault. The novel's chapters are organized around an extended set of anecdotes stretched out across the one-hundred-year course of Edgeworth's life. While contributing to a regional sense of place, *The Innocent Traveller* can also be read as an earnest if frivolous and blandly satirical set-up of late imperial etiquette and mores and the attempts by Vancouver's elites to forge something resembling a cultured, high society in the city.[47]

Fortes has no presence in the book beyond the first pages of "Down at English Bay." Wilson depicts him within a nostalgic if somewhat dross memory of early Vancouver, evoking the happy anomaly of the lone black man on the white pacific outpost:

> Once upon a time there was a negro who lived in Vancouver and his name was Joe Fortes. He lived in a small house by the beach at English Bay and there is now a little bronze plaque to his honour and memory near-by, and he taught hundreds of little boys and girls how to swim. First of all he taught them for the love of it and after that he was paid a small salary by the City Council or the Parks Board, but he taught for love just the same. And so it is that now there are Judges, and Aldermen, and Cabinet Ministers, and lawyers, and doctors, and magnates, and ordinary business men, and grandmothers, and prostitutes, and burglars, and Sunday School superintendents, and dry-cleaners, and so on whom Joe Fortes taught to swim, and they will be the first to admit it. And Joe Fortes saved several people from drowning; some of them were worth saving and some were not worth saving in the slightest – take the man who was hanged in Kingston jail; but Joe Fortes could not be expected to know this, so he saved everyone regardless. He was greatly beloved and he was respected.
>
> Joe had a nice round brown face and a beautiful brown body and arms and legs as he waded majestically in the waves of English Bay amongst all the little white lawyers and doctors and trained nurses and seamstresses who jumped up and down and splashed round him. "Joe," they called, and "Look at me, Joe! Is this the way?" And they splashed and swallowed and Joe supported them under their chins and by their behinds and said in his rich slow fruity voice, "Kick out, naow! Thassaway. Kick right out!" And sometimes he supported them, swimming like frogs, to the raft, and when they had clambered onto the raft they were afraid to jump off and Joe Fortes became impatient and terrible and said in a very large voice, "Jump now! I'll catch you! You jump off of that raff or I'll leave you here all night!" And that was how they learned to swim.[48]

Wilson's depiction of Fortes is fairly innocuous and seemingly inconsequential. But, given *The Innocent Traveller*'s early place in Vancouver letters and Wilson's regional literary pioneering, it operates as a sort of primogenital history and poetics of Vancouver space. Wilson imbues the city with a history. She writes over the text of First Nations occupancy, obscures the contests over space that brought the city to life, and naturalizes the presence of European institutions of governance and social categories. Fortes, too, is conscripted into this pioneer service. The actual labour he performed, of clearing the land of the Vancouver townsite before he settled on English Bay, takes on a metaphorical significance through his appearance in *The Innocent Traveller*: the representation of Fortes in the novel helps to fill a historical vacuum of local space with a narrative of place that creates the initial, tentative markings of a local landscape.

While Fortes recedes from the plot of "Down at English Bay," he maintains a central though passive role in the major conflict in the chapter and, indeed, the entire novel, through Wilson's retelling of a historical incident that shocked late Victorian Vancouver—the so-called "Great English Bay Scandal." According to historian Irene Howard, in September 1899 a "rescue worker" from the Women's Christian Temperance Union (WCTU), one of a handful of moral crusaders trawling the beach on the lookout for unbecoming behaviour, accused the WCTU's president of not only frolicking on the beach in a "semi-nude state" (at that time, "semi-nude," Howard notes, "meant wearing a sleeveless low-necked tunic, without a cloak, boots or stockings") but also "misconduct[ing] herself while in the water with"—"'Nigger Joe,' a bartender," as the worker's own report described our Joe Fortes. The rescue worker was expelled from the WCTU, initiating a series of libel cases that were drawn out over the following years.[49]

In Wilson's rendering of the incident Topaz Edgeworth accompanies her niece Rose to English Bay. While Rose is swimming, Edgeworth encounters Mrs. Hamilton Coffin, on her way to lessons with Fortes. As if anticipating the coming conflict, Wilson is at pains to describe the lack of contact between Fortes and Coffin. Coffin comes to the beach dressed in a "black serge bathing suit" with "no part of her body [displayed] except her face and ears and her arms as far up as her elbows."[50] Both Coffin and Fortes – and Wilson herself – appear acutely aware of the invisible and unspoken codes governing the public intimacy and physical familiarity between black men and white women on English Bay and the necessary performances of an exaggerated, desexualized contact:

> Joe Fortes discussed the motions of swimming with Mrs. Coffin, doing *so* with his arms, and then *so* with his beige legs like flexible pillars, and Mrs. Coffin to the first position. Joe Fortes respectfully supported her chin with the tips of his strong brown fingers. He dexterously and modestly raised her rear, and held it raised by a bit of bathing suit. "How politely he does it!" thought Topaz, admiring Joe Fortes and Mrs. Coffin as they proceeded up and down the ocean.[51]

The following afternoon, Edgeworth attends a meeting of the Ladies' Minerva Club, an institution based on the Atheneum, a white woman's literary society that served as one of the few arbiters of taste and culture in a city whose main activity then (as now) was making money. Coffin's name is advanced for membership. One woman in the club objects. "But *do* the Ladies of the Minerva Club know," asks the woman, "that Mrs. Hamilton Coffin has been seen more than once in a public place, bathing in the arms of a black man?" Edgeworth, "aware of something evil and stupid in the room," finds something within herself and, breaking with her usually reticent, apolitical character, gives a speech in defence of both Coffin and Fortes:

> Ladies . . . I was present yesterday when that admirable woman Mrs. Hamilton Coffin had her swimming lesson from our respected fellow-citizen Joe Fortes. I know that the lady who has just spoken . . . will be quite properly relieved to hear that so far from swimming in the arms of Mr. Fortes, which any of us who were drowning would be grateful to do, Mrs. Hamilton Coffin was swimming in his finger-tips. I feel that we should be honoured to have as a fellow-member so active, progressive, and irreproachable a lady as Mrs. Hamilton Coffin. I therefore beg to propose the name of Mrs. Hamilton Coffin as the tenth member of the Minerva Club.[52]

Edgeworth's speech rouses the members of the Minerva Club, including the one woman who has spoken out against Coffin's membership, to universally endorse the application to the organization.

In the context of a novel in which nothing much happens, where a series of incidents are strung together with little narrative continuity other than that they overlap the temporality of Edgeworth's century-long life, the incident takes on monumental proportions. Its effects are bigger than World War I – which passes by in two quick pages[53] – and, in terms of events, only rivals what emerges as both the climax of the book and of Edgeworth's life: her audience with Queen Mary in Buckingham Palace. As throughout Edgeworth's life, she breaks with the decorum required of the occasion. When the Queen inquires as to the changes in Vancouver over the intervening years since her last visit, Edgeworth releases a stream of irrelevant trivialities concerning her own family.

The two incidents – Edgeworth's audience with the Queen and her defence of Coffin and Fortes – are not unrelated. Edgeworth is of a generation of loyalists to the Crown who bow to pictures of the British monarchy. Wilson's depiction of Edgeworth is a send-up of her parent's mores, even as her critique is tinged with an aura of sentimentality over what was quickly becoming a lost ethic and an obsolete identity. Before her audience with the Queen (which occurs within a chapter titled "Apotheosis"), and in response to criticism from an uncle who chides her behaviour as "colonial," she embraces the term, offering her most conscious and pronounced statement of self-identification in the entire book. "I'm Colonial and I'm proud of it," she asserts, continuing:

> Those who left this country as colonists, and established colonies in the New World have a deal more to be proud of than you who stayed at home and were comfortable . . . a deal too comfortable, I don't mind telling you! It's a word that anyone should cherish and be proud of if they've any sense of history at all, whether they stayed here in comfort or are descendants of those colonists who so nobly landed on those rugged shores.[54]

By combining Edgeworth's momentary social justice with an unreconstructed royalism, Wilson suggests in Edgeworth an apparently contradictory, though internally consistent, logic that mirrors the overlapping and competing claims to space of a not-yet-post-colonial Vancouver and British Columbia – a space whose residents defiantly attempted to preserve as the cultural space of the British Empire even as it was being challenged by nationalist sentiment.

This sensibility repeats itself in Wilson's description of Edgeworth's encounter with Canadian space during her journey across the country to Vancouver. Travelling by rail, that quintessential Canadian nation-builder, Edgeworth is transfixed by the monumentality of the Canadian landscape, the breathless reaches of space and sky. But the narrative production of space in these pages of *The Innocent Traveller* is as much of a narrowly geographic order as it is a way of tying racial and ethnic difference to regional geography, as a way of racializing the production of the local. In Montreal, for instance, Edgeworth's encounter with French-speaking people provides a source of unbridled joy.[55] In Montreal for the first time in her life she meets black people, porters working for the railroad. Edgeworth's surprise at the presence of black people in the city parallels Fanon's disoriented encounter with a white child on the streets of Paris, though without Fanon's critical and self-reflexive interpretations, as the object of the white gaze. "Look!" exclaims a white child upon encountering Fanon. "A Negro."[56] Here is Edgeworth:

> "Ah! Negroes!" exclaimed Aunt Topaz with delight, hastening ahead. "How do you do! How do you do! I'm sure I'm very glad to see you! Have you a wife, yes? And Family? This is a charming surprise!" "Yassum," said the porter, presenting to Aunt Topaz his unusually wide swelling nostrils and preposterously fine set of dazzling white teeth. Aunty gazed at them, admiring. "Splendid!" she said. "Magnificent! Much better than ours! What do you

> use? In Africa I understand they use a stick. It is very efficacious! Or is it diet?"[57]

When Edgeworth reaches the Prairies she sees Aboriginal people "wrapped in blankets, with a plait of hair over each shoulder."[58] When she finally arrives in Vancouver, Asians come into her field of vision. In a letter to a friend, Edgeworth writes of Yow, a Chinese man working as a servant in her household:

> . . . and we have a Chinese cook called Yow with a queue with green silk plaited in to make it longer wound round his head in the house and let down and caught up somehow under his right arm when he walks in the street with Chinese slippers turned up a bit in front and a very good black silk coat and trousers indeed quite expensive with a high neckband. He wears a hat. I can't understand a word he says but he seems very good I'm sure.[59]

While literary critic Arnold Itwaru rightly chides Wilson for drawing on racial stereotypes for her depictions of non-white people, *The Innocent Traveller* not only belies the myths of the empty wilderness colonized solely by Europeans and a Canadian landscape devoid of people of colour, but also presents people of colour as a part of that landscape.[60] Moreover, in *The Innocent Traveller* people of colour appear simultaneously as exotic and naturalized, as both foreign body and indigenous entity, if only because Edgeworth's innocent and oblivious liberalism deflects a more cynical critique.

At the same time Fortes's interactions with whites are entirely with children and women. Yow's are solely with the women of the Edgeworth household. In *The Innocent Traveller* Fortes is not given anything of a life beyond his encounters with "all the little white lawyers and doctors and trained nurses and seamstresses who jumped up and down and splashed round him" at English Bay.[61] Yow's character is more nuanced, though at the same time it is even more blatantly based on a set of racial stereotypes of Asians that conforms to a common knowledge about race and racial difference typical of someone of Wilson's generation and class.[62] Yow is depicted as moody and irascible, more often than not threatening to "killem" the Edgeworth children, filled with contempt for the Edgeworth clan – except for Topaz's great aunt, for whom he has an abiding, though unexplained, platonic love. He is engaged in a continual contest for power with Rachel Edgeworth over the domestic division of labour in the household. He substitutes ingredients in family dinners for no reason other than spite and sets meal times to satisfy his own incessant desire to gamble in

Chinatown. Wilson attempts to delve into the Chinese mind by translating a conversation that Yow has with a cousin, Fooey, from Cantonese into a "simple pidgin." But its half-baked, broken nature suggests that the two men were barely comprehensible to each other in their own language, and its contents are only used to demonstrate Yow's cunning and wily nature. At one point Fooey, perhaps voicing Wilson's own sentiments regarding racial difference, notes how the "two races" – white and Chinese – faced "a great area of fog-like confusion and misconception" in their relations.[63]

Yow and the Edgeworth clan – though this time as the Hastings family – would return in Wilson's 1952 *Equations of Love*, published as the novella *Lilly's Story* in the United States. In *Lilly's Story* the spatialization of racial difference in Vancouver that was only hinted at in *The Innocent Traveller* is made explicit. After fulfilling his housekeeping duties in the Hastings household Yow would "transform himself," shedding, as she writes in *The Innocent Traveller*, "his cloak of West End respectability"[64] and then entering, in *Lilly's Story*, "a different world, a Chinese World."

> His real life now began, and the innocent Hastings family were left to their silly and mysterious occupations. When Yow went to his room he wore a white coat and apron and his hair was plaited in a queue which was wound round his head. When he came out of his room a few minutes later he wore a good black high-necked jacket with trousers to match of expensive material with a faintly brocaded pattern.[65]

Yow would leave the West End, wandering down a neat path that maps the ways in which race and class are separated in the city: from the wealthy, white West End – the home of Joe Fortes – down Robson, down Granville, to Pender Street and Shanghai Alley, the heart of Chinatown. Of Chinatown, Wilson writes:

> One could see them [the Chinese] through the smoke, clustered around tables, squatted upon the floor, all talking loudly in Chinese shorthand. The police did not in those days interfere very much with their pleasures. Shanghai Alley was riddled darkly with gambling dens, one much like the last, all smelling vilely of some kind of smoke, all resounding with voices clacking like typewriters (much argument), no place in which to spend the night. . . . Just around the corner from Shanghai Alley was a restaurant – no, a joint – with Chinese characters on its dark face. Restaurants in Chinatown were not in those days called Mandarin Gardens or Peking Chop Suey and so forth for the benefit of foreigners. There were Chinese customers, and there were Chinese characters, or none, on the windows or doors. The food was good.

> Sometimes there were dried fish or octopuses in the windows. They stayed there a long time and collected dust, as they were a symbol, not to eat, although probably no one would have minded eating them.[66]

By now, Wilson's depiction of this "different world" appears riddled with cliché. Yet it contributed to a romanticized, touristic view of Chinatown – even though she tries to mark it with the stamp of authenticity – while obscuring the historical forces that created Chinatowns in the first place. As Kay J. Anderson has demonstrated, Vancouver's Chinatown did not come about because of some tendency towards Chinese insularity, but because of the effects of white violence and Anti-Asian zoning ordinances in enclaves like the West End, Shaunnessy, and Point Grey that prompted Asian, as well as other people of colour and the working poor, to cluster in Chinatown and the surrounding neighbourhoods that make up what is now known as the Downtown East Side.[67]

In *Lilly's Story* Yow develops an obsession and lust for Lilly Waller, "a white girl with taffy-colored hair who worked in Chinatown" – poor, white, and orphaned at an early age. Yow, "in his dark mind," refers to Lilly as his "lady friend."[68] Lilly shows no interest in Yow until he begins stealing silk stockings and a bicycle from the Hastings family to give to Lilly as gifts. He is soon caught for the thefts. Fearing reprisals from the police, Lilly flees to Comox, a small town on Vancouver Island. There she has a baby out of wedlock, whom she determines to raise in a fashion that would sever her from the depravities of her own class origins. Yow appears to return to the story in a brief encounter later in the novella. Lilly thinks she spies him walking in front of her home and the rush of her past comes to her, literally (and melodramatically) knocking her out. "She had forgot the associates of her vagrant years," writes Wilson, "and here was Yow, the most dangerous, the most violent of them all."[69] But Yow disappears again, leaving the reader to speculate if it was actually him, or Lilly's long-standing anxieties linking criminality, vagrancy, and violence with Asians. According to literary historian David Stouck, in the original version of the story Yow is actually the father of Lilly's daughter, Eleanor. But Eleanor's "Chinese" genes are recessive and her Asian characteristics skip her and only appear when her own daughter is born – at which point, as Stouck notes, "Lilly's world of deceptions is shattered" and Eleanor dies "incredulous, shamed, and heartbroken."[70]

The consequences of Fortes's racialization and sexualization in Wilson's rendering of the Great English Bay Scandal do not, of course, have anywhere near the impact on the narrative of Yow's in *Lilly's Story*, especially in its original, unpublished version. Where the characterization of

Fortes leads to a small but significant moral triumph for Topaz Edgeworth, that of Yow leads to tragedy for Lilly Waller. Furthermore, Yow's characterization is consistent with a broader, historical pattern of racial anxieties amongst Vancouver's whites regarding the presence of Asians in the city and their threat to white power. In the late nineteenth century, this threat appeared in the guise of a "yellow peril"; in the late twentieth, through the transformation of Vancouver into "Hongcouver" – especially because of worries over the impact of an influx of Chinese people (and capital) into the city following the transition of Hong Kong from British to Chinese rule.[71] On the other hand, Fortes's characterization, while based on the minstrel show's American tradition of racist depictions, functions *because* of this Asian threat; his racialization can only be understood with reference to the persistent anti-Asian discourses in the city and the province.

This racial difference is narrated through the production of space in Wilson's writing, through her rendering of a racial geography of Vancouver, whose boundaries overlap a moral space. Racial fear and fantasy are juxtaposed in *The Innocent Traveller* and *Lilly's Story*. Yow's Chinatown, containing the inscrutable and unassimilable Chinese, gambling, smoking opium, eating strange food, crowded into filthy tenements, possibly involved in white slavery – contrasted with Fortes's West End, with his clean and trim cottage on English Bay, inhabited by a lone black man, the solitary Negro, the desexualized Old Darkey nurturing the white race, loyally serving Vancouver's whites. The social distance that saw Fortes confined to a cottage on the periphery of the West End, his interactions with whites limited to contact with women and children, is replicated in the circumscribed position he is given within the narrative of *The Innocent Traveller*: a servant in both life and text, Fortes is more caricature than character, more Negro than black, only existing to aid the moral growth of Topaz Edgeworth and Vancouver's white citizens.[72]

Yet there is a contradiction in Wilson's recasting of the Great English Bay Scandal. While bringing Fortes into the fold of white society, she simultaneously manages to keep him out of it by strictly adhering to the social and sexual codes whose potential transgression caused the scandal, and Edgeworth's momentary eruption of morality, in the first place. Still, Fortes's racial difference is trumped because he is a "fellow citizen" – not only of Vancouver, but of the British Empire. When asked of his nationality, Fortes would reportedly reply, "Me? Ah'm British."[73] He was, of course. There was no Jamaican or Barbadian or Trinidadian nation at the time. But journalists found a way of turning his racial difference into a positive example of black exceptionalism. "Although born of an alien race and color," one writer wrote, "Joe Fortes was British to the backbone." Another said,

"Although black outside," Fortes "was white all through."[74] Fortes is remembered precisely through the qualified incorporation of black subjects into Vancouver society. He embodies a certain kind of race-transcending Britishness despite his imagination within the tropes of the American minstrel show. And most importantly, he was assimilable into Vancouver's white culture in a way that the Asian population – because of the fears generated by their numerical preponderance and their potential economic clout – was not. Fortes could become a mascot because Asians had remained a menace. And in this, we have the essential problem of the imagination of black space in Vancouver and British Columbia.

Negotiating Spaces and Places

Wayde Compton has suggestively addressed this predicament of black space by revising C.S. Giscombe's version of the folk maxim I used to begin this chapter. Compton, as a local inhabiting one of those far-off places that Giscombe evokes, realizes that not only is he, "in American Giscombe's imagination," the "someone else black already there"[75] – but that Joe Fortes, as the prior inhabitant of this space, is Compton's own "someone else black already" *here*. But Compton also admits that he first heard the folk aphorism from a Chinese Canadian friend who told it to him with a slight twist. According to Compton's friend, the aphorism read: "No matter where you go, no matter how far, no matter to what unlikely extreme, no matter what country, continent, ice floe, or island you land on you will find a Chinese family already there." Not only that: "They will be running the restaurant."

By reading his own experience through the spatial grammar of a Chinese diaspora, Compton universalizes what is, at first glance, a racially bound bit of wisdom. He expands its application by moving from a kind of black exceptionalism that sees in the fact of diaspora something unique to black people. By incorporating what is, in essence, the Chinese version of Fanon's Negro – the clause "they will be running the restaurant" – he finds a canny means of negotiating the heavily layered texts of race and racism that define the spaces of blackness even before black space can exist, especially in those contexts where blackness is marginal to the epic historical conflicts over space. Moreover, by locating himself within this other place, Compton invokes a spatial practice, one that Joe Fortes ambiguously symbolizes, that finds a certain critical value in understanding blackness as always foreign to any place – as always remaining the lost tribe of a lost tribe.

Notes

1 C.S. Giscombe, *Into and Out of Dislocation* (New York: North Point Press, 2000), p.10.

2 Dany Laferrière, *Down Among the Dead Men*, trans. David Homel (Vancouver: Douglas and McIntyre, 1997), pp. 92–93.

3 For a sample and introduction, see the later contributions to Wayde Compton, ed., *Bluesprint: Black B.C. Literature and Orature* (Arsenal Pulp Press, 2001).

4 In 2001, according to the Census, British Columbia had 25,465 black people out of a total population of 3,907,735. The total Canadian population consisted of 32, 378,122; blacks made up 662,215 of it. The Chinese (342,665) made up the largest visible minority population in British Columbia followed by South Asians (164,365). See <http://www.statscan.ca>.

5 Frantz Fanon, *Black Skin, White Masks*, trans. Charles Lam Markmann (New York: Grove Press, 1967), p.173.

6 See Sam Greenlee, *The Spook Who Sat by the Door* (London: Allison and Busby, 1969). For Greenlee, of course, "spook" refers to both the racial slur and a covert operative.

7 W.E.B. Du Bois, *The Souls of Black Folk* (New York: Norton, 1999).

8 Ibid., p.10; Wayde Compton, "Introduction," in *Bluesprint*, ed. Compton, p.37.

9 For overviews of the history of blacks in the province, see Rosemary Brown, "The Negroes," in *Strangers Entertained: A History of the Ethnic Groups of British Columbia* (Vancouver: B.C. Centennial '71 Committee, 1971), pp.237–42; and Crawford Kilian, *Go Do Some Great Thing: The Black Pioneers of British Columbia* (Vancouver: Douglas and McIntyre, 1978).

10 Mifflin Wistar Gibbs, *Shadow and Light: An Autobiography, with Reminiscences of the Last and Present Century* (Lincoln and London: University of Nebraska Press/Bison Books, 1995 [1902]), pp.93–109.

11 On Father Divine and his Peace Mission Movement, see Jill Watts, *God, Harlem U.S.A: The Father Divine Story* (Berkeley: University of California Press, 1992).

12 Adele Perry, *On the Edge of Empire: Gender, Race, and the Making of British Columbia, 1849–1871* (Toronto: University of Toronto Press, 2001).

13 Giscombe, *Into and Out of Dislocation*, p.111.

14 Ibid., p.15.

15 This is best demonstrated in a number of recent publications by the region's black writers. See, for instance, David Nandi Odhiambo, *diss/ed banded nation* (Victoria: Polestar, 1988); David Nandi Odhiambo, *Kipligat's Chance* (New York: St. Martin's Griffin, 2004); Lawrence Brathwaite, *Wigger* (Vancouver: Arsenal Pulp Press, 1995); Lawrence Brathwaite, *Ratz Are Nice (PSP)* (Los Angeles: Alyson Books, 2000); Nikola Marin, "Chinese Laundry: One of Those Mysteries You Can't Solve with Just a Dictionary," *West Coast Line*, 22:31.2 (Spring/Summer 1997), pp.52–49; Wayde Compton, *49th Parallel Psalm* (Vancouver: Advance Editions, 1999), and *Performance Bond* (Vancouver: Arsenal Pulp Press, 2004). For surveys of recent black cultural production in British Columbia, see Peter Hudson, "Disappearing Histories of the Black Pacific: Contemporary Black Art in Vancouver," *Mix: The Magazine of Artist-Run Culture*, 22:3 (Winter 1996–97), pp.48–56; and Wayde Compton, "Introduction," in *Bluesprint*, ed. Compton, pp.17–40. On the critique of "anthropologization" in diaspora studies, see David Scott, "That Event, This Memory: Notes on the Anthropology of African Diasporas in the New World," *Diaspora*, 1:3 (1991), pp.261–84.

16 Giscombe, *Into and Out of Dislocation*; C.S. Giscombe, *Giscome Road* (Normal, Ill.: Dalkey Archive Press, 1998). Giscombe discusses claims to "black" space in regards to Douglas and Giscome in the essay "Border Towns, Border Talk," in *Diverse Landscapes: Re-Reading across Cultures in Contemporary Canadian Writing*, ed. Karine Beeler and Dee Horne (Prince George: University of Northern British Columbia, 1996), pp.49–64. See also Roy Miki, "Supplement to *Philly talks 18*," *PhillyTalks.org*, 18 (n.d.), pp.1–2 <slought.org/content/11801>; and Compton's poems "JD" and "Douglas's

Covenant," in *49th Parallel Psalm*, pp.18, 44, and his comments on Douglas and Gibbs in Compton, "Black Writers in Search of Place: A Three-way Conversation about History, Role Models, and Inventing 'The Black Atlantis'" (Interview with Esi Edugyan and Karina Vernon), *The Tyee*, Feb. 28, 2005, March 1, 2005 <http://www.thetyee.ca/Life/2005/02/28/BlackWriters/>.

17 Compton, "Black Writers in Search of Place."

18 Compton, "Douglas's Covenant," in *49th Parallel Psalm*.

19 In Vancouver, within the first hundred years of European settlement and contact, between 90 and 95 per cent of the original Salish population was wiped out. See Leslie Robertson and Dara Culhane, "Introduction," in *In Plain Sight: Reflections on Life in Downtown Eastside Vancouver*, ed. Leslie Robertson and Dara Culhane (Vancouver: Talon Books, 2005), p.16.

20 On the history of Hogan's Alley, see Daphne Marlatt and Carol Itter, *Opening Doors* (Victoria, B.C.: Aural History Program, 1979), pp.56–63, 108–10, 138–44, 169–73; and Andrea Fatona and Cornelia Wyngarten, *Hogan's Alley* (video, 1994). Compton has used Hogan's Alley in his poetry; and while Fatona and Wyngarten's account of Hogan's Alley is of a black queer space, Compton's is strictly heteronormative. See the section titled "Rune" in his *Performance Bond*, pp.111–56, as well as his essay, "Hogan's Alley and Retro-Speculative Verse," in *Unfinished Business: Photographing Vancouver Streets, 1955–1985*, ed. Bill Jeffries, Glen Lowry, and Jerry Zaslove, a special issue of *West Coast Line*, 47:37.2 (Vancouver: Presentation House Gallery/*West Coast Line*, 2005), pp.109–15. Compton is one of the founders of the Hogan's Alley Memorial Project, an organization whose goals, as its name suggests, are to preserve the community's memory. See <http://hogansalleyproject.blogspot.com/>.

21 On the question of erasure and invisibility in Vancouver, especially in Strathcona and the Downtown East Side, see Dara Culhane, "Their Spirits Live within Us: Aboriginal Women in Downtown Eastside Vancouver Emerging into Visibility," *American Indian Quarterly*, 27:3,4 (Summer/Fall 2003), pp.593–609; and Denise Blake Oleksijczuk, "Haunted Spaces," in *Stan Douglas: Every Building on 100 West Hastings*, ed. Reid Shier (Vancouver: Contemporary Art Gallery/Arsenal Pulp Press, 2002). Attempts to reverse the trend to erasure include Marlatt and Itter, *Opening Doors*; Laurel Kimely and Jo-Ann Canning-Dew, *Hastings and Main: Stories from an Inner City Neighbourhood* (Vancouver: New Star Books, 1987); Robertson and Culhane, eds., *In Plain Sight*; and Maggie De Vries, *Missing Sarah* (Toronto: Penguin Canada, 2004).

22 Frederick Ivor Case argues this point in his underread discussion of black Canada, *Racism and National Consciousness* (Toronto: Plowshares Press, 1977). Compton has argued that the future of black British Columbia is racially mixed. See Myler Wilkinson and David Stouck, "The Epic Moment: An Interview with Wayde Compton," *West Coast Line*, 36.2:38 (Fall 2002), pp.130–45.

23 Wilson's books include *Hetty Dorval* (London: Macmillan, 1947); *The Innocent Traveller* (Toronto: Macmillan,1949); *Swamp Angel* (Toronto: McClelland and Stewart, 1954); *Equations of Love* (Toronto: Macmillan, 1952), published in the United States as *Lilly's Story* (New York: Harper & Brothers, 1952); and *Mrs. Golightly and Other Stories* (London: Macmillan, 1962).

24 Ethel Wilson, *The Innocent Traveller* (Toronto: McClelland and Stewart, 1982 [1949]), p.144.

25 "In Memory of Joe," unknown source, possibly *Vancouver Sun*, July 1, 1936.

26 Ruth Greene and Gerald Rusthon, *Personality Ships of British Columbia: Thirty-Seven Illustrated Sea Tales of Canada's Western Ships* (West Vancouver: Marine Tapestry Publications, 1969), p.50. His name also brings to mind Fanon's evocation of African intellectuals grappling with the demands of anti-colonial nationalism as "individuals without an anchor, without a horizon, colorless, stateless, rootless – a race of angels." Of course, Fortes lived before the period of which Fanon was writing, and he was neither an anti-colonial nor an intellectual. See Frantz Fanon, *The Wretched of the*

Earth, trans. Constance Farrington (New York: Grove Press, 1963), p.218.

27 Alan Morley, "Vancouver Loved Joe Fortes, and He Repaid the Love in Full," *The Vancouver Province, BC Magazine*, Sept. 10, 1955.

28 Noel Robinson, "'English Bay Joe' Fortes Most Loved Character This Old West End Has Ever Known," *The Vancouver Province*, Aug. 26, 1932.

29 Greene and Rusthon, *Personality Ships of British Columbia*, p.50.

30 Eric Nicol, *Vancouver* (Toronto: Doubleday, 1978), p.111.

31 Roy Brown, "Joe Fortes, English Bay 'Senor' Was Greatly Beloved Figure," *The Vancouver Sun*, May 12, 1954.

32 Robinson, "'English Bay Joe' Fortes."

33 "Great Crowd at Funeral of Joe Fortes," unknown source, possibly *The Vancouver Sun*, Feb. 7, 1922.

34 Stephen Foster, *Minstrel-Show Songs* (New York: Da Capo Press, 1980), p.16.

35 "You can tell that to Mr. Hitler," one civic booster remarked in the 1940s after noting that the only two sculptures erected by public subscription in Vancouver were to a black, Fortes, and a Jew, David Oppenheimer, the city's second mayor. See "Note to Hitler: Canada Monuments Honor Negro, Jew," *The Chicago Defender*, June 5, 1943.

36 "Negro Champion Barred from Vancouver Hotels," *Atlanta Constitution*, March 11, 1909.

37 Fortes was reportedly writing an autobiography, although no drafts of the document have, as yet, been discovered. See "The Story of My Life: Joe Fortes," *Daily News-Advertiser*, Jan. 19, 1913.

38 Louis Chude-Sokei, *The Last "Darky": Bert Williams, Black-on-Black Minstrelsy, and the African Diaspora* (Durham, N.C.: Duke University Press, 2006), p.3.

39 Robert C. Toll, *Blacking Up: The Minstrel Show in Nineteenth-Century America* (New York: Oxford University Press, 1974), pp.79–80, 187, 244–45. See also Eric Lott, *Love and Theft: Black Face Minstrelsy and the American Working Class* (New York: Oxford University Press, 1993).

40 On these debates, see André Alexis, "Borrowed Blackness," *This Magazine,* 28:8 (May 1995), pp.14–20; George Elliott Clarke, "Contesting a Model Blackness: A Meditation on African-Canadian African Americanism, or the Structures of African Canadianité," *Essays on Canadian Writing*, 63:9 (Spring 1998), pp.1–55; and Rinaldo Walcott, *Black Like Who? Writing Black Canada,* 2nd rev. ed. (Toronto: Insomniac Press, 2003). On the internationalization of the minstrel show, see Chude-Sokei, *The "Last Darky"*; and, with specific reference to Canada, Robin W. Winks, *The Blacks in Canada: A History*, 2nd ed. (Montreal and Kingston: McGill-Queen's University Press, 1997), pp.290–98.

41 Wayde Compton, "Blackvoice and Stately Ways: Isaac Dickson, Mifflin Gibbs and Black British Columbia's First Trials of Authenticity," in *Untold Stories of British Columbia*, ed. Paul Wood (Victoria, B.C.: University of Victoria Humanities Centre, 2003), p.26.

42 Ibid., p.19.

43 Bruce Ramsey, "Vancouver's First Lifeguard: Remembering the Days of 'Old Black Joe,'" *The Province* (Vancouver), March 16, 1964.

44 Ibid.

45 Compton, "Black Voice and Stately Ways," p.20.

46 Wilson, *Innocent Traveller,* pp. vii, 126, 125.

47 For a good historical account of the consolidation of class and racial identity in Vancouver, roughly overlapping the period covered by *The Innocent Traveller,* see Robert A.J. MacDonald, *Making Vancouver: Class, Status, and Social Boundaries, 1863–1913* (Vancouver: UBC Press, 1996).

48 Wilson, *Innocent Traveller*, pp.144–45.

49 Irene Howard, "Shockable and Unshockable Methodists in Ethel Wilson's *The Innocent Traveller*," *Essays on Canadian Writing*, 23 (Spring 1982), pp.107–34. The subtext of race and sex, black and white, beneath the English Bay Scandal would recur more than fifty years later in the death of Clarence Clemons, a black longshoreman beaten to

death by Vancouver police in late 1952. The officers allegedly resented that Clemons's common-law wife, Dolores Dingman, was white. See Ross Lambertson, "The Black, Brown, White and Red Blues: The Beating of Clarence Clemons," *Canadian Historical Review*, 85:4 (December 2004), pp.755–76. See also Wayde Compton, "The New Station," *Performance Bond* (Vancouver: Arsenal Pulp Press, 2004), pp.150–52.

50 Wilson, *Innocent Traveller*, p.149.

51 Ibid., p.150.

52 Ibid., pp.154, 155.

53 Ibid., pp.215–16.

54 Ibid., pp.229–30.

55 Ibid., p.101.

56 Fanon, *Black Skin, White Masks*, pp.111–13.

57 Wilson, *Innocent Traveller*, p.102. On black porters on Canadian railroads see Sarah-Jane (Saje) Mathieu, "North of the Colour Line: Sleeping Car Porters and the Battle Against Jim Crow on Canadian Rails, 1880–1920," *Labour/Le Travail* Spring 2001 <http://www.historycooperative.org/journals/llt/47/02mathie.html> (accessed Jan. 24, 2006). On the element of shock and surprise in the encounter with blackness in Canada, see Katherine McKittrick, "Nothing's Shocking: Black Canada," in her *Demonic Grounds: Black Women and the Cartographies of Struggle* (Minneapolis: University of Minnesota Press, 2006), pp.91–119.

58 Wilson, *Innocent Traveller*, p.116.

59 Ibid., pp.121–22.

60 Arnold Harrichand Itwaru, *The Invention of Canada: Literary Text and the Immigrant Imaginary* (Toronto: TSAR, 1990), p.32.

61 Wilson, *Innocent Traveller*, p.145.

62 David Stouck, *Ethel Wilson: A Critical Biography* (Toronto: University of Toronto Press, 2003), p. 160.

63 Wilson, *Innocent Traveller*, pp.169, 171.

64 Ibid., pp.4, 196.

65 Wilson, *Lilly's Story*, pp.8, 4.

66 Ibid., pp.5–6.

67 See Kay J. Anderson, *Vancouver's Chinatown: Racial Discourse in Canada, 1875–1980* (Montreal and Kingston: McGill-Queen's University Press, 1991).

68 Wilson, *Lilly's Story*, p.2.

69 Ibid., p.155.

70 Stouck, *Ethel Wilson*, p.147.

71 On the cultural and political impact of the influx of Asian capital in Vancouver at the end of the century, see Donald Gutstein, *The New Landlords: Asian Investment in Canadian Real Estate* (Victoria: Porcépic Books, 1990); and Katharyne Mitchell, *Crossing the Neoliberal Line: Pacific Rim Migration and the Metropolis* (Philadelphia: Temple University Press, 2004).

72 Notably, all the people of colour within *The Innocent Traveller* are servants to whites: the black porters, the Chinese household help, Fortes – all except the First Nations people, who sit passive and unperturbed outside of, or behind, Canadian history, while at the same time permanently occupying space. "They've got a right to sit there," Edgeworth's niece comments after chiding her aunt for her unsuccessful attempts to get the "Indians" to speak, "they were here first" (pp.116–17).

73 "Death Calls Joe Fortes, Life Guard," *The Vancouver Sun*, Feb. 4, 1922.

74 Noel Robinson, "Joe Fortes: Children's Friend (An Appreciation)," unknown source, possibly *The Vancouver Sun*, Feb. 6, 1922; G.E. McKee, "Joe Fortes," unknown source, possibly *The Vancouver Sun*, n.d.

75 Wayde Compton, "Response for Philly talks: Giscombe/Mckinnon," *PhillyTalks.org*, 18 (n.d.), pp.24–25 <slought.org/content/11801>.

9

Jenny Burman

Deportable or Admissible?

Black Women and the Space of "Removal"

> The women I see in the years that I have been here are often single, black women and single mothers carrying a huge burden, very few employable skills, little prospect for the future with respect to attracting either stable or employment at much more than a subsistence level, with the burden of child care of young children.
>
> — Justice Casey Hill, 2003, defending lenient sentences in the cases against Marsha Hamilton and Donna Mason, both accused of transporting drugs from Jamaica to Toronto

In Canadian legislation that delineates the various inclusions and exclusions of migration policy, references to deportation have given way to a sanitized language of removal: when "deportable subjects" are removed, they are "removed *to*" their places of origin, or in some cases to a "safe" third country (like the United States).[1] What kind of spatializing move does "removal to" make? For one thing, it commits a displacement or erasure, directing attention away from the nation-state doing the expelling and towards the places of origin, which in complementary discourses are held responsible for the deportables' deviation from being ideal Canadian citizens.[2] After deportation, the "removed to" are then grouped together in the public mind as "deportees" or "returnees," held in fear and suspicion by their supposed countrymen and women. They have been expelled and made into the unbelonging, in their new and old "homes." But the subject position of "deportable" also invites us to examine the condition of deportability independent of the end result ("stayed" or "deported").

The threat of deportation hovers over selected residents, and it has both a disciplinary use, with an element of spatial confinement – both internalized and externally enforced – and an influence on what Carole

Boyce Davies calls "migratory subjectivity."[3] To raise questions about the variable discourses of deportability as they apply to different target groups, in what follows I highlight debates, mostly in the courts, about black Caribbean women residents and the criteria that should govern their incorporation into or expulsion from the nation.[4]

Deportability and admissibility, while they have everything to do with the continuing construction of the national citizenry through its equally integral good and bad subjects, are also part of a spatial assertion of power over Canada as a bounded territory and the transnational movements that challenge or threaten its borders. Admissibility, as it is discussed in the "Inadmissibility and Grounds for Removal" sections of the *Immigration and Refugee Protection Act* (2002), refers to a judgment about people who are both outside Canadian borders and living in Canada while applying for status. A person can therefore be deemed inadmissible while inside, relegated to a space of simultaneous presence and absence. The non-status position places that person in the paradoxical predicament of occupying and not occupying a place in the nation. The gap between the habits of everyday life that add up to residency in a place and the absence of documentation that makes the presence official can be widened or narrowed, depending on whether the person's community is deemed suspect at the time. Questions of spatial entitlement are also embedded in the language of "landed immigrant" status: unlike the "landed gentry" of old, people do not necessarily own land as private property, but partake in a collective ownership of the nation-state's land. The category of landed immigrant is by no means secure given the state powers of detention and deportation laid out by "Danger to the Public and Security Certificate" provisions,[5] but non-status residents of Canada are definitively un-landed and un-entitled. Although they can make a place for themselves in everyday ways, through the development of residency patterns and social, familial, and labour networks, non-status people are prohibited from claiming a legitimate space in the nation. This condition might alert us to the limits of the nation as a conceptual category purporting to contain its constituent population, as well as to the reality of the materially lived national space, full of not-fully-here inhabitants. This contrast between the symbolic and spatial constitution of nation opens up a critically productive in-between space, substantiated by in-between subjects.

Susan Bibler Coutin's ethnography of the "space of non-existence" of undocumented migrants in the United States invites us to think spatially about the spectrum of subject positions that are crucial to the ideological operation of the nation-state, from the necessary but reviled "illegal" workforce to the noble eighth-generation settler-cum-host "Canadian-Canadian."[6]

This spectrum might also be framed as a space of foreclosure, a spatial elaboration of the ways in which the public in "danger to the public" and the national in "national security" are reconstituted through policy to redefine insiders and outsiders, and more specifically to reorganize the divisions between citizen and non-citizen. Such a space is predicated on labile provisions for both expunging undesirables from the nation (and as importantly in many cases, the city) and folding in those judged to be redeemable although in need of reform. Expanding this space in between belonging and unbelonging is a geographic practice not only in the obvious sense that it relies on extranational deportation routes to take care of intranational criminal justice problems, but also in a more metaphorical sense: internal "Others," who become hypervisible when accused of transgressions, are usefully mobilized in political and media discourses as foreign elements so as to subtly outline the ideal citizen of a particular geopolitical moment.

We have seen in the last decade or so a great deal of work in cultural geography and cultural studies-influenced social science research on what David Sibley calls the geographies of exclusion: spaces of marginalization on every scale, from domestic to global.[7] I wonder if the either/or oppositional tendencies of this model – one is either included or excluded – risk simplifying what is in reality a moving terrain with countless positions ranging in stability. I am interested here in considering the conditions of *inclusion* of deportable subjects: the nation-building project needs people who are identifiable at once as deportable *and* as salvageable or in need of patronage. Although we need to examine discourses and policies that construct deportability and admissibility in terms of how they exclude, we also need to understand that related discourses and policies also *include* – they decide effectively that there *is* room for certain people among you, and it is *this kind* of room. Boyce Davies argues in the U.S. context that when we talk about deportation exclusively in terms of criminality, we obscure the way in which the state uses deportation to construct its desirable citizens.[8] She is referring here to the construction of a desirable subject in opposition to the deportee, but I would add that to flex its managerial strength and define itself as a certain kind of host – in command but merciful – the state also needs to retain less desirable subjects.[9]

The connections between the undesirable and the desirable migrant, and the seemingly non-existent but transportable refugee, bring into focus the selective inclusion or integration of Caribbean – mostly black Jamaican – women. Through socio-spatial regulation – which is underwritten by racial-sexual mappings on and of the body – black women are cast as assimilable stock figures in need of sympathy, help, corrective discipline, lessons in family values, and so forth. "Host" gatekeepers in the courts and in the media poise themselves to fold in and manage these women. Court and media-generated discourses have given us the figures of "prodigious procreator," drug mule exploited by Jamaican male dealers, deceptive nanny, destitute single mother caught in pathological black family formations, and straight up "H&C" case (someone whose status claim is evaluated on humanitarian and compassionate grounds). I am concerned with the circulation of these figures as ideal types rather than with the question of how accurately or inaccurately they describe individual circumstances. These discourses do not communicate in a unified voice – they contain moments of empathy in excess of patronizing sympathy, and elements of astute analysis of poverty, racialization, and criminalization[10] – but they do weave together to assert the entitled and authoritative hospitality of the "host." I include examples in which Jamaican women were first ordered deported but then saw the order reconsidered or reversed during the appeal process: appeals are interesting sites of analysis because they are essentially pleas to the host for clemency or mercy that take place after a subject's deportability has been firmly established. On the precipice of exclusion, then, the subject-supplicant hopes for a new arbitrary judgment, a whimsical reversal of an earlier decision, a sympathetic patriarch to opt for reform rather than "removal to." She must accept in exchange further intrusions into her intimate circumstances and moral fibre, as well as sociological explanations of her predicament. The 1999 case of Mavis Baker, for instance, which has been frequently cited as a precedent in later cases, triggered an influential "family values"–related discussion of whether the welfare of children is the most important factor when considering the prospective harm of a removal order, or whether it is simply one important factor among many.[11]

The circulation of media representations is an important dimension of the articulation of a space of removal. One example of a mass media commentary that pathologizes and patronizes black families is a November 2005 *Globe and Mail* editorial headlined "The Many Fatherless Boys in Black Families." It opens with a question and answer: "Who is doing the killing and who is being killed in the wave of reckless public violence that has struck Toronto? Black boys and young men with no fathers in their homes." It then goes on to cite three black men (from Britain, the United States, and Canada) to legitimize the claim that there is a "crisis" and to lodge this crisis in the microcosm of the family, as separate from the socio-economic factors facing black communities in particular diasporic locales.[12] It would be simplistic to posit straightforward socio-economic explanations in response to the editorial's pathologization of black parents, but the piece pays no attention to a wider social setting that saw, for example, the decimation of social programs in Toronto after the cutbacks enforced by the provincial Conservative administration led by Mike Harris (1995–2002). It may be true, as the editorial put it, that "poor neighbourhoods in Toronto are crying out for involved fathers," but it is also true that much more is at play: the neighbourhoods in question (Jane and Finch, St. Jamestown, Regent Park) have underfunded public schools, high unemployment rates, and substandard housing, and their residents are overpoliced and underserviced. It is hard to determine what supports the claim that "an involved father is the best crime-prevention program ever designed"; the nuclear family has never protected cities from violent crime. One cannot help but notice the dissonance between this moralistic treatise on fathers' roles and the negligible attention paid to fathering in the written justifications for court decisions that incarcerate or deport black men, not to mention the mass media coverage of male detainees and deportees. Later the editorial lets the mother share in the blame, when it cites the case of Quintin Davers – fatherless, with a mother who gave birth to seven children – who was jailed for fatally shooting a nightclub bouncer: "Isn't it time someone asked why single women are having seven children?"[13] Here the *Globe and Mail* joins the courts' "host society" spokespeople in the debate over the appropriate family values to be insisted on in a multicultural society; the courts frequently weigh in with opinions regarding how many children are too many, the right and wrong reasons for having children, transnational parenting (long separations between children and parents), and other familial matters.

Clemency, Forgiveness, and Rehabilitation

Canadian discourses of deportability and illegality are deeply gendered: the 1995 *Danger to the Public Act* targeted Jamaican and other Afro-Caribbean men almost exclusively.[14] The significant scholarship on the fear of and desire for black males in North America provides a theoretical framework that we can use to make sense of this issue.[15] Publicized cases in the late 1990s included those of Owen Dale Campbell, who was brought to Canada by his mother at the age of seventeen months – he did not get citizenship and was deported from Toronto to Jamaica in 1996 at the age of twenty-two; O'Neil Grant, eventually cleared of charges related to the Just Desserts robbery-shooting but deported for other minor offences – he had lived in Toronto since the age of nine; and Patrick McKenzie, who was deported in 1999 after living in Canada between the ages of ten and thirty-five, then murdered in Jamaica. McKenzie's parents had his remains flown back to Canada to be buried.

When Frances Henry and Carol Tator document an ongoing "Jamaicanization of crime" in Toronto to describe how a "distancing, othering, and marginalization of Black people, and specifically Jamaicans, is established," they refer primarily to Jamaican Torontonian men.[16] Women as prospective deportees are most publicly discussed when children are involved: in the 1970s, for instance, the case of the "Seven Jamaican Women" admitted to Canada as landed immigrants under a domestic workers' program (in particular, an agreement between Jamaica's Ministry of Labour and Canada's Department of Manpower and Immigration) made its way to the highest courts. The Canadian department had circulated criteria for admissibility into this work program: workers should be between eighteen and forty years of age, single, and have no dependent children.[17] The seven women in question were ordered deported for having omitted information about dependent children. In 1978, along with the advocacy group INTERCEDE, they filed a complaint with the Canadian Human Rights Commission; eventually their deportation orders were overturned. One of the slogans used by other domestic workers and supporters was "good enough to work, good enough to stay."

In the 1990s, the case of *Mavis Baker v. Canada* (Minister of Citizenship and Immigration Canada) garnered a lot of attention because it set a precedent regarding instances in which plaintiffs must be given written reasons for deportation orders. Mavis Baker was a Jamaican national who had worked in Canada without papers for more than ten years and had given birth to four children in the country before being diagnosed with paranoid schizophrenia. She was also said to have four other children living in Jamaica. The 1999 decision by Madam Justice Claire L'Heureux Dubé in her case – requiring written justifications for deportation under certain circumstances – led to indignant commentaries in the mainstream press, with writers complaining that the government should have to justify in writing its actions towards "illegals."[18] When Baker's appeal went forward because of her Canadian-born children, a *National Post* editorial stated: "If Ms. Baker truly believes the welfare of her children is paramount, she would return to Jamaica and reconcile her two sets of children. This logic seems to have escaped the Supreme Court."[19] The original Immigration officer's notes on Baker's case were requisitioned during the appeal, and they reveal an implicit judgment about the number of children Baker had, as well as a broader agenda regarding the kind of host Canada should be:

> [Baker] is a paranoid schizophrenic and on welfare. She has no qualifications other than as a domestic. She has FOUR CHILDREN IN JAMAICA AND ANOTHER FOUR BORN HERE. She will, of course, be a tremendous strain on our social welfare systems for (probably) the rest of her life. There are no H & C [Humanitarian and Compassionate] factors other than her FOUR CANADIAN-BORN CHILDREN. Do we let her stay because of that? I am of the opin-

> ion that Canada can no longer afford this type of generosity. However, because of the circumstances involved, there is a potential for adverse publicity. I recommend refusal but you may wish to clear this with someone.[20]

A 2002 case saw Patricia Sterling's deportation order overturned due to a senior Immigration officer's decision that she had engaged in "prodigious procreation" in order to stay in Canada (she had six children in Toronto, after four born in Jamaica in the 1980s). The officer was shown to have "acted with an appearance of bias"[21] when Sterling applied for permanent residence on humanitarian and compassionate grounds on the basis of her children's status. When the courts rule on "the best interests of the child," they make decisions about the strength of intimate family relations, decisions that often determine whether or not a family is to be separated – such is the reach of the "host" into interpersonal matters.

The shift in Canadian jurisprudence away from the "best interests of the child" as a criterion for humanitarian and compassionate consideration, and towards a more vague policy of treating the interests of the child as one among many factors, including the criminal record of the parents, can be related to the moral campaign portraying migrants and refugees as untrustworthy. This comes amid discussion of "passport babies," children who are allegedly conceived to allow their parents to obtain permanent residency.[22] When the migrant woman's body is too reproductive, it is cause for concern. What if she is only bearing children in order to trick the state into letting her stay? An important connection is discernible here between production (migrant labour), reproduction (the migrant woman's body, harbouring other undesirable subjects), and the space of removal or the geopolitical processes influencing the routes travelled by black women.[23]

In Daphney Hawthorne's deportation case at the Federal Court of Appeal, the official report tells the story of the woman's migration to Canada in 1992 and how she had left her eight-year-old daughter Suzette behind with relatives in Jamaica. For the next several years Hawthorne communicated with and sent money to Suzette, and in 1999 she brought her to Canada. Suzette's residency application was sponsored by her father, who also lived in Canada, but her parents were separated (her father had subsequently married another woman). When Daphney Hawthorne was ordered deported a few years later, because she was Suzette's sole supporter she made an application citing "humanitarian and compassionate" needs. The officer evaluating her application turned it down, arguing that since mother and daughter had lived apart for so long, "their relationship could not have been close and . . . their separation now would not be a major hardship for either of them."[24]

In this case the judge ordered a judicial review, but the officer's initial decision gives a sense of the kinds of decisions that Immigration officers with no psychological or family counselling training are called upon to make. In the review, the judge upholds the illogical determination that because mother and daughter had endured one separation, another would not cause undue hardship: "It was the applicant's choice to leave her daughter for eight years. Therefore, since she had not seen her daughter for that length of time one cannot consider it a major hardship if she were to be separated from her again."[25] To frame the kinds of circumstances that drive transmigrant women to spend long and painful periods apart from their children, during which they often continue to parent, as "the applicant's choice to leave her daughter for eight years" is to show at the very least a high-stakes insensitivity to the plight of women in a feminized global labour force.

Drug transporters, or in the ignominious term mostly reserved for women, "drug mules," have attracted great interest and intense policing over the last decade (as well as some sympathy, since the moving portrayal of Colombian women transporters in the 2004 film *Maria Full of Grace*). Women travelling from Jamaica to Toronto are frequently searched for, and sometimes found carrying, drugs, mostly cocaine, in their baggage or in latex packages that they swallow and thus transport in their bellies. In the United Kingdom, authorities circulate estimates that one in ten Jamaicans is likely to be smuggling drugs; the U.K./Jamaican anti-trafficking initiative called Operation Airbridge is now deploying Ionscan machines in the airports and checking travellers more routinely. Stories in the Jamaican press, for example, identify poor women as being connected to local "dons" as well as important transnational figures like the notorious "Father Fowl," the head of a drug empire.[26]

In selected court judgments in Canada (in this case the Ontario Superior Court of Justice), we see the courts struggling with the issue of drug transporters, who are often prospective deportees. One such case, in 2003, involved Marsha Hamilton and Donna Mason, who were convicted of drug trafficking – they had ingested cocaine-filled pellets and thus imported the drug into Canada. Both of them received conditional sentences of less than two years, which combined partial house arrest and curfews and laid out conditions of residency and association. The question after the conviction of Marsha Hamilton, a Canadian citizen of Jamaican descent, was not whether she was deportable but whether her sentence fit the crime. She was twenty-six at the time of the offence, with three children. Donna Mason, a Jamaican citizen but a resident of Canada since the age of seven, had two children. Court documents identified them as impoverished, black, single mothers, and their trial judge was accused of giving them sentences that were too lenient because he was taking into account broader social issues such as poverty, the disproportionate imprisonment of black women, and the rising drug trade in suburban Toronto (in the words of the appeal, Justice Casey Hill was found to have considered social and structural factors in a manner "inconsistent with the principles of sentencing"). Nonetheless, the judge's 240-page report detailing these and other issues tried to grapple with complicated questions of the transnational drug trade and its reverberations in local working-class neighbourhoods.[27]

These socio-spatial histories and conditions, wherein gender, race, poverty, and deportability intersect with the nation and regional (Caribbean) migratory processes, narrow the inhabitable space of Canada and discipline the subject by circumscribing everyday mobility and micromanaging the criminal deemed reformable. Through spatial confinement, bodies are stabilized to make them less threatening, in a reproduction of a certain colonial logic. Mason, interestingly, was not ordered deported, although Jamaican men with less serious convictions (and Canadian-born children) are frequently deported. The appeal overview states that the judge neglected the question of moral culpability of the individual criminals. That finding appears to be accurate, Mason and Hamilton's expressions of remorse notwithstanding: on the one hand, the judge showed unusual sympathy for the structural conditions contributing to the predicament that the two women found themselves in, as well as a refreshing unwillingness to continue to punish those at the bottom of the drug trade pyramid disproportionately; on the other hand, he handled them as infantilized victims who could not be held responsible for their actions. In the first hearing of the case, Justice Hill assembled testimony and reports describing the relatively low recidivism rate of women convicts, based on the research of Margaret Shaw; the disproportionate rate of arrest and incarceration of black men and women, especially for petty drug-related offences;[28] and the ineffectiveness of harsh sentencing on deterring drug importers, based on the research of a criminologist. I should make clear that I am not invoking an ideal scenario in which the courts would be able to ethically assess moral culpability and weigh it against socio-economic conditions: the courts, the prisons, and the legislation governing deportation are part of the same racializing system of criminalization. Further, I am opposed to the use of deportation as a punishment for criminal offences. What I am trying to shed light on here is the "host's" performance of authority over black migrant bodies, which involves far more complex power plays than forcible expulsion.

The Contagion of a Black (Woman's) Body

Radhika Mohanram writes of black bodies that they have been historically marked as static or immobilized, and embodied in a way that links them essentially to the landscape. She notes the traditional "discursive incarceration" of the black "native" in colonial discourse, and points to Fanon's well-known observation that the "black man" is pure representation: he is pulled out of an embodied corporeal schema and thrown into a historical-racial context (this is from the oft-cited "Look mama, a negro!" passage in *Black Skin, White Masks*).[29] It is perhaps the colonial association of the non-white body with her place of origin that makes the in-between body of the transmigrant woman (and the travelling "drug mule" in particular) provoke anxiety. With "drug mule," we have the connotation of a non-reproducing body – the mule – used for unnatural purposes, and an opaque body that might be concealing something illegal. In the United Kingdom's Operation Airbridge, talk of the estimated one in ten Jamaicans entering the country carrying drugs (and often in their bellies) raised the spectre of leagues of hollowed-out black bodies with cocaine-filled condoms where their digesting lunches should be. When we look at the two examples of women alleged to procreate for passports and women drug transporters, we see the historical objectification of the black female body playing out across the sites of suspiciously filled and suspiciously hollow bodies: threatening vessels both.

In the 1999 case of *Richards v. Canada*, the federal court debated the question of whether Darnette Richards constituted a danger to the public.[30] Richards had moved to Canada in 1987 at age twenty-two to live with her grandmother, who eventually sponsored her, and she was convicted in 1989 and 1997 for transporting first marijuana and then cocaine from Jamaica to Toronto. Because of those two convictions, Ministerial opinion deemed her to be a danger to the public and she was ordered deported. The factors that the courts and eventually the appeal judge who stayed the order took into consideration were Richards's role as a primary caregiver to her ailing grandmother, her expressions of remorse and narrative of being used or exploited (tricked the first time, and threatened the second), her moves towards improving her circumstances (she was progressing towards a college diploma), and her pregnancy with a baby fathered by a landed immigrant with no criminal record. The judge engaged in some discussion of whether convictions alone are enough to name someone a danger to the public, citing a previous case that determined the need for convictions to be supplemented by a reasonable projection of threat.

It is clear that Ministerial opinions, based as they are on forecasting future dangers, rely on a great deal of arbitrary and subjective interpretation. Given the deportation option, they are not obliged to place much hope in rehabilitation. However, the scripted gender roles that make courts more or less likely to grant clemency are discernible in a comparison of the cases of women and men with drug convictions.[31] Once Richards was made comprehensible as the stock figure of caregiver – there is, after all, a long tradition in Canada of drawing Caribbean women to migrate as domestic workers and nurses, if not of easily granting them citizenship – and woman exploited by drug-runners, she could be easily deemed "forgivable." Further, forgiving her and reincorporating her are ultimately as valuable as rejecting her, because it contributes to the host's projected image as being in measured, rational control of the inside/outside boundary, and as capable of forming and reforming subjects. These cases suggest how racialized and "deviant" migrant women are folded into the nation-state project through a power dynamic that joins stern but forgiving host to contrite, rehabilitable feminized guest.

Mariana Valverde and Anna Pratt and Sherene Razack discuss the general climate of suspicion facing racialized citizens and prospective citizens in the 1990s. Valverde and Pratt detail the moral campaign against refugee applicants and immigrants that involved a shift in the portrayal of Somali residents – from victims to "masters of confusion" intent on taking advantage of Canada's lax refugee system and social welfare net – and that saw Jamaican residents targeted for heavy policing, detention, and deportation in the wake of the Just Desserts shooting in Toronto.[32] In addition to the *Danger to the Public* legislation that sought to root out criminals and send them "home" – buttressed by the new mandate of the Canadian Security and Intelligence Service (CSIS) to focus on "transnational criminal activity" – there was much discussion of migrants' draining/defrauding of public resources, framed as a wily exploitation of host-nation largesse. The Toronto Police apparently cited Jonathan Swift on their website: "honesty hath no fence against superior cunning."[33]

Razack describes the performance of one judge as "imperial patriarch" in the court case of a Canadian-born woman of colour, a lawyer, accused of falsifying immigration-related documents for her clients. Razack also writes about the experience of sitting in the courtroom as a racialized immigrant subject, whose body in the room – implicitly positioned by the staged battle between unscrupulous and degenerate immigrants and noble and civilized white state representatives – "bridged the gap between personal bodily knowledge and the romantic-metaphoric idea of the nation."[34] Her observations point to everyday instances that reveal the model of the nation-state as capacious container to be illusory. The routes leading outward are as important to the nation as the integrity of its perimeter, whether they lead to actual destinations for deportables or sites of migrant origin that contaminate certain residents.

Many researchers point out a change in popular discourses linking crime to ethnicity: the roots of crime are blamed increasingly on "culture" or national origin rather than on "race."[35] This particular mode of criminalization affects how race is spatialized: in an old move reinvented for a new hybridized social reality, the contaminant is externalized at the moment of its deepest implication and entanglement. An extranational site's "culture" is blamed when "Canadian culture" is at its most heterogeneous and unidentifiable or slippery. Henry and Tator give several examples of press coverage that blames much urban crime on "Jamaican culture."[36] From the *Toronto Sun*: "Colour is not the issue here or in most black-on-black crimes. Culture is the issue. Jamaican culture." From *The Globe and Mail* comes the suggestion of self-censorship: "What everyone knows but no one says in polite company is that the gun-and-drugs culture is heavily Jamaican, and it's spinning out of control."[37]

The role of admission and expulsion policies in the ongoing formation of a deserving Canadian "public" has been widely recognized. The internal management of racialized bodies through policing, surveillance, and incarceration tells a story of selective inclusion and continually reenacts state power over its "not-quite citizens." The impact of such invasive scrutiny on the everyday lives of the legalized and illegalized has been usefully discussed through the idea of precarity – temporary, precarious, migrant work – and the analysis of the instability characterizing life as a deportable.[38] Significantly, the Latin root of "host" is *hostis*, one of whose meanings is "enemy." Legalized forms of belonging, such as citizenship, permanent residence, and work visas, then, are something like gifts from the enemy: they are always weighted with historical injustices, fraught with tensions and expectations, and more precarious than they might seem. Much has been written since 2001, adding to an already existing literature, on the formation of individual and communal suspect identities.[39] As far as racialized dangerous criminals and terrorism suspects are concerned, however, these figures are generally gendered as male. Women occupy a different role: they are not immediately threatening to the community at large. The kinds of things they are targeted for – dishonesty, moral turpitude, bad mothering – tend to contribute to a fear of difference and immorality, constructing the black body as a contagion that intrudes on "normal" society.

Katherine McKittrick writes, "The black woman is thrown into a seemingly static and paradoxical place – she is both outside modernity (disenfranchised, speechless, irrational, (un)definable, all flesh), and inside modernity (thus signifying what proper modern subjects are: not her, not black, not black and female)."[40] Here I have been interested in fleshing out, with the examples of certain Canadian court cases that pit the governing body of the state against the micromanaged but ungovernable body of the racialized migrant woman, the conditions of deportability and admissibility as articulated by a patriarchal host system. The host is, of course, not a singular figure, but a constellation of forces and spatializing processes – incarceration, management through surveillance, deportation – that sets into motion complex power dynamics with vulnerable "guests." The host, disembodied, is sometimes cast as a merciful, magnanimous, and whimsical benefactor, sometimes as a diseased creature hosting parasites and looking for an antigen as a means of self-protection. Black migrant women are among the stock figures whose spatial in-betweenness and "chaotic bodies"[41] make their expulsion from nation-space and their reintegration equally important to the besieged authority of the host.

Notes

1 The term "deportable subjects" comes from Carole Boyce Davies, "Deportable Subjects: U.S. Immigration Laws and the Criminalizing of Communism," *South Atlantic Quarterly*, 100:4 (2001).

2 An example of such a complementary discourse is the mass media coverage in Toronto of a putative "Jamaican culture of violence" that is periodically blamed for the city's increase in gang activity and/or gun violence. Francis Henry and Carol Tator, "Racial Profiling in Toronto: Discourses of Domination, Mediation, and Opposition," in *Report for Canadian Race Relations Foundation* (March 2003), cite numerous newspaper articles that contribute to the scapegoating of Jamaicans.

3 Boyce Davies, "Deportable Subjects."

4 I should emphasize that I am a lay reader of the court documents cited in this chapter, and can claim no expertise in my readings. I bring them in as public domain narratives that flesh out some of the stories told by journalists or policy critiques undertaken by scholars. The Canadian Legal Information Institute offers a valuable online information service detailing the cases under discussion here <www.canlii.org>. The cases I cite are primarily drawn from the Canadian Legal Information Institute website and are referenced accordingly.

5 "Ministerial Danger Opinions" allow for the deportation of Convention refugees deemed a "danger to the public," but they were used in the 1990s to target and deport Afro-Caribbean non-citizen male residents suspected of criminal activity; security certificates are deployed to deport permanent residents or foreign nationals believed to pose a security threat. See "Keeping Canada Safe," Canada Border Services Agency, Government of Canada <www.cbsa-asfc.gc.ca/newsroom/factsheets/2005/jansafe-e.html, 2005>.

6 Susan Bibler Coutin, "Illegality, Borderlands, and the Space of Nonexistence," in *Globalization under Construction: Governmentality, Law and Identity*, ed. Richard Warren Perry and Bill Maurer (Minneapolis: University of Minnesota Press, 2003); Eva Mackey, *The House of Difference: Cultural Politics and National Identity in Canada* (Toronto: University of Toronto Press, 2002).

7 David Sibley, *Geographies of Exclusion: Society and Difference in the West* (New York and London: Routledge 1995).

8 Boyce Davies, "Deportable Subjects," p.950.

9 Scholars researching Canadian illegalization and racialization processes have found Foucaultian concepts of governmentality useful for their attention to the constitution of deserving and undeserving subjects. See Wendy Chan and Kiran Mirchandani, eds., *Crimes of Colour: Racialization and the Criminal Justice System in Canada* (Toronto: Broadview Press, 2002); Mariana Valverde and Anna Pratt, "From Deserving Victims to 'Masters of Confusion': Redefining Refugees in the 1990s," *Canadian Journal of Sociology*, 27: 2 (2002).

10 This is true of court decisions in different areas related to race, crime, and/or poverty. The discussion of racism and racial profiling by police in the 2003 case of *Peart v. Peel Regional Police Services* – in which Garfield Peart and Earle Grant sued the police for profiling and physical abuse – is a fascinating attempt to reckon with the structural conditions giving credence to the plaintiffs' case. It takes very seriously sociological research reports and expert testimony by Dr. Agard, a black psychologist specializing in trauma relating to racial discrimination, although it also ultimately places the onus on the plaintiffs to prove deliberate racist behaviour on the part of two individual officers – hard to do in the face of the latter's denials and the absence of witnesses or recordings. *Peart v. Peel Regional Police Services*, <http://www.canlii.org/ca/cas/fca/2002/2002fca475.html>. See also *Peart v. Peel Regional Police Services*, 2003, CanLII 42339 (ON S.C.).

11 It was ruled to be the latter, and Baker was eventually deported. See Canada, Supreme Court of Canada, *Baker v. Canada* (Minister of Citizenship and Immigration), 1999 <http://www.canlii.org/ca/cas/scc/1999/1999scc41.html>.

12 Editorial, "The Many Fatherless Boys in Black Families," *The Globe and Mail* (Toronto), Nov. 26, 2005.

13 Ibid.

14 For a discussion of gender and deportability in Canada, see Nicholas De Genova, "Migrant 'Illegality' and Deportability in Everyday Life," *Annual Review of Anthropology*, 31 (2002).

15 The critical debates that emerged during and after the Whitney Museum's 1994 exhibition on the black male offer one good sample of this scholarship: Thelma Golden, ed., *Black Male: Representations of Black Masculinity in Contemporary American Art* (New York: Whitney Museum of American Art, 1994). See also Patricia Hill Collins, *Black Sexual Politics: African Americans, Gender, and the New Racism* (New York: Routledge, 2004).

16 Henry and Tator, "Racial Profiling in Toronto," p.20.

17 Anne Bayefsky, "The Jamaican Women Case and the Canadian Human Rights Act: Is Government Subject to the Principle of Equal Opportunity?" *U.W.O. Law Review*, 18 (1979–80), p.467.

18 Finbarr O'Reilly, "Dangerous Opinions," *National Post* (Toronto), Jan. 18, 2001.

19 Editorial, "Separation Anxiety," *National Post*, July 13, 1999.

20 *Baker v. Canada*, "Factual Background," 1999 <http://www.canlii.org/ca/cas/scc/1999/1999scc41.html>.

21 Janice Tibbetts, "Judge Overturns Deportation," *Calgary Herald*, May 10, 2002.

22 An interesting case in Ireland in 2002 tested the nation's commitment to a traditional Catholic pro-children family values. "Baby O" was the fetus of a Nigerian refugee claimant who was fighting her deportation order partly on the grounds that her baby would face unsafe conditions in Nigeria because of high infant-mortality rates. Prior to the economic boom that made it a viable "host society," Ireland had legislated protection for the parents of Irish-born (in the North or South) children as part of the Good Friday Agreement with Northern Ireland. This left the door open for the protection of refugee claimants (who had given birth in Ireland) until their children reached eighteen

– but it also caused much debate and contributed to an anti-migrant backlash. Baby O's mother was ultimately unsuccessful and was deported, but the case is cited by refugee advocates as one that laid bare the hypocrisy of the government where fetuses and children are concerned. The case is described in Fionnuala Quinlan, "Pregnant Woman Could Be Deported within Days," *Irish Examiner*, Jan. 19, 2002 <http://archives.tcm.ie/irishexaminer/2002/01/19/story21432.asp>.

23 Katherine McKittrick, "'Who Do You Talk to, When a Body's in Trouble?': Marlene Nourbese Philip's (Un)Silencing of Black Bodies in the Diaspora," *The Journal of Social and Cultural Geography*, 1:2 (2000), p.227.

24 *Hawthorne v. Canada* (Minister of Citizenship and Immigration) <http://www.canlii.org/ca/cas/fca/2002/2002fca475.html>. See also [2003] 2 F.C. 555, 2002 FCA 475.

25 Ibid.

26 Mark Wignall, "Crews, Criminality, and the Drug Link," *Jamaica Observer*, Aug. 5, 2004. British police identified Owen "Father Fowl" Clarke as the head of a drug empire that distributed in the United Kingdom but was administered in Jamaica. Clarke, allegedly protected by the Jamaican police, was arrested in 2004 in the United Kingdom and sentenced to eleven years in prison.

27 See <http://www.canlii.org/on/cas/onca/2004/2004onca11260.html> for the full report. *R. v. Hamilton*, 2004, CanLII 5549 (ON C.A.).

28 The *Report of the Commission on Systemic Racism in the Ontario Criminal Justice System*, cited in the judgment, states that the black to white ratio of imprisonment for trafficking/importing drugs is 22:1.

29 Radhika Mohanram, *Black Body: Women, Colonialism, and Space* (Minneapolis: University of Minnesota Press, 1999), pp.11, 26; Frantz Fanon, *Black Skin, White Masks,* trans. Charles Lam Markmann (New York: Grove Press, 1967), pp.109–140.

30 See Federal Court of Canada, *Richards v. Canada* (Minister of Citizenship and Immigration) <http://www.canlii.org/ca/cas/fct/1999/1999fct10743.html>, 1999, CanLII 8234 (F.C.).

31 For comparative reference, see the case of Jeffrey Hugh Williams: *Williams v. Canada* (Minister of Citizenship and Immigration), 1997, 1 F.C. 431 <http://reports.fja.gc.ca/fc/1997/pub/v1/1997fca0037.html>.

32 In April 1994 Georgina Leimonis was killed in the course of a robbery-shooting at an upscale Toronto café, Just Desserts. The suspects were black Jamaican-born men, the victim a white Canadian-born woman. The ensuing media coverage focused heavily on Jamaican criminality, and follow-up government legislation (*Bill C44*) targeted Caribbean-born black men for deportation. See Valverde and Pratt, "From Deserving Victims to 'Masters of Confusion,'" p.139.

33 Valverde and Pratt, "From Deserving Victims to 'Masters of Confusion,'" p.139.

34 Sherene Razack, "Making Canada White: Law and the Policing of Bodies of Colour in the 1990s," *Canadian Journal of Law and Society*, 14 (1999), pp.167–70.

35 In addition to Valverde and Pratt, "From Deserving Victims to 'Masters of Confusion,'" see Chan and Mirchandani, eds., *Crimes of Colour*.

36 Henry and Tator, "Racial Profiling in Toronto."

37 Peter Worthington, "Profiling Essential to Fighting Crime," *The Toronto Sun*, Oct. 31, 2002; Margaret Wente, "Death, Guns and the Last Taboo," *The Globe and Mail*, Oct. 29, 2002.

38 Michelle Lowry and Peter Nyers, "Roundtable Report, 'No One Is Illegal': The Fight for Refugee and Migrant Rights in Canada," *Refuge*, 21: 3 (2003); Peter Nyers, "Abject Cosmopolitanism: The Politics of Protection in the Anti-Deportation Movement," *Third World Quarterly*, 24: 6 (2003); Rinaldo Walcott, *Black Like Who? Writing Black Canada*, 2nd ed. (Toronto: Insomniac Press, 2003); De Genova, "Migrant 'Illegality' and Deportability in Everyday Life."

39 Anna Pratt, *Securing Borders: Detention and Deportation in Canada* (Vancouver and Toronto: UBC Press, 2005); Michael Collyer, "Secret Agents: Anarchists, Islamists, and

Responses to Politically Active Refugees in London," *Ethnic and Racial Studies*, 28:2 (2005).

40 McKittrick, "'Who Do You Talk to, When a Body's in Trouble?'" p.226.

41 Ibid.

10

Sonjah Stanley Niaah

Mapping Black Atlantic Performance Geographies

From Slave Ship to Ghetto

It's my brother, my sister.
At the bottom of the Atlantic Ocean there's a
railroad made of human bones.
Black ivory
Black ivory
— Amiri Baraka

Amiri Baraka's poetry provides an essential backdrop to the people whose music I will be discussing here, as well as to the performance practices – dances, rituals – that take place around the music and the conditions of repression and exploitation under which the performers live. So too does a statement by South African actor John Kani, who says that a repressive society produces "some kind of gangrene within you . . . that eats your soul, that forces you to save your soul. I couldn't really say that a repressive society would result in creative art, but somehow it does help, it is an ingredient; it acts as a catalyst to a man who is committed."[1]

Black forms of music and their corresponding performance practices have deeper continuities than are readily apparent in movement, musical, and celebratory patterns. Crucially, these deeper continuities have not been fully explored by such disciplines as ethno-musicology, geography, or cultural studies. Based on data gathered over twelve years' participation in Jamaica's dancehall music performance and over six years of research, I want to expand my reading of New World performance practices to other black performance genres. Essentially, an analysis of dancehall's macro- and microspatialities reveals spatial categories, philosophies, and systems, thereby delineating what is best captured by the term "performance geography." Here I want to apply performance geography to black performance practices that range from the middle passage slave-ship dance limbo to the ghettoes where the blues, Kingston's dancehall, and South Africa's kwaito emerged. Out of the marginal space of the ghetto, performance cultures have consistently challenged the very contexts that militate against their emergence.

What is performance geography? By performance, I mean physical, mental, emotional, and spiritual activity that enacts a human existence, specifically in the "black Atlantic" space between violation, ruptured roots, and self-reconstruction; it is a requirement for life. Like the enslaved who arrived at Kingston Harbour, Jamaica, after the ordeal of the middle passage in the seventeenth and eighteenth centuries, inner-city youth survive the challenges of the urban experience through their strategies of performance (voluntarily or not). Further, with renewed interest in space and its implied discourse of spatiality spawned by the works of Michel Foucault, Edward Soja, and others, I see performance geography as building on the work of Catherine Nash and Nigel Thrift on the role of performance, specifically embodied practices, in cultural geography.[2] This work looks at how people living in particular locations give those locations identity through performance. Bearing in mind that this is work in progress, I see it as a mapping of the locations used, the types and systems of use, the politics of their location in relation to other sites and other practices, the character of events/rituals in particular locations, and the manner in which different performances/performers relate to each other within and across different cultures.

My analysis of performance geography in the context of blackness, and of the New World and its middle passage history, invokes Paul Gilroy's concept of the black Atlantic as a counterculture of modernity. But there are ways in which I depart from that reading even as my work continues that tradition. Despite the criticisms from Don Robotham on the lack of attention to material forces, Peter Sutherland on the virtual absence of examples from Latin America, Africa, and the wider Caribbean in the formation of the transatlantic black culture, and Norman Corr Jr. and Rachel Corr on the absence of the middle passage history of suffering as a reference in the construction of black Atlantic scholarship,[3] I concur with Gilroy, who states:

> In the space and time that separate Robert Johnson's "Hellhound on my Trail," the Wailers' exhortation to "Keep on Moving," and the more recent Soul II Soul piece with the same name, the expressive cultures of the black Atlantic world have been dominated by a special mood of restlessness. These songs . . . evoke and affirm a condition in which the negative meanings given

> to the enforced movement of blacks are somehow transposed. What was initially . . . a curse – the curse of homelessness or . . . enforced exile – gets repossessed. It becomes affirmed and is reconstructed as the basis of a privileged standpoint from which certain useful and critical perceptions about the modern world become more likely. . . . I want to suggest that it . . . represents a response to successive displacements, migrations, journeys . . . which have come to constitute these black cultures' special conditions of existence.[4]

Geographically themed, Gilroy's work speaks to a spatial imperative in the black experience in terms of restlessness, homelessness, displacement, migration, and other journeys. I would like, on a point of convergence with Gilroy, to continue the unearthing of New World performance, indeed of popular culture and space in the tradition of Kamau Brathwaite, Wilson Harris, and Geneviève Fabre, who have etched clear images of the slave-ship dance limbo in black Atlantic scholarship. Space is an important element in New World performance.

The limbo dance highlights the importance of not only the historical but also the spatial imagination. Emerging out of the lack of space available on the slave ships, the slaves bent themselves like spiders. Incidentally, the lack of space is also obvious to the visitor of slave castles such as Elmina Castle, with low thresholds that the enslaved navigated to move from dungeon to holding room to the "door of no return" (now renamed the "door of return") before boarding the slavers.[5] Consistent with certain African beliefs, the dance reflects the whole cycle of life. The dancers move under a pole that is gradually lowered from chest level, and they emerge on the other side, as their heads clear the pole, as in the triumph of life over death.[6] The slave ships, like the plantation and the city, reveal(ed) particular spaces that produce(d) magical forms of entertainment and ritual.

This historical continuity is evidenced in how movement patterns like the limbo were preserved throughout the last three centuries, emerging among the Jamaican Maroons, twentieth-century Jamaican tourist entertainment, and within Trinidad as a wake dance.[7] Crucially, limbo also appeared in Jamaica's dancehall culture as one of the popular dance moves of the year 1994. Limbo holds memory and marks continuity among performance practices of the New World. Firstly, limbo calls our attention to the dance movement and to the space (its limits and potential) in which the movement was (and still is) performed. Secondly, it is a "ritual of rebirth"[8] that goes beyond the slave ship of the middle passage; it has also been linked to puberty and war rituals within Africa, to Kongolese cosmology in particular, as well as funeral rites.[9] Similarly, the plantation dances and urban dancehall events evoke memories of celebratory events held within spatially restricted, heavily policed, and marginal settings. What I have done in previous work is to set up a conversation between limbo as dance, space, system, and symbol to look at the parallels, the common genealogy, spatially and performatively, with dancehall performance in order to develop my case for the use of a spatial argument.[10] I extend that work here.

A look at the scholarship on and common genealogy of the blues, dancehall, and kwaito reveals that some of the same comments have been made about the performers, lyrics, role, performance practices, raison d'être, and aesthetics. What else can be said of the link between dancehall, the blues, and kwaito? I will not historicize the main elements of these forms (see chapter 3 here); rather, I want to provide a brief description of them, focusing on analyzing their spaces of performance, their venues, and the stories they tell about the meaning of celebration.[11]

The Politics of Space in Dancehall Culture

The name "dancehall" has a spatial nuance. It first flourished in the 1950s in Jamaica around the consumption of the emerging popular music, especially in the Kingston Metropolitan Area, and its name derives from the exclusive yards/halls/lawns in which dance events were mainly held. It is to be understood first of all as the space in which adults meet to consume, celebrate, entertain, and affirm group identity.[12]

In my early research my use of space as a holistic category for analyzing dancehall performance led to an examination of the venues, the events that occurred in those venues, and the culture of celebration in Jamaica, as well as the dance movement as an underexplored aspect of dancehall culture since the 1950s. I developed a classification scheme based on characteristic features, degree of commercialization, permanence, and hierarchy, and, associated with these elements, analytical categories, recurring metaphors, spatial descriptors, and philosophies that characterize the evolution of popular dancehall culture in Jamaica.[13] There are important stories about space in dancehall culture (see Table 1). Most notably, dancehall occupies multiple spatial dimensions (urban, street, policed, marginal, gendered, performative, liminal, memorializing, communal), which are revealed through the nature and type of events and venues, and their use and function. Most notable is the way in which dancehall occupies a liminal space between what is celebrated and at the same time denigrated in Jamaica, and how it moves from private community to public and commercial enterprise. Further, the way in which the urban gendered body creates space and status through performance in spite of the odds characteristic of life at the edge of survival is indicative of the role and importance of celebratory performance cultures. Then too, beyond the multiple spatial dimensions are spatial philosophies, such as that of boundarylessness, which is revealed in the way that "boundedness" translates into "unboundedness," freedom, journey, contest, and transformation.

Are the characteristics of spatial use, the philosophy and transformatory nature of dancehall culture and its evolution, similar for the blues or kwaito? What do they have in common in terms of performance space? From the Saturday night slave dance, to blues, dancehall, and kwaito, music and dance performances have been central to black life. Following from Gilroy's statements on the mental, physical, and philosophical journeying and displacement across the black Atlantic, I now turn to the spatial dimensions of the blues and kwaito to explore the common genealogy of the slave-ship (limbo), plantation (slave dance; blues), and ghetto (dancehall; kwaito) performance spaces.

Table 1
Summarizing Dancehall's Spaces

A. Spatial Divides	B. Spatial Systems	C. Spatial Descriptors (analytical tools)
personal/communal	ritual	liminal
body (home/room) ghetto area (urban, street, pub, yard)	memory	real/imagined
private/public	economy	contested/contesting
exclusive/inclusive	politics	marginal/legitimate
closed/open; inner/outer	performance	nomadism
anonymity/visibility	identity	limitless/boundaryless/transnational
female/male	aesthetics	transformatory
autonomous/policed	violence	siege

The Space and Ethos of the Blues

Why the blues? Blues busters, blues dance (popular entertainment for the youth based on the sound-system culture), blue beat (what ska came to be called), and Clue J and the Blues Blasters are just some of the indications of the obvious influence that the blues has had on Jamaican culture.[14] The early importance of the blues is also evident in the *Gleaner* advertisements that announced the latest blues records for sale, as on July 26, 1924, when they heralded tunes such as "Mobile Blues" and "Limehouse Blues," among others. There were many copies of American big bands, with accompanying "fake books" that contained the musical repertoire, a sign of heavy U.S. popular musical influence on Jamaica from the 1930s to 1950s.[15] Blues was played in the dance hall before rhythm and blues, and by the 1960s ska had developed as a combination of rhythm and blues and Jamaican forms such as mento. There is also the lingering influence of the blues in rhythm and blues, which was dominant in the 1950s and continues today in the work of U.S. artists rotating on the Jamaican airwaves.

Outside of the historical links, are there any common features in these musical flows? What is the blues, and how did it move from place to place in the early twentieth century? Around the late nineteenth century thousands of black migrants experienced and took advantage of their "out-of-placeness"[16] to travel from place to place through the South, in search of work or a sense of new self. In the context of troubles and problems of the everyday, blacks in the U.S. Delta region created their music. Some think of the blues as "ain't nothing but a good man feeling bad." The blues is about being human, and is seen as an "anodyne for suffering that leaves the musician or listener feeling good again."[17] The experience of American blacks is bound up in the blues – poverty, political disenfranchisement and legal segregation, and the violence of lynchings, beatings, and shootings are articulated in the musical and intellectual writings of the performers. The blues as a form of expression highlighted such issues as frustration, lack of love, loneliness, anger, life in the slums, rejection – many of them universal themes. Blues is also used as a way of playing jazz, and sometimes blues is synonymous with jazz.[18] Most importantly, the blues culture is defined, according to Michelle Scott, as the "various forms of communication and the creation of community that occurred in such recreational environments as saloons, vaudeville houses, tent shows, juke joints, and street corners. In these spaces, blues music became more than just entertainment, but music of self-definition and personal liberation."[19]

I am interested in the space of the blues. The context in which early New World dance and later blues and jazz emerged gives some indication of the space and conditions in which enslaved Africans had their entertainment. Based on the New Orleans "Black Codes," the enslaved had Sundays off and many used the day to dance, sing, and play instruments in Congo Square (c. 1804–20). Hundreds of enslaved performers were escorted to the Square, where local authorities supervised their performances. Policed spaces of performance were legitimized by segregation laws (c. 1894). Formerly privileged Creoles lost their jobs as performers due to these laws, while blacks gained employment to play music in the saloons and dance halls, at which older brass bands were the staple. Black performers were also to be found playing in minstrel shows, circuses, travelling roadshows, medicine shows, vaudeville shows, and carnivals.

The restrictions on black subjects in the blues era[20] stimulated innovative ways of maintaining the culture and ritual of the dance hall. Since licences for operating dance classes were relatively easy to get, venues such as Drake's Dancing Class by day were transformed into New York's Jungle's Casino by night. This Casino was a cellar, without fixtures or furnishing; liquor was stashed behind the unconcealed coal bin in the event that the venue was raided. Under the guise of dance classes, patrons danced up a storm doing two-steps, waltzes, schottisches, the metropolitan glide, mule walk, and gut stomp dances.[21]

The blues brings into this mix interesting locational or situational elements by virtue of its point of origin in the Delta region.[22] Alan Lomax, David Grazian, and Amiri Baraka explicitly acknowledge that space and place are critical to an understanding of the blues, as are its origins in slavery.[23] The Delta, the swamps of New Orleans, and Chicago's Southside are regional key points that illustrate how the blues has a home with authentic symbols and icons. It originates from the field hollers, chain-gang chants, choruses of road builders, clearers of swamps, lifters and toters, and anger of work songs rooted in the African singing tradition. Beale Street in Memphis is an important site of popular blues. The Mississippi Delta region is home to many blues giants, including Muddy Waters, Howlin' Wolf, and B.B. King.[24] Song titles attest to the importance of place. For example, a significant number of popular recordings highlight key sites of blues memory: "Memphis Blues" (1912), "St. Louis Blues" (1914), "Beale Street Blues" (1916), Jelly Roll Morton's "Kansas City Stomp" (1938), Bessie Smith's "Gulf Coast Blues" (1923), "Louisiana Low Down Blues" (1924), "Jail House Blues" (1923), and "Florida Bound Blues" (c. 1925), and Count Basie's "Going to Chicago" (c. 1938). While a lyrical analysis reveals that location was not always a strong reference point in these kinds of songs, the use of place as an important signifier (for an imprisoning lover from St. Louis or escape from the condition of the South, for example)[25] highlights the different ways in which place is inscribed in selfhood and a sense of community.

The places of importance also include highways and streets, certain yards, and verandas, with the memories and myths of the blues bound up in certain locations. It was thought that blues music came from the back alleys, the equivalent of the lanes of early Kingston, and portrayed the ways of the alley, its lifestyle.[26] Stephen King makes reference to the blues crossroads at the intersection of highways 61 and 49, which run through the Delta.[27] It is said that this is where Robert Johnson, a foundation bluesman, sold his soul to the devil in return for his musical genius. The street is also an important site. In dancehall culture the streets are overtaken when music and dancing at a particular venue spill onto the street; in Kingston the street at the corner of Pink Lane and Charles, for example, has been a well-known venue from the 1950s to the present. Violin player Jim Turner describes Beale Street as "a song from dawn to dawn."[28]

What is distinct about the blues is that its emergence is in displacement, "out-of-placeness," transport and travel, touring and migration, flows and networks. The concept of travelling roadside blues (the title of one of Robert Johnson's songs) encapsulates the nomadism in blues performance. Like the movement of Jamaican mento bands in the 1940s and 1950s, itinerant Delta blues men traversed the Delta region up to the 1930s using trains, trucks, and carts. Gertrude "Ma" Rainey, for example, according to Baraka, "toured the South for years with a company called the Rabbit Foot Minstrels and became widely known in Negro communities everywhere in America."[29] Indeed, modes and symbols of travel in the Delta region were racialized: "In many Delta towns, a railroad track serve[d] as an obvious physical symbol of racial demarcation," and crossing it was regulated.[30] The nomadic street-corner performers were another important feature of the displacement. The visually impaired Lemon Jefferson, for example, characteristically moved from place to place with guitar in hand. The travel and experience on the road led to a kind of professionalism, a geography of learning that predates distance education. The best-known musicians were wanderers and migratory farm workers. In a way, restless feet produced "placefulness" in the music.

As a popular site, juke joints (or honky tonks) were commonly associated with the machines that supplied music when there were no live bands.[31] Jukeboxes were usually located in the middle of the joint's floor. This is not the main source of the meaning of these places, however. The Gullah word *jook* or *jog*, meaning disorderly or wicked, derives from the Banbara or Wolof of the Niger–Congo West African region.[32] *Jook house* means disorderly house – combining a brothel, gaming parlour, and dance hall with a roadhouse or tavern providing music and drinks. Jukeboxes, invented in the 1930s, began to provide music in the houses that did not have their own bands. Some juke joints were also on plantations, occupying a policed space. For example, McKinley "Muddy Waters" Morganfield, a tractor driver (credited with being one of the key originators of urban blues music), supplemented his income by operating a juke joint that was located on a plantation.[33] Juke joints were constantly raided by the county sheriff and deputies or the city police. They were often the site of fights, complete with knife wounds or fatalities.

According to Baraka, you had to go to the "gutbucket cabarets" to hear real blues. These were the lower-class venues where tripe or chitterlings, the delicacy of pig guts, was served. These chitterlings (chitlins) appear under a different name in the South African context.

While the blues developed and was consumed in a more commercialized setting, it also maintained a strong presence in the more marginal/informal lounges and shacks (including many impromptu jam sessions), the street corner, at barbecues (family or public picnic events), roadhouses, and private and semi-private parties. Chicago was the northern point of the Illinois Central Railroad, which covered the Delta's North/South route. Migrants to Chicago came from Mississippi, Louisiana, Alabama, Arkansas, and Tennessee.[34] The constant movement of bodies, music, and performers within these multiple, informal, organic spaces (juke joints, streets, cities) was an imperative produced by the condition of oppression. Even as the spaces were policed, performers defied the legal restrictions and continually produced new ways of maintaining black cultural identity.

Urban blues came to be more strongly associated with the formal setting of clubs and ballrooms such as the House of blues, a modern replica of southern juke joints, and the Savoy Ballroom. In 1926 the Pelican (on Gravier and South Rampart streets) was opened, becoming New Orleans' newest and largest state-of-the-art dance hall. Being equipped with female and male sanitary conveniences with attendants in waiting, free telephone, lounges, dance floor, and smoking room made the Pelican a superior facility. Kansas City, like Clarksdale and Memphis, had its own ballrooms, such as the Pla-Mar, Fairyland Park, and Frog Hop. Southside Chicago's Grand Terrace was also a popular ballroom. Clarksdale's clubs included the Dipsy Doodle, while New Orleans had the Monarch as well as Animale Hall, known for the behaviour of its (inebriated) patrons, who started numerous fights. Too often raids had to be requested to round up the rioters. Popular theatres were venues available in the urban areas and included, at the highest level, Carnegie Hall.

Ballrooms like the Savoy, which was first opened in March 1926 on

Lenox Avenue and 140 and 141 streets in Harlem, were among the most prestigious venues. The Savoy, whose dance floor was the length of a city block, with double bandstands to house two orchestras, occupied a two-storey pink building sporting mirrored walls, a marble staircase, and a ten-thousand-square-foot wooden floor that had to be replaced every three years due to excessive wear. It hosted regular dance contests. This was one of the highest expressions of the blues making and taking space. The ballroom was open to the public (black and white) for a minimal cover charge. Large Christmas events were popular and consistent with the proliferation of various dance events that had long been held around holidays on the plantations. Weekends were popular, with Saturdays often packed from corner to corner with strutting, swinging, shouting, shifting, rolling, hopping, dragging, bouncing, shouting, bumping, shaking, grinding, stomping, twisting, shuffling patrons. Blues dancing was at its highest level of execution and improvisation at such venues, with old and new moves on display. In the words of Duke Ellington from the recording containing the same line: "It don't mean a thing if it ain't got that swing." Blues people are "dance-beat-oriented people."[35] As spaces of dance there were famous moves such as the lindy hop ("a creative, energetic, free-spirited" dance with a partner, executed with bent knees and including various kicks), the Charleston,[36] Suzy Q, truckin', mambo, big apple, slow drag, jitterbug, fishtail, mooche, collegiate shag (created by college students), and Carolina shag. West Coast swing and jive evolved from the lindy hop.

A high degree of spectator involvement, revelry, and celebration around dance made the ballroom into a temple, according to Albert Murray: it was a sort of ritual space. The blues musical pandemic that swept America from 1926 to 1960 ensured the viability of venues that, like the Savoy, served as a "comprehensive elaboration and refinement of communal dancing."[37] New modes of community are built through dance, and rituals are performed. Blues musicians were simultaneously (as they played) "fullfiling a central role in a ceremony that was at once a purification rite and a celebration, the festive earthiness of which was tantamount to a fertility ritual" and "a ritual of purification and affirmation" as well as a ritual of resistance and resilience.[38] Although the dance hall does not appear to conventional ritual workers/preachers as the locale for a purification ritual, Murray acknowledges that the rituals of voodoo/vodun (the madams, snake doctors, fortune tellers) are integral to the ceremony. Dance-hall proprietors are aware of the purging atmosphere that dance floors provide for what Murray calls "the baleful spirits."[39] Of course, early perceptions of blues music mirror perceptions held of dancehall music by purists who hold the Judeo-Christian moral ethic as the high-water mark of spirituality. Blues was thought to be devil music, not music of the church or of God. The church as a space and religious aesthetic has a relationship with the blues in the history of those blues stars who had to go to church and were not even permitted to go to the weekend blues. "Ma" Rainey, W.C. Handy, and Jelly Roll Morton, among numerous others, have blended the conventions of the Protestant church musicians with their own practice.

Blues events, according to Murray, celebrated specific occasions: "victory in combat, sports, and other contests," and "achievements in business, politics, and the arts." They also celebrated "traditional events such as birthdays, marriages, graduations, and all the seasonal and official red-letter anniversaries."[40] This tendency mirrors the celebratory ethos of both dancehall and kwaito.

At the highest commercial level are blues clubs (such as Chicago's B.L.U.E.S.) that are not seasonal or ephemeral, and (since the 1960s) contemporary blues festivals, along the order of Jamaica's Sunsplash or Sumfest,[41] that receive funds from corporate sponsors and boost the tourism industry, especially of Tennessee and Mississippi. The celebratory spaces housing blues festivals serve three purposes: the homecoming (a sort of pilgrimage to home) or honouring of musicians (dedicated to the memory of performers); the preservation of blues culture; and integration/racial harmony.[42] Such commercial festivals include the B.B. King Homecoming Festival, Mississippi Delta Blues and Heritage Festival (c. 1979), Sunflower River Blues and Gospel Festival (c. 1993), Highway 61 Blues Festival (c. 2002), King Biscuit Blues Festival (c. 1985), and the Chicago Blues Festival. But even commercial activity has not been exempt from state intervention. Even when festivals were small-scale events (c. 1980s) and not well attended, law enforcement officers seemed to plague them. As festivals proliferated throughout the 1990s with high levels of corporate sponsorship, and civic and state support, they began to represent high levels of commodification by capitalizing on the resurgence of blues in the 1960s. Just how organic community events in mostly marginal spaces become viable commercial activity is an important dimension of the transformation of space achieved through black Atlantic performance culture.

An examination of blues performance through the lens of space shifts the focus from linear, musical, lyrical, or celebrity analyses to incorporate other perspectives, theoretical orientations, histories, and national contexts. Without referencing fixed points of origin, I have shown that the blues and dancehall share a common spatial imagination: they refer to the production and consumption of culture within policed, marginalized, ritual spaces, in the context of displacement, disenfranchisement, and state intervention. This relationship between place, performance, and identity extends beyond national contexts to a wider diasporic space of musical trajectories. It is in this context that I now turn to kwaito.

Shebeens, Kwaito Street Bashes, and Politics

Why kwaito? What is kwaito? The influence of South African music on the Jamaican calypso/mento fusion is highlighted by Timothy White in *Catch a Fire* as a cross-fertilization "producing around the late 1940s and early 1950s an aggressive amalgam that also contained South African elements and a percussive tack similar to the Highlife music of Nigeria."[43] It is a symbiotic process of cross-fertilization, however, and the influence of Jamaican music on kwaito has hardly been probed. Jimmy Cliff, Bob Marley, and Peter Tosh have significantly influenced the African musical landscape, Zimbabwe and South Africa in particular. Of course Africa's look to the diaspora has seen the influence of early tours by vaudeville and ragtime performers, which spawned a whole new culture of music production culminating in a distinctive South African jazz and the colloquial renaming of townships like Sophiatown as "Little Harlem." Significantly, American jazz is more popular in South Africa than in any other African country, which is due, according to David Coplan, to the existential parallels.[44] In this regard, though, my focus on kwaito does not privilege the musical hegemony that obtains in the flow of music from the U.S. musical empire to the rest of the world. Instead I focus on how kwaito speaks to and about dancehall, an African diasporic community of music creators and their influence, and the broader black Atlantic spaces of performance.

Kwaito's similarities with dancehall are political, musical, social, and cultural. Dancehall emerged around the 1950s and 1960s as an activity pioneered by the lower classes, a generation seeking political independence from Britain. Kwaito emerged in the era of a democratized South Africa, a new freedom era. As with the 1980s accusations about dancehall's "slackness"[45] character (mostly from international critics) juxtaposed with the neo-liberal approach of the Jamaica Labour Party government, kwaito has been branded with the same empty lyrics that have been thought to flourish under neo-liberal macroeconomic rule. Both are seen to have taken cues from the trends of new governments that supposedly gave rise to the advancement of personal wealth, and glamorized gangster lifestyles. Themes in kwaito and dancehall music are also similar: social commentary about crime and violence, anti-politics, sexuality/sexual prowess, socially conscious songs about AIDS awareness, and violence against women in an era of increased gang rapes of women, especially in South Africa.

Kwaito's genealogy reveals a musical potpourri: antecedents such as

(1950s) Marabi nights, *Mbaqanga* or jive (a musical experience around traditional songs heard in the shebeens), Kwela (1950s), *Mapantsula* (lower-class culture c. 1980s, characterized by large groups of male dancers in synchronized movements very much resembling the 2002 rise of male dancing crews in Jamaica), Bubblegum (1980s), township jazz, Afro-pop and Western music such as rhythm and blues, jungle, hip hop, house, ragga (short for "raggamuffin," raga is the name by which dancehall is sometimes known, especially in Europe), and rap.[46] Coplan in particular has explored the cross-cultural dimensions of kwaito, specifically the focus on a reading of the Atlantic as a musical space of exchange.

Kwaito forged new identities that went beyond an apartheid South Africa burdened by a history of isolation. It has distinct styles of dancing, performance, fashion, and language (mostly township slang and indigenous languages). Unlike the protest music of Hugh Masekela, Miriam Makeba, and Dolly Rathebe, among others, kwaito, like the 1980s emergence of dancehall music, is thought to be apolitical,[47] with what is often misogynist content focused on girls, cars, and partying, and sexually explicit dance moves. The general opinion is that its arbiters seek to dissociate themselves from agony, struggle, conflict, and exploitation, that they exhibit "a culturated degree of estrangement"[48] from the generation X that fought for the end of apartheid. As Thandiswe of Bongo Maffin fame stated in an interview, kwaito is "about the energy of the time, post-independence youth expressing their freedom and excitement about everything being so brand new."[49]

This theme signals a movement into a new iteration of youth culture, ghetto youth culture – a culture linked to city life and not the rural backward and seemingly unprogressive life of grandparents.[50] Siswe Satyo says that the performative language and ethos of kwaito are "about throwing off the shackles of archaic rules imposed by some village schoolmaster or mistress. It is a benchmark of 'sophistication and creativity' within the peer group."[51] Kwaito stars are a new generation. They include M'du, Arthur, Oskido, Lebo, Mzekezeke, Mafikizolo, Mandoza, Mzambi, Chicco, Zola, and groups such as Boom Shaka, Bongo Maffin, Trompies, Aba Shante, and Genesis.

Kwaito is seen as the "true music" of the new South Africa rainbow nation, born when Nelson Mandela was released.[52] It defines a generation, and is prominent on popular television programs and in advertisements, films, websites, and magazines, and on radio waves, in fashion – a signifier for today's freedoms. Considered the music of township youth, it is a black dance-music genre blending various musical cultures, and it at once signifies "age and locale."[53] Between 1999 and 2004, 30 per cent of all hit songs were kwaito tunes, and an analysis of the music industry suggests that 31 per cent of all adults are part of the kwaito nation.

Kwaito is as ubiquitous within South Africa as dancehall music is in Jamaica. The music pumps out of minibus taxis, clubs, radio bashes, shebeens, and parties. Technology has reordered the spaces of its production and consumption, making it possible for a kwaito recording to be produced from start to finish by one or two persons in one location, and consumed in another. Distance is inconsequential and space is about flows; the local/global influences feed each other. Kwaito is beyond the sound economies, racialized "spatialities and temporalities of apartheid" (to borrow a characterization of township life from Achille Mbembe, Nsizwa Dlamini, and Grace Khunou).[54] It allows, like dancehall and the blues, for the circulation of another "version" of local text, space, and the everyday, a sort of "transnational/cosmopolitan performance."

While its appeal is to youth, its purchase is clearly understood by the older generation, evidenced by its incorporation into political campaigns to mobilize voters. This usage is similar to the incorporation of the popular Rastafari symbolism and Rastafari-inspired music, as well as dancehall music, into election campaigns of political parties in Jamaica.

Johannesburg and its surrounding townships, in particular Soweto, contain important sites of memory for kwaito. The township is associated with high levels of danger for the average black South African youth: high murder rates, police harassment, hardship, and squalid conditions. A visual representation of Soweto's poor neighbourhoods would feature horse-drawn carts, dirt surface roads, mud-brick homes, barefoot children, and intense overcrowding. In the 1930s, for example, few of the standard services existed in townships like Soweto and Sophiatown. Roads, lighting, and water were non-existent. Families survived on low wages earned in mines and on the illegal brewing of beer by women.

This system of deprivation induced a whole culture of survival, of which music was only one form of expression. By the 1950s, beer, music, and dancing came together especially on weekends around the "shebeens" – the name usually given to unlicensed houses that sell alcoholic drinks. The Shebeen Queen's house was cleared of furniture and, for a modest entrance fee, patrons were treated to live music, beer, and stew. As in the blues juke joints, where chitterlings were served, and as in dance halls in Jamaica, where "mannish water" made from goat innards was an important part of the fare, so too in Soweto the lowly tripe was elevated to a delicacy in the social sessions referred to as "tripe parties." Tripe is especially popular because it is understood to be "useful for overcoming hangovers and recovering from Sunday drinking."[55] Sometimes shebeen parties went on all night.

Shebeens can be understood as sites of control, spaces of surveillance and closure, especially under apartheid. But dance and music performance constructs an alternative political, spatial, and cultural narrative for the shebeen, an identity inconsistent with dominant political interests. Lara Allen, invoking and expanding work by James Scott, points out that music inherently has "hidden transcripts" that carry private meanings made public by the medium of transmission.[56] By virtue of the transmission to various audiences, musical messages transgress and rebut hegemonic discourses, which is a sharp departure from modernist conceptions of leisure (including the consumption of music), which see pleasure as its only utility.

One glaring opposition to such constructions is the way in which dance halls, shebeens, and juke joints construct a politics of enjoyment even as everyday experience militates against that state of being. The existence of enjoyment assaults and mocks the oppressive everyday and those who construct and maintain it. Enjoyment can reduce the potential to incite violence against the self and community because it channels energies in a pleasurable way. Where plantation, township, and ghetto folk are left to self-destruct in the quagmire of oppression, they mock that oppression by surviving in its face. Thus the very spaces created for consumption and production of cultural forms and access to pleasure constitute sites of political power for that practice and the people who create them.

Different types of shebeens attracted different audiences: the "respectable" versus the very "low class." Shebeens also served as meeting places for activists during apartheid. There is a contemporary parallel here in the rude boys, gang members, and dons who sometimes meet in Jamaica's dancehall sessions to (symbolically) taunt or rival other gangs and police officials by their very presence, though not necessarily to plan insurrection. Many of these participants are wanted men, and numerous raids on dance sessions are thought to have occurred as a result of gunmen, rude boys, or dons hiding in the dance hall.

Shebeens still form an important part of today's social scene. Haile Stone, in her research on shebeens, notes the role they play in contemporary South Africa: they "serve a function similar to jook joints for African-Americans in the rural South."[57] They are a social institution that builds a sense of community and group identity. Shebeens shaped the city's cultural geography, cutting across class, but shaped by blacks. They are also called taverns and today are legally operated, mostly by men rather than women. They host young adults in the eighteen to twenty age cohort, typically having facilities such as tables, chairs, and decorated dance floors.

"Kwaito is steeped in the ghetto," Maria McCloy writes.[58] The music draws its sustenance from the ghetto and generates dialogue with other ghettos around the world. With kwaito, urban youth could spend their nights in clubs rather than remain outside under curfew – the context in which kwaito emerged. Youth gangs are a real part of the everyday life of the ghetto, and they are also role models for youth who aspire to gain material wealth quickly.[59] But wealth achieved from the music has fostered upward mobility and stimulated out-migration from South African ghettos. Kwaito, like the blues and dancehall, provides a way out of the township or ghetto even as it forms the source from which the music has its sustenance. One artist named himself Zola after the area in Soweto he came from. In the ghetto the street is an important site: on weekends streets are taken over by jams or bashes, where aspiring actors try to woo audiences and attract the attention of producers. The street is the first stage for many aspirants.

There is much more to kwaito, though, and I want to focus on its connections with Jamaican reggae/dancehall style. Simon Stephens, for example, argues, "Kwaito's appropriation of the ragga vocal style and aspects of modern European dance music is a direct result of black South African exposure to these." The appropriation is a strategy employing "symbols of a black cultural ecumene and resistance."[60] But this is a simple way of stating what is a deeper relationship that takes in, on the one hand, conversations between Africa and its diaspora, and, on the other, the black Atlantic, Jamaican reggae musicians, and the South African liberation struggle.

The first kwaito group was Boom Shaka, and it is no coincidence that its leader, Junior Dread (Junior Sokhela, a street boy from the Hillbrow area), had a long relationship with Jamaican music through his uncle. According to Junior:

> I've been a reggae fan since I was young because I had an uncle, and my uncle was an MK soldier. So what he did, he used to play Bob Marley but he loved Winston Rodney [also known as Burning Spear]. They loved Burning Spear, Culture [Joseph Hill], and he had like Mutabaruka, I-Roy, and U-Roy. . . . I used to hear all of them when I was young and I didn't know, but I got so interested, because he used to play them loud and they wouldn't allow us to play any music which we want, so because it was his radio we had to listen to his music. So he'd put on a Prince Fari album and play it like non-stop everyday. So we'd be singing to that and I got used to it, I started imitating it. By that time as a youth I was still confused: I used to do break dancing, ragga, and do football, everything [but] I just loved music.[61]

Similarly, a telling statement by Stoan, a member of the South African group Bongo Maffin, explained the kind of conversation taking place across the Atlantic musicscape about aspiration, transformation, and the politics of progress and freedom. Stoan states: "When kwaito started, we had aspirations. We wanted to be like hip hop and ragga, like all the other forms of urban music that also came out of the ghetto and became huge."[62] Elaborating, Stoan added:

> If we had to look at any other example of black people off the continent who have found their essence, it's Jamaicans. For us, for South Africans after the curtain was lifted, after we could see other things besides what was presented to us on television which was blacksploitation movies and stuff like that, buffoons, you know the picture of us. Any other successful picture of a black man was him behaving like a caricature of himself. So Jamaicans brought another element to a picture we had of us as an out of body experience. Yeah, so I think you'll find that a lot of people, you know, have been touched by the culture, in South Africa, within ten years. Jah Seed has also really spread his influence. Let me tell you a story. He started Djing [deejaying] in Yeoville at a place called Tandor with Andy, the Admiral, this is his white selector and he used to do this, he used to "wheel" the tunes, you know, and people used to complain he'd be playing a tune and just as the people are going crazy he'd stop the tune and wheel it, "you know massive mi tune nice yuh play it twice." And I go to him, you know Apple, South Africa is different man, you just gotta play the song and people gotta enjoy it. And he's like "No, a Stone Love, dem affi learn bwoy, if a tune nice yuh affi play it twice man. Now, wheel an' come again." By the end of that year, not even, within six months people on the dance floor were the ones now screaming out "Wheeeeeel, pull up man, wheel that tune an' come again."[63]

Stoan's invocation of the ghetto as the space of creation and identity can be viewed against the backdrop of its use within sociology and anthropology. Ulf Hannerz contextualizes ghetto as an "anti-euphemism" for inner-city or slum, indicating the poor rundown conditions but also the "nature of community and its relationship to the outside world," ethnicity, family ties, and other factors that keep people living in the same space, ultimately producing a ghetto lifestyle.[64] What is different about early ghettos like the one Hannerz studied and contemporary ones, particularly in Jamaica, is that their "status as communities" is not necessarily determined by a strong dependency on relationships with outsiders who dominate and jobs that are found on the outside, for example. Fundamentally, economic and political self-sufficiency is low relative to non-ghetto communities. What exists, in addition to high unemployment and economic support – maintained sometimes through illicit activities around the trade in illegal substances, weapons, and certain entertainment ventures, and with little movement inwards or outwards on a daily basis by the majority of its citizens – is the proliferation of bonds of internal solidarity around music and dance. There is a transnational news and migratory network that the music and dance operate in, a sort of World Wide Web distributing news of struggles and victories of daily life through music and the tangible links through travel among ghetto citizenry via Brixton, Bronx, Lagos, and Soweto.

The spaces of kwaito are varied and can be viewed, like dancehall and blues venues, on a continuum from community to commercial, based on the nature and type of events they host. Kwaito music is heard in refurbished warehouses, university stadiums, clubs, parks, semi-private and private parties, festivals, stage shows and street bashes, train stations, and free concerts hosted by record companies and attracting sponsorship from multinational corporations like Pepsi-Cola. Events are most common in the summer and are used to celebrate public holidays, commemorative occasions, birthdays, anniversaries, victories after a soccer match, and marriages, and to conclude interment rites.

The street bash was the most ubiquitous in the early period and still exists today. Street bashes have always been held in contravention of state laws, and during apartheid they were raided, although police officers were afraid of the townships after dark. The street is transformed into an event when the sound system is set up and people gather for the evening. These are the common weekend township bashes, which do not attract a cover charge. Clubs, on the other hand, attract cover charges and range in the class of their clientele and location. Clubs such as Tandor and Rockefellars in Yeoville, Horror Café (which has reggae/dancehall music on Thursday nights), Enigma and Sanyaki in Rosebank, and the Stage in Randburg are all in the greater Johannesburg area. Major centres such as Cape Town, Durban, and Pretoria have numerous clubs spotting the nightscape.

In a sense, kwaito has achieved in ten years what the blues didn't and dancehall has recently achieved: there are solid artists who own recording studios, are producers and DJs, and own record labels and video production companies. They travel the world on tours, and occupy soundscapes that are simultaneously local, national, regional, and transnational. Oskido, a DJ and a producer with his own record label and video production company, has played within Africa, Europe, and the United States. A good example of this is the recent travel itinerary of Bongo Maffin: they have toured the United States twice, played at "Reggae on the River" in California, opened for Basement Jaxx in Central Park at "Summer Stage," opened for Yellow Man at Sounds of Brazil (SOBs) in New York, played at the International Day of Peace concert at the Coliseum in Rome (on a stage shared by Ray Charles and Khaled in 2002), opened for Femi Kuti at Hollywood Ball in California, and played at small clubs in Germany and other European and United Kingdom destinations.

Like dancehall, dancing has given kwaito increased appeal. Dance moves were popularized by the first kwaito group, Boom Shaka, which continues to create moves, like "Chop di grass," done to honour the men who cut grass when highways are being constructed.[65] Dancing girls provide a motivation for men to go to kwaito parties and stage shows. Boom Shaka explains that their dancing is African and comes from the *Kwasa Kwasa* urban dance of Zaire, a dance that is popular among South African youth and performed mostly in the shebeens to kwaito music. Dance moves are sexy and have included the Butterfly, the *Squga* (get down) dance named after Mzekezeke's recent "song of the year," Madiba jive (after one of Mandela's famous moves on his release from prison), Chicken (from the 1980s, mimicking moves of the chicken), Copetsa, Sekele (a circle dance, traditional), CODESA (from Convention for a Democratic South Africa, the name given to the negotiations around the reconstruction period), Bason (named after the whites thought to be involved in the killing of blacks with the HIV virus), and Tobela (Boom Shaka's song of the same Sothu name meaning "thank you," a greeting fashioned into a dance resembling dancehall's "Signal the Plane"). Like Jamaican dance moves, these steps offer a window into the everyday life of South Africans while adding to the global conversation about meaning and representation and embodiment. DJs and producers have suggested that over fifty dance moves, building on traditional as well as regional dance influences, have been created since kwaito's emergence.

With a healthy dance culture, there are contestations over the display, size, and form of the female body as a site onto which many inscriptions about propriety, work, ethics, and morality have been written; and it is a site in which gender relations are being revised. In an interview Coplan explained the point he made in his 2005 article about the complex renegotiations in gender relations. In reference to a music video by his favourite kwaito group, Trompies, Coplan described the story depicted:

> There's a beauty contest at the bar and the contestants, some of them are *fohloza* [a word coined to mimic the sound made by fat moving on a woman's body] and some of them are spaghetti, very thin, and we know that society favours spaghetti nowadays, you have to be thin. But the band is not having it. As the girls are introduced across the stage, every time there's a biggish one they're all going "wow, look at her!" or "look at that one, look at her," only for the big ones and they are ignoring the slender ones. So they have

> their beauty contest: first, second, and third prize are taken by the big ones and the spaghettis lose out. And then these girls who won the contest they leave the club with members of the band who are admiring them. . . . Of course it was hugely popular because first of all, a lot of our ladies do tend to be on the larger side and they can't manage the spaghetti look. Second of all it was just reversing the social stereotype that, you know, to be beautiful you must be thin, so the band was turning that upside down.[66]

These discourses are, of course, not unique to kwaito. Hip hop and dancehall have mature conversations about the place, nature, beauty, and power of woman, of woman as whore, wife, sweetheart, diseased, and virtuous, as well as of the conniving woman.

Millennial Indaba My Children! The Atlantic as Drum

What is the significance of this trajectory, these similarities, the links, the common genealogy? Why performance geography versus cultural history? What I have shared with you is an alternative way of looking at performance through space, particularly through the black Atlantic as space, a musical and performance space. Dancehall, kwaito, and the blues are racialized performance sites of contestation, travel, and transience, transcendence and boundarylessness, pleasure and ritual, innovation, hybridity, and social integration that have fed each other and continue so to do. Their citizenry simultaneously enact, reclaim, reconnect, and renew self and diasporic cultural identity. Like dancehall and the blues, kwaito constitutes a more recent site of "psychic relocation" (using Allen's term), embodying questions of and paths towards making space, of making a new self and nation, a process that is also taking place within various sites in the black Atlantic world.[67]

Putting this into language closer to home, Brathwaite's notion of nation language helps us understand what happens out of the affirmation that Jamaican patois speaks through us, of us, and for us to the world of growing converts who, especially in Japan, learn patois before or instead of English – propelled by the distance education provided by reggae and dancehall music. In the case of music it is diasporic language transmitted through performance.[68] Performance, like spirituality, can be seen as a network linking us to the source of existence through ritual, our inner selves, and each other across different terrains, nations, and identities. It tells stories about deep connections.

Around the beginning of this century Wole Soyinka made a plea for a millennial *indaba* – an important conference – to be held on U.S. soil.[69]

Soyinka, as an exiled citizen of Africa and a citizen of the diaspora, actively contemplated the relationship between the children of the diaspora and those on the continent. Soyinka spoke of the "oceans of ignorance" that "still separate the general black population from the mother continent." He argued that a "percussive impact is required, a mammoth-scale, extended event that celebrates and contextualizes both the African past and contemporary reality." A millennial *indaba* was what Soyinka posited as the way of achieving this goal – through conferences, exhibitions, film, performing arts, and celebration – all to promote exchange. This was his vision for bringing in the new era and closing the past.

The terrain of these performance geographies, and especially kwaito, suggests an alternative way of viewing the millennial *indaba*. The sounds of the Caribbean, especially those of Jamaica that have travelled to the United States (depending on your chronology or depth of research), influenced the emergence of the blues, which in turn influenced the music of Jamaica and South Africa. The South, like the rest of Africa, has been influenced by the diasporans in both the United States and Jamaica. There is a large network of travel and cross-fertilization through which exchange and learning helped wash away Soyinka's "oceans of ignorance." The millennial *indaba*, albeit the *indabas* that have occurred in South Africa and other countries, has been achieved using what ordinary people have always had – the common impulse to create, to perform, despite the odds, in marginalized circumstances.

Therefore, I start where I began: at the bottom of the Atlantic are the tracks of black ivory laid down throughout the years of the middle passage slave trade. The ivory is moving to the beat of a triangular trade in reverse, bones flowing with the rhythms back to Africa. As our ancestors had little space in which to perform, so too did their offspring, as evidenced in the blues, dancehall, and kwaito. In instances in which performers have had to create space to meet their need to celebrate in the face of oppression and repression, the adoption of a philosophy of limitless space and boundarylessness allows for the reclamation, multiplication, and transcendence of space. This is what performers have achieved in the spaces and places in which repression propels struggle.

Notes

1 John Kani is quoted in David Coplan, "God Rock Africa: Thought on Politics in Popular Black Performance in South Africa," *African Studies*, 64:1 (2005). I would like to acknowledge the role of all our forebears who were a part of those struggles to create, live, and name their place in the world, and, importantly, those who died trying to pre-

serve the cultural history of performance practices. Funding for the project to gather data in South Africa was made possible by the award of the Rhodes Trust Rex Nettleford Fellowship in Cultural Studies (2005). I would like to acknowledge the contributions of Wilma Bailey, Deborah Hickling, Lorna Smith and Aggrey Brown, Herbie Miller, and Jalani Niaah to the work presented here. I would also like to thank the crew in South Africa who made the gathering of data easy and phenomenal. To David Coplan, Christopher Ballantine, Lara Allen, Gavin Steingo, Xavier Livermon, Yaa Asantewaa, Ras Sepho, Ashifashabba, DJ Jerry, Stoan, Arthur, Oskido, Junior Dread, and Nutty Nys – your contributions have been invaluable. Much of the material here was first presented as the Twelfth Annual Distinguished Philip Sherlock Lecture, Feb. 27, 2006, at the University of the West Indies, Mona Campus.

2 Catherine Nash, "Performativity in Practice: Some Recent Work in Cultural Geography," *Progress in Human Geography*, 24: 4 (2000), pp.653–64; Nigel Thrift, "The Still Point: Resistance, Expressive Embodiment and Dance," in *Geographies of Resistance*, ed. Steve Pile and Michael Keith (London: Routledge, 1997), pp.124–52.

3 Don Robotham, *Culture, Society and Economy: Bringing Production Back In* (London and Thousand Oaks, Cal.: Sage, 2005); Peter Sutherland, "In Memory of the Slaves: An African View of the Diaspora in the Americas," in *Representations of Blackness and the Performance of Identities*, ed. Jean Rahier (Westport, Conn., and London: Bergin & Garvey, 1999), pp.195–212; Norman Corr Jr. and Rachel Corr, "'Imagery of Blackness' in Indigenous Myth, Discourse, and Ritual," in *Representations of Blackness and the Performance of Identities*, ed. Rahier, pp.213–34.

4 Paul Gilroy, *The Black Atlantic: Modernity and Double Consciousness* (Cambridge, Mass.: Harvard University Press, 1993), p.111.

5 Personal observation, Elmina Castle, Cape Coast, Ghana, Nov. 9, 2003.

6 Molly Ahye, "In Search of the Limbo: An Investigation into Its Folklore as a Wake Dance," in *Caribbean Dance from Abakuá to Zouk: How Movement Shapes Identity*, ed. Susanna Sloat (Gainesville: University Press of Florida, 2002), pp.247–61.

7 Ahye, "In Search of Limbo," pp.247–61.

8 Geneviève Fabre, "The Slave Ship Dance," in *Black Imagination and the Middle Passage*, ed. Maria Diedrich, Henry Louis Gates Jr., and Carla Pedersen (New York and Oxford: Oxford University Press, 1999), pp.33–46.

9 Maureen Warner-Lewis, *Central Africa in the Caribbean: Transcending Time, Transforming Cultures* (Mona: University of the West Indies Press, 2003), pp.242–43; Ahye, "In Search of Limbo," pp.250–54.

10 See Sonjah Stanley Niaah, "A Common Genealogy: Dancehall, Limbo and the Sacred Performance Space," *Discourses in Dance*, 2:1 (2004), pp.9–26, for a first look at this in the context of New World dancehall culture and the slave-ship dance.

11 In doing this I use a combination of secondary sources (newspaper articles, scholarly papers, biographical data, interviews) and primary data collected from periods of research in Jamaica and South Africa, where I employed interviews, case studies, and participant observation in addition to an analysis of posters, tickets, flyers, maps, Internet sources, and television broadcasts.

12 See Sonjah Stanley Niaah,"Kingston's Dancehall: A Story of Space and Celebration," *Space and Culture*, 7:1 (2004), pp.102–18; and Stanley Niaah, "Kingston's Dancehall Spaces," *Jamaica Journal*, 29: 3 (2006), pp.14–21.

13 See Stanley Niaah, "Kingston's Dancehall: A Story of Space and Celebration"; and Stanley Niaah, "Making Space: Dancehall Performance and Its Philosophy of Boundarylessness," *African Identities*, 2: 2 (2004), pp.117– 32.

14 The Blues Busters was the vocal group popularly in the top ten musical charts in Jamaica, with regular bookings at musical showcases at the Majestic and Carib theatres.

15 U.S. big bands refer to the blues and jazz bands that emerged around the 1930s. Some twenty to thirty bands that played mento and jazz existed in Kingston by the 1940s, all of them modelled on American big bands. Rhythm and blues refers to the popular

black American musical genre that found favour with Jamaicans around the 1950s in the sound-system dances.

16 I prefer to use the term out-of-placeness to highlight the sense of being out of place, out of a place to be and becoming.

17 Both quotations are from Jimmie Rodgers, quoted in Peter Puterbaugh, "Pain for Gain: The Blues Is Purely American Music," *Attache*, December 2005, pp.39–43.

18 I use the blues as an umbrella term with the recognition that there are various sub-genres: country blues, electric blues (which is credited to Muddy Waters, who electrified Delta blues in urban Chicago, c. 1947–55), Delta blues, soul blues, and so on. The distinction between urban and country blues is, of course, their spaces of operation. Country blues is played and consumed in the juke joints and roadhouses around which blues culture developed and was expressed. Bessie Smith, for example, moved from being a street performer to a theatre headliner as part of the transition from country blues to urban blues. Muddy Waters moved from rural Mississippi to Chicago in 1943. See Peter Rutkuff and Will Scott, "Preaching the Blues: The Mississippi Delta of Muddy Waters," *Kenyan Review*, 27:2 (2005), p.129. See also chapter 3 here for an elaboration on the political economy of blues geographies; and Clyde Woods, *Development Arrested: The Blues and Plantation Power in the Mississippi Delta* (London and New York: Verso, 1988).

19 Michelle Scott, "The Realm of a Blues Empress: Blues Culture and Bessie Smith in Black Chattanooga, Tennessee, 1880–1923," Ph.D. dissertation, Cornell University, Ithaca, N.Y., 2002.

20 By blues era, I mean between the period 1930–50, which marked the emergence and proliferation of blues music.

21 Amiri Baraka (Leroi Jones), *Blues People: Negro Experience in White America and the Music That Developed from It* (New York: William Morrow & Co., 1968 [1963]), p.108.

22 See Alan Lomax, "I Got the Blues," *Common Ground*, 8:4 (1943), pp.38–52.

23 David Grazian, *Blue Chicago: The Search for Authenticity in Urban Blues Clubs* (Chicago and London: University of Chicago Press, 2003); Baraka, *Blues People*.

24 Stephen King, "Blues Tourism in the Mississippi Delta: The Functions of Blues Festivals," *Popular Music and Society*, 27: 4 (2004), pp.455–75.

25 Albert Murray, *Stomping the Blues*, 25th anniversary edition (New York: Da Capo Press, 2000 [1976]), p.66.

26 Murray, *Stomping the Blues*, p.50.

27 King, "Blues Tourism in the Mississippi Delta," p.466.

28 Quoted in Shane White and Graham White, "Strolling, Jooking and Fixy Clothes," in *Signifyin(g), Sanctifyin', and Slam Dunking: A Reader in African American Expressive Culture*, ed. Gena D. Caponi (Amherst: University of Massachusetts Press, 1999), p.435.

29 Baraka, *Blues People*, p.89.

30 King, *Blues Tourism in the Mississippi Delta*, p.472.

31 During the 1890s recordings became popular primarily through coin-in-slot phonographs in public spaces and by 1910–20 had become the mass medium for popular music; but it was orchestral and classical instrumental music that was most recorded at that time and could therefore be played by the phonographs. By the 1930s jukeboxes emerged to satisfy the dwindling phonograph market and could be found in roadhouses and taverns or juke joints. Every U.S. innovation finds its way to Jamaica, and the juke box is no different. In the 1960s my own grandfather purchased a jukebox, which provided the music for various weekend dances organized by my aunts and uncles.

32 See Juliet Gorman's work on the etymology of "jook" at <http://www.oberlin.edu/library/papers/honorshistory/2001-Gorman/jookjoints/allaboutjooks/etymology.html>.

33 Rutkuff and Scott, "Preaching the Blues," p.140.

34 See Ralph Eastman, "Country Blues Performance and the Oral Tradition," *Black Music Research Journal*, 8:2 (1988), pp.161–76.

35 Murray, *Stomping the Blues*, pp.148, 189.

36 Thought to have been an Ashanti dance, the Charleston emerged in the United States during the blues dancing era and bears similarities with Jamaica's butterfly dance.

37 Murray, *Stomping the Blues*, p.17.

38 Ibid., pp.17, 38, 42.

39 Ibid., pp.23, 24.

40 Ibid., p.17.

41 Sunsplash and Sumfest are the premiere summer reggae festivals in Jamaica.

42 King, *Blues Tourism*, p.457.

43 Timothy White, *Catch a Fire: The Life of Bob Marley* (New York: Henry Holt, 1991 [1983]), p.17.

44 David Coplan, "Born to Win: Music of the 'Black Atlantic' Revisited," paper presented at the National Art Festival, Grahamstown, South Africa, July 6, 2005, p.11.

45 In Jamaica "slackness" in this context refers to lyrics about women's body parts, or display of women's sexuality, whether through lyrics or dance moves. It is also used interchangeably with vulgarity to refer to licentious behaviour, especially among women.

46 For an ethnomusicological history of South Africa, see Coplan, "God Rock Africa," pp.9–27; and Lara Allen, "Kwaito Versus Crossed-Over: Music and Identity during South Africa's Rainbow Years 1994–99," *Social Dynamics*, 30:2 (2004), pp.82–111. For a review of the scholarship on kwaito, see Gavin Steingo, "South African Music after Apartheid: Kwaito, the "Party Politic" and the Appropriation of Gold as a Sign of Success," *Popular Music and Society*, 28:3 (2005), pp.333–57.

47 This criticism has also been levelled at dancehall. However, like dancehall's politics, kwaito's politics are seen in the discourses about safe sex and the AIDS pandemic. Steingo, "South African Music after Apartheid," warns that kwaito's rejection of politics as a stance is political, and that there is a new politics of riches beyond the struggle realized through opportunities made available through music.

48 See Sarah Nuttall, "Stylizing the Self: The Y Generation in Rosebank, Johannesburg," *Public Culture*, 16:3 (2004), p.451.

49 Maria McCloy, "Mama Africa Meets the Kwaito Generation: Interview with Musicians Miriam Makeba and Thandiswe," July 2000 <http://www.unesco.org/courier/2000_07/uk/doss24.htm>.

50 Cf. Stephens, "Kwaito"; Allen, "Kwaito Versus Crossed-Over," p.140; and Sizwe Satyo, "Kwaito-Speak: A Language Variety Created by the Youth for the Youth," in *Freedom and Discipline: Essays in Applied Linguistics from Southern Africa*, ed. Elaine Ridge, Sinfree Makoni, and Stanley G.M. Ridge (New Delhi: Bahri, 2001).

51 Sizwe Satyo, "Kwaito-Speak," p.141.

52 See World Economic Forum, *South Africa at Ten: Perspectives by Political, Business and Civil Leaders* (Cape Town and Pretoria: Human and Rousseau, 2004), p.156.

53 Allen, "Kwaito Versus Crossed-Over," p.86.

54 See Achille Mbembe, N. Dlamini, and G. Khunou, "Soweto Now," *Public Culture*, 16:3 (2004), p.500.

55 Cf. Mbembe, Dlamini, and Khunou, "Soweto Now," p.501.

56 Lara Allen, "Music and Politics in South Africa," *Social Dynamics*, 30:2 (2004), pp.1–19.

57 See Haile Stone's seminar paper on shebeens <www.history.und.ac.za/Sempapers/stone2001.pdf>.

58 Maria McCloy, "Kwaito," *UNESCO Courier*, July 2000, p.1.

59 David Coplan, interview with author, July 2005.

60 Simon Stephens, "Kwaito," in *Senses of Culture: South African Culture Studies*, ed. Sarah Nuttall and Cheryl-Ann Michael (Oxford: Oxford University Press, 2000), p.257.

61 Interview with the author, July 2005. Boom Shaka's recording "Words of Wisdom" is influenced by U-Roy.
62 McCloy, "The Kwaito Story" <http://www.rage.co.za/issues43/ >.
63 Interview with the author, July 2005.
64 Ulf Hannerz, *Soul Side: Inquiries into Ghetto Culture and Community* (Chicago: University of Chicago Press, 2004 [1969]), p.11.
65 Junior Dread says he is the first guy in South Africa to do ragga music.
66 Interview with the author, July 2005.
67 Allen, "Music and Politics in South Africa."
68 Kamau Brathwaite, *History of the Voice: The Development of Nation Language in Anglophone Caribbean Poetry* (London: New Beacon Books, 1995 [1984]).
69 Wole Soyinka, "A Millennial Indaba," c. 2000 <http://www.edofolks.com/html/pub34>.

James A. Tyner

11

Urban Revolutions and the Spaces of Black Radicalism

The concept of urban public spaces – of streets, parking lots, shopping malls, and parks – pervades numerous discussions in geography, planning, and related disciplines, and these studies provide insight into the contestation of public spaces and the "right" to the city.[1] Indeed, as Henri Lefebvre suggests, revolutionary events generally take place on the street – in public spaces.[2] These public spaces, then, are the sites of contestation, regulation, and resistance.

Space is thus not an inert stage upon which society is played out. Instead, space is produced through the interactions of ideas (or discourses) and practices. Conceptually, Lefebvre's work is especially informative. Lefebvre suggests that spaces can be divided into two basic forms: representations of space and representational spaces. Representations of space include those spaces conceived by planners, bureaucrats, and other professionals. As Andy Merrifield explains, representations of space reflect "the arcane models, signs, and jargon used and transmitted by these 'specialists.'" These "abstract" spaces, moreover, are the dominant spaces of any society, intimately tied to the relations of production.[3] Specific examples include various urban revitalization schemes and the subsequent demolition of neighbourhoods; the placement of major highways; and the construction of public housing projects.

Representations of space can be materially demarcated, as in the erection of signs, walls, and fences. Enforcement can be further ensured through collective action and the threat, if not actual use, of force. The imposition of Black Codes following emancipation, for example, and the later Jim Crow laws were attempts to fix the meaning of space, reflecting a hegemonic cultural norm (white supremacy, for example). Spaces in this sense were colour-coded and imbued with particular racialized meanings.

The dominance of representations of space, though, is far from complete. The hegemonic control of space is always open to exposure, confrontation, reversal, and refusal through counterhegemonic practices.[4] Indeed, if African Americans had accommodated themselves to segregation and discrimination without protest and resistance, there would have been no need to pass laws to sustain the colour-caste system.[5] The alternative spaces – representational spaces – are conceived by and acted upon by artists and activities, poets and protesters. Representational spaces are the spaces of resistance and protest.

The history of cities and of thinking about cities has periodically been marked by an intense interest in the transformative role of urban social movements and communal action.[6] Along this line Don Mitchell argues, "The idea of public space has never been guaranteed; it has only been won through concerted struggle, and then, after the fact, guaranteed (to some extent) in law."[7] However, geographers and other social scientists have directed minimal attention to the spatial struggles of black radical movements.

This concern with place and space serves as the catalyst for my conceptualization of black radicalism, the radical political thought of the Black Power movement. Although I cannot do justice here to the full variations of that movement, I intend to highlight the salience of geography to the political thought of the movement by discussing the issues of integration and communal separatism. As I argue elsewhere, Malcolm X and, later, the Black Panther Party articulated crucial alternative spatial conceptions of urban politics and social justice.[8] The Black Power movement was about the reappropriation of space – the cry of "Black Power" represented a demand for an urban revolution. The urban revolutionary thought embedded within black radicalism included their desires to claim and reimagine the city; by extension, this remaking of urban space was foundational both for civil and human rights.

Black Radicalism

The civil rights movement – or, as Manning Marable writes, the "Black Freedom Movement" – was a series of crucial civil, political, social, and economic battles that took place between 1945 and 1975.[9] But these battles also took *place*. Ruth Wilson Gilmore, to this end, argues, "A geographical imperative lies at the heart of every struggle for social justice."[10]

Black radicalism is about alternative geographies, of social and spatial transformations; black radicalism is about the remaking of spaces.[11] It is, in effect, about constructing new societies through progressive action. Robin Kelley argues that the conditions and the very existence of social movements enable participants to imagine something different, to realize that things need not always be this way. It is this imagination – this ability to construct new spaces – that Kelley terms "poetic knowledge." Kelley explains that in the poetics of struggle and lived experience, in the utterances of ordinary folk, in the cultural products of social movements, in the reflections of activists, we can discover the many different cognitive maps of the future, of a world not yet born. He concludes that the most radical art is not protest art but works that take us to another place, that envision a different way of seeing, perhaps a different way of feeling.[12]

Much of African American history, as Mumia Abu-Jamal explains, is rooted in a radical understanding that America is not the land of liberty, but rather a place of the absence of freedom, a realm of repression and insecurity.[13] Indeed, as Marable asserts, "Black consciousness was . . . formed in response to the omnipresent reality of racist violence that generations of African Americans experienced in their daily lives."[14] This accounts for the critical commentary of the United States that was expressed so passionately, so forcibly, by Malcolm X.[15]

In post–Second World War America, Malcolm X viewed the spaces of America not as a dream but as a nightmare. He did not in 1963 – unlike Martin Luther King Jr. – see a Promised Land, one where the white racists could be redeemed. America was not a bright City on a Hill illuminating the world in all its glory. Rather, America was a hypocrisy, a place of dreams deferred and promises not kept.[16] In his "Ballot or the Bullet" speech delivered at the Cory Methodist Church in Cleveland, Malcolm X told his audience:

> I'm one of the 22 million black people who are victims of Americanism. One of the 22 million black people who are victims of democracy, nothing but disguised hypocrisy. So, I'm not standing here speaking to you as an American, or a patriot, or a flag-saluter, or a flag-waver – no, not I. I'm speaking as a victim of this American system.[17]

King himself warned about the possibilities – or perhaps, to some, the nightmare – of black nationalism and subsequent revolution. In his polemical "Letter from Birmingham City Jail," King produced what Adam Fairclough called "the most widely-read, widely-reprinted and oft-quoted document of the civil rights movement."[18] King's warning was deeply personal, touching at the soul of America. He wrote: "We know through painful experience that freedom is never voluntarily given by the oppressor; it must be demanded by the oppressed." King's writing had a sense of immediacy. He explained, "There comes a time when the cup of endurance runs over, and men are no longer willing to be plunged into an abyss of injustice where they experience the blackness of corroding despair." How is it possible to wait when, in the words of King:

> . . . you have seen vicious mobs lynch your mothers and fathers at will and drown your brothers and sisters at whim; when you have seen hate-filled policemen curse, kick, brutalize and even kill your black brothers and sisters with impunity; when you see the vast majority of your twenty million Negro brothers smothering in an airtight cage of poverty in the midst of an affluent society; when you suddenly find your tongue twisted and your speech stammering as you seek to explain to your six-year-old daughter why she can't go to the public amusement park that has just been advertised on television, and see tears welling up in her little eyes when she is told that Funtown is closed to colored children, and see the depressing clouds of inferiority begin to form in her little mental sky, and see her begin to distort her little personality by unconsciously developing a bitterness toward white people; when you have to concoct an answer for a five-year-old son asking in agonizing pathos: "Daddy, why do white people treat colored people so mean?"; when you take a cross-country drive and find it necessary to sleep night after night in the uncomfortable corners of your automobile because no motel will accept you; when you are humiliated day in and day out by nagging signs reading "white" and "colored"; when your first name becomes "nigger" and your middle name becomes "boy" (however old you are) and your last name becomes "John," and when your wife and mother are never given the respected titled "Mrs."; when you are harried by day and haunted by night by the fact that you are a Negro, living constantly at tiptoe stance never quite knowing what to expect next, and plagued with inner fears and outer resentments; when you are forever fighting a degenerating sense of "nobodiness"; then you will understand why we find it difficult to wait.[19]

The cup of endurance, indeed, did run over. By the mid-1960s a radical break had appeared, marked by the urban rebellions that occurred in many cities across the country as well as by the assassination of King in 1968. In 1964, 1965, and 1966 violent outbreaks took place throughout the United States: in Watts, New York City, Cleveland, Chicago, Philadelphia, Rochester, Jersey City. By 1967 over 120 major and minor uprisings had been registered; over eighty people – mostly African Americans – had been killed within these rebellions. It was this social context of mass disorder and urban chaos, according to Abu-Jamal, that provided for the rise of the Black Power movement.

Ironically, the call for "Black Power" in the mid-1960s, with its antecedents in the Nation of Islam, the demands of Malcolm X, and the existence of urban unrest in Northern cities, was first thrust into the spotlight in the South. In 1966 James Meredith, the first African American graduate of the University of Mississippi, staged a 265-mile "march" through the South to challenge fear and to encourage black voter registration. Somewhere along the Tennessee-Mississippi border, Meredith was ambushed and hit by a shotgun blast. As Meredith recovered, civil rights leaders, including representatives of the Student Nonviolent Coordinating Committee (SNCC), the Congress of Racial Equality (CORE), and the Southern Christian Leadership Conference (SCLC), planned to continue with his March Against Fear. Disagreements arose, however, as to the message that was to be forwarded through the march. Some, like Stokely Carmichael – the newly elected chair of SNCC – seized the opportunity to call for black solidarity and to actively resist oppression. In the process, white participation would be de-emphasized. Carmichael, a veteran of civil rights protests in the South, was influenced by the self-defence messages of Malcolm X and Robert Williams. He believed that African Americans needed to promote black pride and self-defence, and to actively and overtly challenge white supremacy. Other leaders opposed this separatist-leaning approach and demanded a march based more on integrationist principles. Roy Wilkins and Whitney Young, leaders of the National Association for the Advancement of Colored People (NAACP) and Urban League, respectively, hoped to utilize the march to raise support for President Lyndon Johnson's civil rights bill.[20]

During the march, as Jeffrey Ogbar describes it, state troopers, using tear gas and clubs, attacked activists. Refusing to sit idly by, SNCC organizer Willie Ricks demanded that African Americans abandon pleas for white acceptance and adopt a strategy of "Black Power." Carmichael joined in, shouting: "The only way we gonna stop them white men from whipping us, is to take over. We been saying freedom for six years and we ain't got nothin'. What we gonna start saying is Black Power."[21] As Ogbar concludes, the call for Black Power by Ricks and Carmichael was a reaction to, and acknowledgement of, an emergent political consciousness. But their words and actions were also part of a longer, and more geographically expansive, effort to wrest social justice from an oppressively racist society. Marable explains:

> The state of being critically self-aware involves a fundamental recognition that many common practices of daily life retard one's development. As racialized populations reflect upon the accumulated concrete experiences of their own lives, the lives of others who share their situation, and even those who have

died long ago, a process of discovery unfolds that begins to restructure how they understand the world and their place within it.[22]

How then are we to articulate the particularities of the Black Power movement? Initially, we must turn our attention to the details of urban-based concerns. In Northern and Western cities, for example, de facto rather than de jure segregation was largely the norm. Whereas many of the Southern-based civil rights campaigns were predicated on integration (for example, lunch-counter sit-ins, school desegregation), a prime focus articulated by the urban-based black radicals was the control of their own communities rather than integration into white communities.[23] Northern segregation, as explained by Jeanne Theoharis, operated differently. Public spaces in the north were not legally separated, although in practice the end result was just the same. African Americans continued to encounter discrimination and prejudices in movie theatres, public restrooms, hotels, and restaurants. Equally if not more pressing, though, was the existence of systemic inequalities in education, employment opportunities, and governance. Schools, housing, and jobs were allocated based on strict racial hierarchies.[24] The particularities of locally based racist practices required specific methods – but the more general political objective of equality remained constant. We must keep this continuity foremost in mind when discussing the geographies of black freedom struggles.

The Urban Context of Black Power

Planners and politicians have historically viewed U.S. cities as economic engines. In part this condition is derived from the existence of two "circuits of investment capital" that find prominence in urban areas. A primary circuit entails an investment of capital in manufacturing activities. Capitalists hire workers to manufacture commodities, which are then sold at a profit. These profits are subsequently used for further investment in manufacturing activities. Owing to various economies of scale (localization and urbanization economies, for example), capitalists often concentrate their activities within urban areas. A secondary circuit hinges on real estate investment – purchases of land specifically facilitate profit and capital accumulation. Speculators may, on the one hand, invest in property with the expectation of an appreciation in value; on the other hand the owners may develop the land for residential or commercial use. In either case, the circuit is "complete" when the investor actualizes a profit and subsequently reinvests the monies into more land-based projects. As sites of capital accumulation, therefore, cities have fuelled local and national economies.

African Americans have had an uneasy relationship with the modern American capitalist city. During the Great Migration, hundreds of thousands of African Americans left the South to follow the "American Dream" in the Northern and Western industrializing cities. However, the attainment of the American Dream was often far from forthcoming. Komozi Woodard identifies the early twentieth century as being marked by "increasing class formation, rapid urbanization, unprecedented ghetto formation, and anticolonial unrest." Moreover, he suggests that as blacks migrated to the North, they were not absorbed into white America; instead, they developed a distinct national culture and consciousness.[25] The spaces of the African American ghetto bore little resemblance to the spaces promised by the American Dream. Too often the "green pastures" turned out to be concrete fields with forests of cramped project buildings.

Abu-Jamal suggests that "ghettos are not natural growths," adding, "They are legal constructs that are the fruit of the long-held beliefs and practices of segregation."[26] Segregation both by custom and by law contributed to the spatial formation of the "black ghetto." Increased population densities, institutional neglect, legal restrictions, and violence and intimidation all contributed to the concentration of African Americans in impoverished spaces. State-prescribed segregation, for example, limited the prospects of African Americans for economic advancement. From Baltimore to Richmond, from Norfolk to Atlanta, residential segregation ordinances were passed that prevented the "free" movement of African Americans. Residential segregation became translated materially in the sense that attempts by African Americans for self-improvement and entrepreneurship were limited. By restricting the rights of African Americans to buy and sell property in response to market opportunities, or to gain access to housing loans and credit, segregation placed a ceiling on their ability to accumulate wealth and improve their physical environment.[27]

The black ghetto also resulted from a broader geographical restructuring of economic activities. During the 1940s and 1950s, for example, cities were on the decline. According to David Wilson, suburbanization was seen as a solution to a 1940s national economic malaise and uncertain postwar social order. Weak local and national economies needed bolstering. Consequently, planners, policy-makers, and politicians viewed suburban property development, utility extension, housing construction, and mortgage lending as strategic solutions to capitalist concerns. Government programs such as the Federal Housing Administration and Veterans Affairs mortgage loan programs, as well as various local tax abatement programs, fuelled the consumption of land and housing, and contributed to the production of buildings and neighbourhoods far from city cores.[28] In turn the geographical restructuring of manufacturing jobs from central cities to the suburbs contributed to the impoverishment of inner-city residents. On the one hand, African Americans were often economically unable to purchase households in suburban areas. On the other hand, those African Americans who were able to afford new homes were often prevented from doing so by zoning laws and other racist practices. African Americans, in effect, were spatially trapped.

Inadequate transportation systems likewise worked against African Americans and other inner-city residents. Reliant on public transportation, many individuals were unable to take advantage of relocated economic opportunities in the suburbs. In short, the spatial structure of the city and suburb often worked against African Americans.[29] While the suburban idyllic came to represent the American Dream, urban areas – and especially the industrialized cities of the North and West – came to be seen as blighted areas.

Cities were not entirely neglected, however. During the 1950s, but especially throughout the 1960s, various levels of government did make efforts to retain the wealth-creating potential of urban areas. These policies and programs emerged not out of any genuine concern for the welfare of inner-city residents, but rather as a means of recapturing urban economic bases and tax bases. Local and federal governments began, in the late 1940s and early 1950s, to promote massive public housing and urban renewal schemes. David Wilson notes that in 1940 fewer than twenty U.S. cities contained public housing; after 1955, though, housing programs gained a new sense of urgency. Between 1949 and 1967, more than 600 public housing projects were launched in some 700 cities. By 1970 over 450 public housing projects had been built in U.S. cities.[30]

The social costs of urban renewal and public housing schemes were enormous. Blighted buildings and neighbourhoods were to be razed and replaced by more "optimal" land uses. In the process, entire neighbourhoods were destroyed, replaced with drab housing projects, or office high-rises, or left vacant. Wilson relates that the programs demolished many more homes than they built and displaced more people and activities than they relocated. One infamous case is that of Buffalo's Ellicott project. Begun in 1954, the scheme – within ten years – displaced 2,200 African American families in a 161-acre area and provided only six new single-family homes.[31]

As urban areas were being destroyed by capitalist-motivated government programs, African American youths and households were identified as contributing factors to "urban decay." Wilson notes that suburbanization and city decline accelerated after 1967. Suburban areas gained over eighteen million people and more than three million jobs; cities, conversely, experienced substantial population and tax base declines. Wilson also points out that the urban rebellions of the 1960s, notably in Newark, Chicago, Los Angeles, Gary, Detroit, and Cleveland, "activated a sense that minorities had grown restless and volatile." He argues that the mainstream (white) media represented cities as places controlled by delinquents and other socially undesirables. African Americans, as represented in the media and government reports, dominated city streets, scared away whites and investment, and deepened ghetto formation.[32]

It is no coincidence that the Black Power movement emerged within this context of the struggle for U.S. cities. The words of Malcolm X, H. Rap Brown, and Huey Newton all fed into the dominant discourses of "black-on-black" violence, gang warfare, and the black militant. Consequently, these discourses were inseparable from the image of black radicals who rejected the liberal integrationist schemes of the dominant society and refused to acknowledge their place in capitalist society.

The urban revolution of black radicals, including Malcolm X and those who followed, was predicated, then, on a political-economic understanding of socio-spatial relations. Eschewing the traditional "integration/segregation" dichotomy, these black radicals advocated a variation of separatism, one that I term *communal separatism*.[33] By this I mean separate communities, such as black towns, wherein African Americans retain political, economic, and social control of their surroundings. This contrasts with *transnational separatism*, which refers to the literal return of diasporic peoples to the African homeland. The concept of communal separatism is important in that it highlights the political-economic dimension of the integration/segregation dichotomy. Integration, for these black radical intellectuals, was a capitulation to domination. Access to and control of resources are what mattered.

Socialism, Communalism, and Black Power

The Black Power movement was first and foremost an urban revolution. Malcolm X and his ideological heirs (such as Huey Newton, Eldridge Cleaver, and H. Rap Brown) advocated revolution because they believed that fundamental transformations of racism were not possible within the existing capitalist system. As Brown explained:

> America is a country that makes you want things, but doesn't give you the means to get those things. . . . America says you got to have money to live and to get money you got to have a job. To get a job, you got to have an education. So along comes a Black man and he gets a worse than inferior education so he can't qualify for a job he couldn't get because he was Black to begin with and he's still supposed to eat, keep his family together, pay the rent and buy an Oldsmobile.[34]

What emerged – in the speeches and writings of Malcolm X, Huey Newton, H. Rap Brown, and others – was a powerful critique of capitalism forwarded by these black radical intellectuals. This critique, moreover, was predicated on an assemblage of socialist, communal, and spatial concepts and based on the apparent contradictions of capitalist accumulation within the urban ghettos.

As a starting point, consider the place of integration in the struggle for black equality. The efficacy of integration was seriously questioned by many African Americans who lived in the North and West, in cities without legally sanctioned racial oppression but where de facto policies were nonetheless brutal, direct, and efficient in subjugating black people.[35] Indeed, Malcolm X and others understood that residential segregation was buttressed by economic integration. Socially, African Americans were "placed" in segregated neighbourhoods. Racist techniques, including redlining, were used to maintain a physical separation of peoples. And yet the capitalist system permitted – indeed encouraged – the unidirectional economic integration of the ghetto. Whites were permitted to buy land, set up shops, and profit from the spatial entrapment of African Americans. To "integrate" into such a system was to placate a racist and classist hegemony.

Black radicals differentiated, economically, between *segregated* spaces and *separate* spaces. African Americans, while consigned to inferior and segregated living spaces, were still readily available as a reserve supply of cheap (and trapped) labour. Moreover, segregated spaces did not preclude whites from capital investment opportunities in African American areas. Segregated spaces, far from being separate spaces, were – economically speaking – highly, though unfairly, integrated. It is for this reason, in part, that black radicals were opposed to the idea of integration. As H. Rap Brown explains, "What they [whites] didn't understand was that none of us was concerned about sitting down next to a white man and eating a hamburger."[36]

Black liberation was not based on integration; indeed, integration would – according to many black radical intellectuals – preclude liberation. According to Brown, "Integration was never our concern." He explains,

"You cannot legislate an attitude and integration is based upon an attitude of mutual acceptance and respect between two racial or cultural groups in the society." Yet, as Brown notes, "White people got hung up on integration. Segregation was the problem and the elimination of segregation was the solution, not integration. It was the unequal nature of segregation that Black people protested against in the South, not segregation itself."[37]

Black solidarity and communal separatism were, however, foundational to the demand for Black Power. For Malcolm X, integration without a change in the underlying attitudes of a racist system was a hollow prospect. Malcolm X understood, on the one hand, that integration served a symbolic function that reproduced white supremacy. Whites – as the normative group – were (and are) seen as naturalized. In a relational process, blacks are the marked "Other," to be refracted against the unmarked white. It did not matter if blacks lived next to whites if the basic structural and institutional conditions remained unchanged (and unchallenged). That is one reason why separation appeared to be attractive. On the other hand, Malcolm X perceived both segregation and integration as exploitative and oppressive to African Americans. H. Rap Brown likewise argued, "When a race of people is oppressed within a system that fosters the idea of competitive individualism, the political polarization around individual interests prevents group interests."[38] The route to achieve human dignity and self-determination, therefore, was through communal separatism, articulated not as a back-to-Africa movement but rather as a political, social, and economic revolution of the American capitalist system.

Following the revolutionary writings of Frantz Fanon, advocates of Black Power recognized what other integrationist-minded leaders often did not, namely that those in power would not willingly relinquish control. Consequently, Black Power proponents such as Carmichael, Wilkins, Brown, and Newton were intolerant of appeasing white liberals with language that whites approved. To these radicals, it mattered little if whites liked the words "Black Power."[39] This explains, likewise, the demands for revolutionary change. As Malcolm X said:

> It's impossible for a chicken to produce a duck egg. . . . A chicken just doesn't have it within its system to produce a duck egg. . . . The system in this country cannot produce freedom for an Afro-American. It is impossible for this system, this economic system, this political system, this social system, this system, period. . . . And if ever a chicken did produce a duck egg, I'm quite sure that you would say it was certainly a revolutionary chicken![40]

Socialist in orientation, Black Power proponents focused on structural changes and a redistribution of the ownership of production. Mitchell points out that the "right to the city" entails not simply a just distribution of goods and opportunities, but also social control over the means of distribution.[41] These were the lessons learned and taught by Malcolm X. This is what was required in the remaking of American space – an urban revolution to overturn the racist structures that defined the country.

Communal separatism was apparent in the practices of Newton and the Black Panther Party. Neighbourhood programs, including the petitioning for community control of the police, the teaching of black history classes, the establishment of health clinics, and the investigation of incidents of police brutality: all related to the promotion of black solidarity, self-defence, and self-determination. As such, the Black Panther Party, and related organizations, exhibited a combination of political philosophy with material programs.

The Contestation of Space

Discussing the emergence of Black Power, Abu-Jamal writes:

> Armed resistance to slavery, repression, and the racist delusion of white supremacy runs deep in African American experience and history. When it emerged in the mid-1960s from the Black Panther Party and other nationalist or revolutionary organizations, it was perceived and popularly projected as aberrant. This could only be professed by those who know little about the long and protracted history of armed resistance by Africans and their truest allies.[42]

Geographers have paid scant attention to the political geographies of black radical intellectuals and, specifically, the Black Power movement. And yet a contestation over space was prominent in the varied approaches to the black freedom struggle. The arguments of Malcolm X, Huey Newton, H. Rap Brown, Stokely Carmichael, and scores of other black radical intellectuals were about the material inequalities that existed within the segregated spaces of the United States. They critiqued a hypocritical system that promoted integration as part of the American Dream but in reality was a further technique that served to subjugate African Americans. The existence of segregation would not be resolved through integration, because integration was yet another tool of the oppressor, one that retained the basic inequalities in society – namely the ownership of production – while permitting economic exploitation to continue.[43]

Integration policies, according to these intellectuals, deprived African

Americans of their fundamental right of self-determination. To integrate into a white supremacist society was to negate the spaces of African Americans. If they were to adopt the norms, values, and nomenclature of the dominant society, African Americans would cease to exist as a people. As such, integration contributed to the dehumanization and displacement of African Americans just as strongly as segregation policies. In neither case were African Americans in control of their own communities and, hence, their self-determination.[44]

Lefebvre concludes:

> A revolution that does not produce a new space has not realized its full potential; indeed, it has failed in that it has not changed life itself, but has merely changed ideological superstructures, institutions or political apparatuses. A social transformation, to be truly revolutionary in character, must manifest a creative capacity in its effects on daily life, on language and on space.[45]

A revolution for black self-determination was required – and put forward by groups such as the Black Panther Party. Only through the autonomous control of public and private resources would it be possible for African Americans to achieve self-determination and self-development. Black radicalism – and specifically the Black Power movement – was (and continues to be) about producing a space for social justice.

Notes

1 Eugene McCann, "Race, Protest, and Public Space: Contextualizing Lefebvre in the U.S. City," *Antipode*, 31 (1999), p.167. See also, for example, Don Mitchell, *The Right to the City: Social Justice and the Fight for Public Space* (New York: Guilford Press, 2003); Mona Domosh, "Those 'Gorgeous Incongruities': Polite Politics and Public Space on the Streets of Nineteenth-Century New York City," *Annals of the Association of American Geographers*, 88 (1998), pp.209–26.

2 Henri Lefebvre, *The Urban Revolution* (Minneapolis: University of Minnesota Press, 2002), p.19.

3 Andy Merrifield, *Metromarxism: A Marxist Tale of the City* (New York: Routledge, 2002), pp.89–90.

4 Wolfgang Natter and John Paul Jones, "Identity, Space, and Other Uncertainties," in *Space and Social Theory: Interpreting Modernity and Postmodernity*, ed. Georges Benko and Ulf Strohmayer (Oxford: Blackwell, 1997), p.150.

5 George Fredrickson, *Black Liberation: A Comparative History of Black Ideologies in the United States and South Africa* (New York: Oxford University Press, 1995), pp.98–99.

6 David Harvey, *Spaces of Capital: Towards a Critical Geography* (New York: Routledge, 2001), p.188.

7 Mitchell, *Right to the City*, p.5.

8 James A. Tyner, "'Defend the Ghetto': Space and the Urban Politics of the Black Panther Party," *Annals of the Association of American Geographers*, 96 (2006), pp.105–18; James A. Tyner, *The Geography of Malcolm X: Black Radicalism and the Remaking of American Space* (New York: Routledge, 2006).
9 Waldo E. Martin Jr., *No Coward Soldiers: Black Cultural Politics in Postwar America* (Cambridge, Mass.: Harvard University Press, 2005), p.5.
10 Ruth Wilson Gilmore, "Fatal Couplings of Power and Difference: Notes on Racism and Geography," *The Professional Geographer*, 54 (2002), p.16.
11 Tyner, *Geography of Malcolm X*, p.8.
12 Robin D.G. Kelley, *Freedom Dreams: The Black Radical Imagination* (Boston: Beacon Press, 2002), pp.9–11.
13 Mumia Abu-Jamal, *We Want Freedom: A Life in the Black Panther Party* (Boston: South End Press, 2004), p.14.
14 Manning Marable, *Living Black History: How Reimagining the African-American Past Can Remake America's Racial Future* (New York: Basic Civitas Books, 2006), p.16.
15 For more on Malcolm X, see George Breitman, *The Last Year of Malcolm X: The Evolution of a Revolutionary* (New York: Schocken Books, 1968); Eric Wolfenstein, *The Victims of Democracy: Malcolm X and the Black Revolution* (London: Free Association Books, 1989); Louis A. DeCaro Jr., *On the Side of My People: A Religious Life of Malcolm X* (New York: New York University Press, 1996); Louis A. DeCaro Jr., *Malcolm and the Cross: The Nation of Islam, Malcolm X, and Christianity* (New York: New York University Press, 1998); Kwame Natambu, *The Life and Work of Malcolm X* (Indianapolis, Ind.: Alpha Books, 2002).
16 Tyner, *Geography of Malcolm X*, p.11.
17 Malcolm X, *Malcolm X Speaks*, ed. with prefatory notes by George Breitman (New York: Grove Weidenfeld, 1965), p.26.
18 Adam Fairclough, *Martin Luther King, Jr.* (Athens: University of Georgia Press, 1995), p.79.
19 James M. Washington, ed., *A Testament of Hope: The Essential Writings and Speeches of Martin Luther King, Jr.* (New York: HarperCollins, 1991), pp.292–93.
20 Jeffrey O.G. Ogbar, *Black Power: Radical Politics and African American Identity* (Baltimore: Johns Hopkins University Press, 2004), pp.61–63.
21 Quoted in Steven Lawson, *Civil Rights Crossroads: Nation, Community, and the Black Freedom Struggle* (Lexington: University of Kentucky, 2005), p.149; see also Ogbar, *Black Power*, pp.72–75.
22 Marable, *Living Black History*, p.36.
23 Tyner, "Defend the Ghetto," p.106.
24 Jeanne Theoharis, "Introduction," in *Freedom North: Black Freedom Struggles Outside the South, 1940–1980*, ed. Jeanne Theoharis and Komozi Woodard (New York: Palgrave Macmillan, 2003), p.3.
25 Komozi Woodard, *A Nation within a Nation: Amiri Baraka (LeRoi Jones) and Black Power Politics* (Chapel Hill: University of North Carolina Press, 1999), pp.6, 23.
26 Abu-Jamal, *We Want Freedom*, p.58.
27 Fredrickson, *Black Liberation*, p.128.
28 David Wilson, *Inventing Black-on-Black Violence: Discourse, Space, and Representation* (Syracuse, N.Y.: Syracuse University Press, 2005), pp.22–23.
29 Geraldine Pratt, "Reproduction, Class, and the Spatial Structure of the City," in *New Models in Geography: The Political-Economy Perspective*, ed. Richard Peet and Nigel Thrift (London: Unwin Hyman, 1989), p.93.
30 Wilson, *Inventing Black-on-Black Geography*, p.25.
31 Ibid., pp.26–27, 28.
32 Wilson, *Inventing Black-on-Black Geography*, pp.30–31.
33 Tyner, *Geography of Malcolm X*, p.115.
34 H. Rap Brown, *Die Nigger Die! A Political Autobiography by H. Rap Brown (Jamil*

Abdullah Al-Amin) (Chicago: Lawrence Hill Books, 2002), pp.18–19.

35 Ogbar, *Black Power*, p.20.

36 Brown, *Die Nigger Die!* p.55.

37 Brown, *Die Nigger Die!* pp.55–56, 124. Geographers, too, have been "hung up" on the concept of integration. Numerous statistical indices have been developed, all ostensibly to "measure" the social distance between racialized groups and to "determine" the degree of assimilation between the groups. For intellectuals such as Malcolm X and H. Rap Brown, however, numbers weren't needed to demonstrate the existence of racial oppression and exploitation. Every incident of police brutality, every lynching, was evidence of race-based geographies of injustice.

38 Brown, *Die Nigger Die!* p.16.

39 Ogbar, *Black Power*, p.77.

40 Malcolm X, *Malcolm X Speaks*, pp.68–69.

41 Mitchell, *Right to the City*, p.32.

42 Abu-Jamal, *We Want Freedom*, p.29.

43 Tyner, *Geography of Malcolm X*, p.79.

44 Ibid., p.162.

45 Henri Lefebvre, *The Production of Space*, trans. Donald Nicholson-Smith (Oxford: Blackwell, 1991), p.54.

12

Rinaldo Walcott

Homopoetics

Queer Space and the Black Queer Diaspora

for Brian Williamson

The spaces for black masculine performance in contemporary North American popular culture are actually few. Despite the overwhelming impact that black popular culture, especially its masculinized version(s), has had on, and continues to have on, North American popular culture generally, black men occupy a strange and queer place in that milieu. The spaces for the performance of black masculinity are largely characterized by musical cultures, fashion – or more accurately, style – and an urban bad-boy aesthetic that tends to limit black men to performing a small number of roles concerning their manhood. Even though small, these roles nonetheless have had a tremendous impact on how non-black men also perform their masculinity – either in concert with black men or in opposition to them. Black men who fashion identities beyond, or contradictorily in relation to, those limited roles are misread in all kinds of ways, and at the extreme they sometimes become victim to violence from all sorts of men (black included) who, in a racist society, perceive them to be a danger and a threat.

The prevailing demand, then, is that black men must be knowable not only to themselves, but also, most importantly, to others. That is, they must fit preordained scripts of which often they (as individuals) had little or no part in drafting; still they must struggle to live up to or to deny and evade these limited versions of masculinity. Various perceptions of black masculinity consequently place an enormous amount of pressure on black men to conform to the limited roles offered them. All of this is not to say that many black men do not take great pleasure in performing those limited roles, and they can and do, in fact, simultaneously produce new and disturbing versions of these roles. The more recent invention or performance of the homothug is evidence not only of how others attempt to delimit black men, but also of their own complicity with what the black feminist Patricia Hill Collins, in *Black Feminist Thought*, long ago identified as "controlling images": visual and ideological representations deployed to control the perception and assessment of black women in a negative fashion. Black men's complicity with controlling images in regard to themselves indicates the ways in which stereotypes about black masculinity have been internalized and performed as the essence(s) of their identities. Images like the homothug, the stud, the drug dealer, and the gangster, many of them dangerously and damagingly negative, become *them*. Partly in complicity with the ideology behind "controlling images," black men perform these images of themselves in numerous spaces in North American contexts; in queer spaces and milieu those images have come to be some of the most defining representations of black men. And yet in urban queer space, right alongside the homothug, for example, is the long-standing stereotype and evidence of the actual black drag queen (of which I shall say more later).

However, this chapter reads for and demonstrates how black gay men in Toronto's gay ghetto fashion selves that draw contradictorily on a range of black diaspora identifications and ephemera to continually undermine and remake the always potentially hegemonic white queer space. Reading for how style, music, gesture, and stereotype work to remake queer space simultaneously demonstrates how these same practices invoke a black queer diaspora through ephemeral identifications with other assumed, imagined, and invented black spaces. This chapter is an against-the-grain reading of how black gay men understand their positions within queer space. In short I mean to demonstrate that black gay men assume and make use of a margin in queer space but in doing so they actually occupy more than a margin – centre/margin language is just not an adequate descriptor for the negotiation and articulation of race, space, difference, and queerness in this particular context.

Black Queer Diaspora

The black queer diaspora is an invention that cuts across numerous boundaries. It allows for multiple and conflicting identifications based upon a shared sense of sexual practice and the ongoing machinations of racialization, especially anti-black racism. Significantly, the black queer diaspora functions as a network of borrowing and sharing of cultural expression, products, language, and gesture. This cross-border, outernational sharing and identification work to produce particular kinds of kinship relations that keep both in play and at bay suggestions that black queer practices are aberrant, anti-black, not as fully developed as Euro-descended practices, and so on. Thus the black queer diaspora is a counterweight to forces, both white and black, that position black queer sexuality as either non-existent or in need of spokespeople on its behalf. In this way, then, the black queer diaspora functions simultaneously as an internal critique of black homophobia and a critique of white racism.

Some time ago, a long-time black gay activist speaking at a public meeting in Toronto pointed out that in the early 1980s, if you wanted to find black gay men in Toronto you had to go to New York, Buffalo, Detroit, and even sometimes Washington, D.C. The claim of this activist was an interesting assertion based on a mountain of anecdotal evidence. On reflection his claim can allow us to make sense of black queer life in Canada from the past to the present, and probably even the future. Black queer life in Canada is diasporic and transnational. By this I mean that black queer life borrows and shares across national borders to constitute itself locally. Black queer life thus refuses national designation as its originary site of identification and instead casts its lot with black queers transnationally.

The question of who and what circulates in socio-spatial patterns is in part one way of constituting the black queer diaspora. Thus a representative list might include but not be limited to Isaac Julien, Marlon Riggs, Audre Lorde, Pat Parker, Barbara Smith, June Jordan, and James Baldwin, among many other people, films, books, and music, and a range of political arguments and debates, gestures, signs, and styles. This queer diaspora ephemera and its bodies (constituted as the real and symbolic names above) make assumptions about blackness strange. In other words, a black queer diaspora works to unhinge blackness from an assumed and oft-times unquestioned heterosexuality. In this way a black queer diaspora remakes the boundaries of the black diaspora, not only making its reach more inclusive of the unruliness that is diasporic blackness, but also raising difficult concerns and questions for the category of blackness. So while black queers and black heterosexuals share a common historical past, how that past is understood and utilized in relationship to contemporary injustices can oftentimes be quite different. Thus I am in part suggesting that the black queer diaspora comes into being through the circulation of people, texts, films, oral narratives, and other forms of ephemera that work as a way of fashioning an imagined diasporic community inside a much larger, but tension-filled and ambiguous, diaspora community.

Gayatri Gopinath has explored the ways in which diaspora needs queerness and queerness needs diaspora. In her view diaspora is to nation what queerness is to heterosexuality. The making and unmaking of each concept in the face of its seeming “Other” open up the terrain for exploring the various assumed contexts of marginality. Diasporas exist because they exceed national boundaries, with the nation being understood as the norm. Queers too exist as the excess of heterosexuality, with heterosexuality being understood as the norm. In each case the "abnormal" actually allows for a pinpointing of the limits of the normal. Both diaspora and queer allow for different kinds of relations – kinship and otherwise – to emerge. Thus these formations as both conceptual and actual sites of belonging, identity, and identification have socio-political, cultural, and economic implications of great magnitude.

Take as an example two sites of queer expressivity in Toronto. The first is GLAD (Gays Lesbians of African Descent) and the second is Blockorama, a festival of black queer culture. Each of these sites operates across various boundaries to constitute black queer subjectivities across nations and sexualities and racisms. GLAD is a group that largely focuses on "continental queer Africans in Toronto," and Blockorama stakes out space in the annual Toronto Pride parade to produce a queer cultural expression that stretches from "Trinidad to Ghana" and "Philly to Toronto." Both groups act to bring into existence, through various bodies, expressions, politics, and ephemera, a range of identificatory positions around which black queers can coalesce – even if only momentarily, even though I would strongly suggest that these are not short moments of identification. These two organizations work to make black queer diasporic subjecthood possible and evident. The two organizations extend the space of continental Africa and its diaspora into Canada, and by so doing reconfigure and respacialize geographies of history, desire, and identification, in the process producing "new kinship" relations.

Queer Spaces, Black (Male) Bodies

The proliferation of queer spaces in most urban North American centres means that black queer people can find themselves living more socially intimate lives with white queer North Americans than might have been the case in the past. In particular, gay villages (or gay ghettos) in large urban centres have become sites for the co-mingling of cross-racial and monoracial forms of various social and intimate pleasures. This close contact between groups that under other circumstances might not share a common space of pleasure and intimacy allows for a number of crucial social changes and historical legacies to emerge in the verbal, stylistic, and gestural economies of queer ghettos. The shorthand logic of gay ghettos is that there are spaces of community based on sexual practices and that other kinds of social categories of identity take a back seat to that of sexual identity. Considerable scholarship in the past decade has demonstrated that in North America the category of gay has largely come to stand in as the archetypal white, middle-class male.[1] This acknowledgement, at least in the literature, has meant that in the small and intimate geographies and space of queer identities, numerous racial, gender, and class skirmishes are taking place. What I want to do here is in part to explore how black queer men respond to those skirmishes through cross-border ephemeral identifications.

Thinking about black queer diaspora space might seem to some to be a project fraught with an identity politics that is considered no longer useful. I am attempting to do something quite different about identity politics. In fact, I am interested in identity and black queer identities as those identities work to create forms of anxiety for an imagined and assumed white queer Canadianness. I am concerned with the spatial politics and forms of knowledge claims made by black gay men in Toronto's gay ghetto (Church Street), about their imagined position within that queer geography and space. One of the best ways of mapping the evidence of black queer men in Toronto's queer space is to chronicle their lives in the bars. The space of the bar and its geography of sex, labour, and commerce place black men in very interesting roles. The performances commanded require that we pinpoint the site of the performance, whether commerce, labour, or sex (which can be both of the previous) and that we pay socio-political attention to how black men find space, make space, and occupy space in the changed dynamics of post-liberated queer urban ghettos – as encapsulated by the shift from drag queen to homothug.

The evidence of black queers and queers of colour is one that continually has to be written into the post-Stonewall history despite their presence at the now mythic historical beginning of the contemporary gay and lesbian movement. Black queers and queers of colour find themselves caught between Eurocentric queer histories and homophobic communities that seek either to deny their presence or to view them as if in a perpetual state of progressive development. But interestingly enough, it is in fact this paradox of either not existing or being in a state of perpetual development that allows black queers the opportunity to develop "languages" and styles uniquely theirs. These styles infiltrate and in many cases become central parts of what we can now call the "mainstream" queer community – meaning that these styles cross over into whiteness. When such crossovers occur, what often goes missing is the antecedent blackness of the style – it is reinvented as "white." The most famous and probably most contested of these styles is disco, but there are more contemporary instances as well.

Anthony Thomas has made a trenchant critique of the missing

history of house music now that it has crossed over.[2] House was a black gay invention that was produced and expressed in Chicago's black gay clubs (in particular the Warehouse) until it went global. These days it is almost impossible to find any urban centre with a queer nightclub scene that does not feature house at some point in its musical programming. Like disco before it, house occupies a central place in queer communities' economies of pleasure and thus its very existence brings at least the trace of blackness to the centre of queer communities. Brian Currid, who has done the most detailed investigation of house and its relationship to other black music, such as rap, and to queer identities and communities, argues: "House thus re-figures the operations of race and class within constructions of gay identity providing an alternative narrative in which gay black men are not marginalized, but central to the history of gay community and identity." Currid further states that when one reads the centrality of house to contemporary urban queer communities, an "alternative to unilinear white middle class understandings of queer history" emerges.[3] Currid's insights inform much of what follows here.

Black bodies, even when small in numbers, have a tremendous impact on queer communities. I want to stress, however, that this impact must not be read as exceptional but only as something in accord and relation to the impact that black peoples generally have on the wider North American culture. In queer space black bodies take authorial ownership of black cultural expressions of all sorts, and this taking of authorial ownership places black queer bodies in a paradoxical and contradictory site of being both tastemakers and outsiders. In the geographies of gay male Internet dating and "hook-ups," black gay men's bodies represent both desire and repulsion. This dynamic is in part the contradictory impulses of the place that black queer men hold in economies of desire in queer communities, where the myth of the "big dick" still rules even while black queer men are rejected because they do not possess that which is the most prized possession in queer settings – white skins.

Thus, when Charles Nero asked "why are gay ghettoes white?" his question carried a certain urgency concerning the place of black queer men in urban queer spaces. Both Nero and Martin Manalansan have turned their attention to how acts of gentrification affect the lives of black queers and queers of colour, especially poor and working-class queers in the United States.[4] Critiques of how the alterations of physical and built space are used to control black queers, queers of colour, and other poor and "undesirable" bodies in gay ghettoes demonstrate how the archetypal gay white middle-class male figure comes into being and can be an empirical reality. Additionally, such scholarship also points to the terms under which some queers become acceptable and others do not. In Nero's case, he identifies the idea of the black gay man as an imposture as being central to how the lives of black men are circumscribed or pushed outside of gay neighbourhoods. Manalansan, though, has demonstrated how "narratives of crime" in a post-9/11 United States have come to limit and delimit queer space for those racialized as not white. Thus both Nero and Manalansan offer assessments of urban queer space and its attendant politics that we should pay close attention to.

Both scholars concentrate on the politics of gentrification as a signal for how racialized poor queer bodies have been excised from the "we are family" discourse of the contemporary gay and lesbian movement. Their insights concerning how that racialized excision works are underwritten by a critique of how black queers and queers of colour understand and make sense of their ambivalent and ambiguous relationship to "queer citizenship" at the beginning of the twenty-first century. It might be anecdotally suggested that since the new queer citizenship is fundamentally based upon class, consumption, and whiteness, queers of colour are forced or pushed into finding other ways of engaging their "queer citizenship." Significantly, Nero and Manalansan are both fundamentally engaged in a political-economy critique at a time when much of global capitalism has successfully reoriented human life into the regimes of global neo-liberal imperatives.

Still, while acknowledging the importance and necessity of this critique, I want to shift the ground a little bit and turn to the arena of culture. While it is necessary to state that culture is not outside the regime of neo-liberal reordering, culture takes on a different valence in that regime. It is safe to say that there is in fact a culture of neo-liberalism, and I am going to focus on how black queers respond to that culture. Specifically, their everyday acts of refusal reposition them inside queer communities and they are therefore implicit to the making and unmaking of these particular cultural geographies. In "Black Men in Frocks: Sexing Race in a Gay Ghetto (Toronto)," I argue for what I call a multicultural and Creole space for black queer life in Canada.[5] My argument is based upon the small numbers of black queers present in Toronto, but recognizes the enormity of the impact of those numbers. Thus these spaces bring with them different and multiple ways of performing blackness, queerness, and maleness. The interconnection and the resulting tensions mean that these spaces are not neutral spaces devoid of all of the other socio-political and cultural politics implicit in the larger society. I hope to demonstrate that black queer men hold a larger place in this queer culture than is often assumed and that quite often black queer men are complicit in the production of queerness, in its representative forms as whiteness.

However, before I turn to a case study of Toronto and black queer presence I want to discuss a somewhat different notion of multiculturally queer. The dominance of multiculturalism as a frame for thinking about Canadian identity is only about thirty-five years old, but it has become a central aspect of how most Canadians think about themselves and the nation. In Terry Goldie's introduction to *In a Queer Country* he writes of queers: "We who claim a different sexual identity might live in our own world, that indefinable space which could be called 'queer country.'"[6] Goldie does not proceed to say that this queer country exists inside another country – let's call it a straight country – but he does suggest that queer country is not an entity unto itself. In Goldie's contribution to that collection of articles – "Queer Nation?" – he quickly moves from queer country and queer nationalism to Canadian nationalism or, more generously, desires for Canadian nationalism. He writes: "Canadians are at once less flamboyant and yet more respectful of variety than their American neighbors." Goldie's multicultural Canadian trace is evident in the use of the word "variety."[7] He then offers a reading of the TV comedy classic *Kids in the Hall*, particularly the work of gay actor Scott Thompson. What is most striking about Goldie's claims in the "Queer Nation?" essay is that while recognizing that some Canadian values "have caused homosexual Canadians great trauma," he writes in regard to what he calls Canadian values in the context of a Thompson joke and a lesbian anecdote: "The anecdote and Thompson's skit don't refuse homosexual difference from mainstream Canada, but do present an ambivalent respect for certain Canadian values, particularly tolerance."[8] What troubles me about Goldie's queer country is that I do not recognize it as my country.

Nero's and Manalansan's critiques of queer space can be helpful here because their work speaks to very local geographies of which the nation becomes the ultimate experience of those geographies. The evidence of tolerance that Goldie reads in both of his examples as constituting a nod to Canadianness is not a tolerance that those marked as not white can lay claim to as a part of something we might call Canadianness. Rather, intolerance seems more to mark the terms of Canadianness from the later point of view. Thus, we (Goldie and I) share the same geographic space or territory, but we inhabit it in such radically different ways that recognizing such a space as "the same" or ontologically connective becomes almost impossible.

Subsequently, by the time Goldie gets to what he calls "multiculturally queer?" (always with a question mark) he has reproduced the normative Canadian nation in all its various mythical guises. "Multiculturally queer?" is, significantly, the last section of his essay, reproducing a particular linear construction of the nation (that now familiar trajectory of movement from colony to multicultural modern nation-state). I do not read this linearity as ironic. Rather, I am interested in Goldie's use of toleration as a signal of Canadianness because I think it speaks to something important about the ways in which inclusion in national practices and discourses works.

Fortunately, included in *In a Queer Country* is an essay by Gary Kinsman that offers a much more nuanced reading of the Canadian nation-state. Kinsman is clear on reading for the various ways in which state policies and narratives create complex and shifting positions of exclusion and inclusion. Simultaneously he is also clear that much queer organizing in the Canadian context reproduces the inclusion/exclusion model for a range of tolerated and not tolerated identities. Kinsman points out that a systematic study of Canadian state formation would point to how various forms of oppression are embedded in the making of the state. Drawing on queer legal theorist Carl Stychin, Kinsman writes: "According to his insightful investigations of the intersections of nation, sexual identity, and rights discourse, Canadian state formation may be able to address social differences through its recognition of difference and tolerance of diversity."[9] But this does not mean that such addresses are always ultimately useful and liberating. Kinsman is intent on proving, and he does demonstrate, how Canadian state formation is an anti-queer project. He thus further adds, "This does not mean, however, that lesbians and gay men have not been able to exert agency and win gains within these state relations. Hegemony has never been total or secure. We have made important gains, but these gains have been limited."[10]

Kinsman's analysis is informed by a radical critique of the ways in which the market or late capitalism has impacted the formation of the nation-state and thus the sometimes partial toleration of once reviled identities, like queer identities. But his analysis suggests that toleration, rights talk, or the social and political gains that have been made are not sufficient and that those gains only shore up the state's already inequitable project. He concludes, "In the end, we need to organize against the state form itself, which is based on constructing a series of relations that stand over and against people in our everyday lives, and that actively prevent us from gaining democratic control over the social circumstances of our lives."[11] Kinsman thus provides insights on Canadian nation-state formation as a practice of oppression that is often mirrored in lesbian and gay political organizing itself, and in part helps to explain why the archetypal white gay male figure also operates so unchallenged in the Canadian public sphere as well.

Black queers could choose the relative "queer citizenship" that liberal

Canada offers with its rights to queer marriage, among a range of other protected rights. But once they do so, at the microlevel they become the multicultural or no-white ethnic "Others" of the queer family, much in the manner that Goldie writes of them. Instead, black queers in Canada recognize blackness as multicultural and transnational, and they organize and draw from such sources in their building of community. In this way black queers make kinship relations an outernational experience that much more accurately fits their everyday contexts. Black queers in Canada thus more firmly identify with black queers globally than with the white queer paradigm that now understands sexuality as just yet another multicultural category to be managed by the state through various forms of legislation.

Toronto: A Case Study

Currid offers music as a central mode for thinking about black queers and the (dis)function of the queer "we are family" discourse. His analysis centres black queers in one of the central economies of contemporary queer life and its spaces of performance. In the Toronto queer economy of pleasure, and in this specific case, music culture, two black men – Rolyn Chambers and Gairy Brown – dominate and operate in a very interesting fashion to produce queer community as essentially white, which leads inescapably to the irony of black men offering to white men ways of performing white queerness. In the local magazine *Fab*, which is billed as a publication devoted to the party scene, one of the central columns is written by and overseen by party-reporter Chambers. In his column "Deep Dish" Chambers provides a written and photographed collage of the previous week's party events (mostly local but sometimes out of town as well). The photos take up most of the inches of the column space. Most but not all of the photos are of white, young men out partying. "Deep Dish" dishes out a "humorous" caption for each of its photos, and the narrative element of the column reports on which events were successful and which were not, essentially party gossip. "Deep Dish" sets a standard for the places to be seen, but it especially sets a standard for taste – the places to be seen at and the kinds of fashion/dress and body types that are desirable.

Similarly, when it comes to places to be seen, Gairy Brown, a local promoter and "party stylist," produces those sites. Brown's parties are the places where masses of white queer bodies groove to the latest sounds and songs of queer pop life, all against backdrops imagined and dreamed up by him. As an especially important figure in the local queer circuit scene, Brown produces shows that shore up a certain kind of whiteness for contemporary white urban queers. These parties, which tend not to have a very large black queer participation, nonetheless have elements of blackness that underwrite their sense of attraction to their audiences. While one might argue that figures like Brown and Chambers give white queer audiences what they want, I would suggest that something much more subversive is at stake: the ways in which black queer men continue to be the barometer of queer taste. Indeed, black queer men are the producers of desire, fashion, and style – imaginative conduits of queerness – even when those tastes are conditioned to produce white-on-white desire. This is queer life, after all. The ambiguous position that these black queer tastemakers hold *remakes* queer economies of pleasure and by so doing also produces queer geographies in ways that are both darkly visible and invisible. But equally important, these figures have a significant impact on queer economy – particularly its financial side – which is especially significant when most queer businesses still cater to the economies of pleasure – bars and clubs. The case of Brown and Chambers can be replicated across numerous North American urban centres where black queer men function as style and tastemakers across various communities.

To further illustrate how black queerness works to ambivalently racialize space and configure relations of race and class within archetypal white gay ghettoes, the space of entertainment, especially dance clubs, can again offer us much insight. I know of no free-standing black gay clubs in Toronto. As opposed to definitively black clubs, "black nights" at general-population gay clubs have characterized the scene in Toronto. But once a "black night" is advertised, the club basically becomes a black gay club. The taint of blackness means that even one "black night" gives a club space the reputation of being a "black club" so that the place and space become firmly associated with black bodies, even if the place is not occupied by black bodies on every night of its operation. Association and affiliation with blackness always seem to blacken. In such situations black men and the non-black men who love them occupy space in the queer ghetto that is associated with both repulsion and deep levels of psychic attraction because those spaces become sites of a queer-community imagined tastemaking. These black spaces are often posed as queer imposture sites, but yet these imposture sites operate to have an impact on everything from styles of dress to music. Thus one of the central ironies is that spaces of black queer "imposture" also function as the reservoir of all queer desire.

The question of how notions of the black gay imposture work to fashion queer space is particularly clear in the performance of the homothug. This "new" figure operates as tastemaker, bringing hip hop's cross-cultural-style dominance to queer communities and simultaneously also bringing along the old and lingering stereotype of the dangerous black male who could potentially commit murder. The deep attraction to this figure across racial lines in queer urban space tells us much about the contradictory ways in which pleasure plays itself out in sexuality and how different racialized subjectivities are implicated in those pleasure-making ways.[12]

Contradictions, Identifications, and Pleasure-Making

Every Sunday when I go to Church – that is, Church Street, in Toronto's gay ghetto – I am greeted by a set of contradictions, identifications, and pleasure-making that confirms the "marginalized centrality" of black queer men to contemporary queer culture. The contemporary successes of the gay and lesbian movement have co-terminously happened alongside an attempt to produce the queer community as different but the same. Much of the work of making queer just another state-sanctioned multicultural category has been to weed out or make less apparent and sometimes even invisible all those members of queer communities who would cause great dissonance for hetero-normativity and its authorizing of post-liberation queer life. Thus sex radicals in particular have been increasingly marginalized in queer communities. Similarly, drag queens, who have been both the post-Stonewall bond of queer community and its simultaneous shame, have come into and gone out of vogue – straight acting is more sought after than any hint of effeminacy on queer Internet cruise sites.

These kinds of observations set a number of contradictions into play. At the local bar I frequent every Sunday, for instance, three black drag queens usually perform for a crowd that is 95 per cent white male. These three queens do a medley of pop songs, which they interpret with various dresses and gestures. The audience that awaits them every Sunday is extremely appreciative. It is almost as if this particular audience is trying in some way to push against the tide of a certain kind of homo-normativity that would have queers just be like everyone else, except for a practice of sex, which they will never publicly speak about. The drag queens seem to deliver every single Sunday. However, I would point out that as these drag queens deliver a certain kind of respite for the ongoing banality of straightening out queer life by re-queering gay and lesbian life – not to mention black life – they also centre and decentre whiteness in the gay ghetto in important ways.

The humour that the black queens engage in is almost always race-based. The humour positions blackness in opposition to whiteness, but when it does so it is never in relation to a simple and easy domination of black bodies by white ones; rather, it is always in the context of how whiteness takes its advantage from domination, and how that domination comes with an expense of some kind. The humour of the drag queens, whether it is a black queen doing a Celine Dion song or proclaiming to be a "redneck woman," is meant to constantly undermine and show up the absurdities of race and racial categories. These queens push at the limits of the racial imagination in their performances, making whiteness appear an absurd claim to identity and desire. On the stage they become desired authorizing subjects, collecting numerous tips from adoring white fans while subjecting whiteness and sometimes blackness to a sense of absurdity. As one lip-synching queen likes to put it when she doesn't know the words of the song, "Who you think I'm fooling? You know this ain't real."

Notes

1 See Suzanna Walters, *All the Rage: The Story of Gay Visibility in America* (Chicago: University of Chicago Press, 2001); and Katherine Sender, *Business, Not Politics: The Making of the Gay Market* (New York: Columbia University Press, 2005).
2 Anthony Thomas, "The House the Kids Built: The Gay Black Imprint on American Dance Music," in *The Greatest Taboo: Homosexuality in Black Communities*, ed. Delroy Constantine-Simms (Los Angeles and New York: Alyson Books, 2000).
3 Brian Currid, "'We Are Family': House Music and Queer Performativity," in *Cruising the Performative: Interventions into the Representation of Ethnicity, Nationality and Sexuality*, ed. Sue-Ellen Case, Philip Brett, and Susan Leigh Foster (Bloomington and Indianapolis: Indiana University Press, 1995), p.173.
4 Charles Nero, "Why Are Gay Ghettoes White?" in *Black Queer Studies: A Critical Anthology*, ed. E.P. Johnson and M. Henderson (Durham, N.C.: Duke University Press, 2005); Martin Manalansan, "Race, Violence, and Neoliberal Spatial Politics in the Global City," *Social Text*, 84–85 (2005), pp.141–55.
5 Rinaldo Walcott, "Black Men in Frocks: Sexing Race in a Gay Ghetto (Toronto)," in *Claiming Space: Racialization in Canadian Cities*, ed. Cheryl Teelucksingh (Waterloo, Ont.: Wilfrid Laurier University Press, 2006).
6 Terry Goldie, "Introduction," in *In a Queer Country: Gay and Lesbian Studies in the Canadian Context*, ed. Terry Goldie (Vancouver: Arsenal Pulp Press, 2001), p.1.
7 Terry Goldie, "Queer Nation?" in *In a Queer Country*, ed. Goldie, p.9.
8 Ibid.
9 Gary Kinsman, "Challenging Canadian and Queer Nationalisms," in *In a Queer Country*, ed. Goldie, pp.209–10.
10 Ibid., p.210.
11 Ibid., p.227.
12 See Rinaldo Walcott, "The Struggle for Happiness: Commodified Black Masculinities, Vernacular Culture, and Homoerotic Desires," in *Pedagogies of Difference: Rethinking Education for Social Change*, ed. Peter Trifonas (New York: Routledge Falmer, 2003).

Appendix

Letter from the Rastafari Community of Shashamane to UN Secretary General Kofi Annan, June 27, 2001*

Shashamane is the gift land granted to the Black people of the world wishing to return to Africa by His Imperial Majesty Emperor Haile Selassie I in 1931. This land grant is originally 500 hectares of fertile land, located between two rivers – the Malkoda River and Shashamane River, The land was formerly issued through the administration of the Ethiopian World Federation (EWF).

Some of the earlier settlers, who came and occupied the land, are still here after over thirty years. The majority of whom have come from Jamaica, America, and other Caribbean Islands, and also other countries. Three generations have occupied the land grant spanning the decades that saw the King of Kings reign, the aftermath when the Derge seized power, and most recently the transition of power to the current Ethiopian Government. By and large the greater numbers of those who have responded to this call are members of the Rastafari faith.

During the period of the Derge, a large portion of the land was confiscated and a small portion of (11) eleven hectors was returned and distributed to 18 families who remained on the land during this period. The Oromos population has occupied a large portion of the land, and no new land has been issued from that period until now, even though there has been a steady and growing increase of Rastafari population (man, woman, and children), who have still responded to this call of Repatriation, since 1992 (after the fall of the Derge), and since the Centenary year Celebration of His Imperial Majesty until this present time.

Current Situation: Although the Ethiopian Government has tolerated the Rastafari community presence and the Oromos know that this is land set aside for the African at home and abroad. Those who have chosen to live in Shashamane, have no legal document, nor official recognition, even though a percentage of children have been born each year on the land grant and are still considered not legal citizens and are expected to pay

---

* See chapter 2, p.31.

Residents fees annually once they have reached a certain age. We have no Legal Representation who could represent the Rastafari community and help with our interest on an Official legal level. Each and every family and individual has to secure themselves and their own interest in any possible manner.

The following information listed are some of the main issues and immediate conditions that face the Rastafari community to date and to which we would like your assistance in helping the Rastafari community to address.

A. LEGAL CITIZENSHIP

The majority who leave the West and return to live in Ethiopia came to be accepted as Africans/Ethiopian with rights to Citizenship. We therefore desire to have full legal status and to be recognized as citizens of Ethiopia, with all the privileges and rights to live, work and travel freely as Ethiopians.

B. ASSISTANCE IN RE-ESTABLISHING THE LAND GRANT

The Land Grant was originally granted by Emperor Haile Selassie in 1931, to the Black people of the world (Africans abroad and at home) wishing to return to Ethiopia. The grant was again highlighted through the Administration of the EWF (Ethiopian World Federation), an Organization, which is to carry out the task of distribution of the land to those who return to Ethiopia.

We therefore request and require your assistance in reactivating this important organ with the power to function and operate legally and officially towards fulfilling its original task as administrators of the land grant.

C. DUTY FREE CONCESSIONS

In order to establish a strong, viable and self-sufficient community here in Ethiopia, it is very important that the Rastafari community be able to convey materials into the country, such as variety of machinery, tools, musical equipment, and all other variety of foreign materials needed for development without having custom taxes.

Currently this is exactly the case we are experiencing, these materials can help us develop the community. We are therefore requesting assistance that can allow tax-free status in order to clear materials coming through customs.

D. REPATRIATION AND REPARATIONS

This is the issue for African descendants that were removed from Africa, exploited, and subjugated to slavery, a great injustice and now have chosen to return and re-establish ourselves in Africa as legal citizens, with the opportunity to develop our community.

Contributors

Jenny Burman is Assistant Professor of Communications in the Department of Art History and Communication Studies at McGill University, Montreal, where she teaches in the area of transnational cultural studies. Her research focuses on non-status activism, the diasporization of Canadian urban space, and the traffic of goods and people joining Canada and the Caribbean.

Carole Boyce Davies is Professor of English and African–New World Studies at Florida International University, Miami. She is the author of *Black Women, Writing and Identity: Migrations of the Subject* (1994) and *Claudia Jones . . . Left of Karl Marx: The Politics and Poetics of a Black Communist Woman* (2007). Other publications include *Ngambika: Studies of Women in African Literature* (1986), *Out of the Kumbla: Caribbean Women and Literature* (1990), *Moving Beyond Boundaries* (1995), *The African Diaspora: African Origins and New World Identities* (1999), and *Decolonizing the Academy: African Diaspora Studies* (2003). She is general editor of *The Encyclopedia of the African Diaspora* (2007).

Peter James Hudson is a doctoral candidate in American Studies at New York University. He is the editor of *North: New African Canadian Writing*, a special issue of *West Coast Line*, and has published essays in *Prefix Photo*, *Transition: An International Review*, and *Chimurenga*.

Babacar M'Bow is International Program and Exhibit Coordinator at Broward County Libraries Division, Fort Lauderdale, Florida, and focuses on cultural studies with an emphasis on Africa and African diaspora arts. His publications include *Splendors of Trinidad and Tobago: The Art of Carnival* (2000), *Haiti: From a Legacy of Freedom to an Explosion of Cultures* (2001), *The Soul of Black Folk: Africa and the African Diaspora* (2003), *The Descent of the Lwa: Journey through Haitian Mythology* (2004), *Benin: A Kingdom in Bronze* (2005), and *Roots: The Idea of Modernity in Contemporary Haitian Art*.

Katherine McKittrick lives in Toronto and teaches gender studies, critical race studies, and indigenous studies at Queen's University, Kingston, Ontario.

Her interdisciplinary research examines questions of socio-spatial justice in the black diaspora – particularly through creative texts (poetry, music, fiction). She is the author of *Demonic Grounds: Black Women and the Cartographies of Struggle* (2006) and is researching the writings of Sylvia Wynter.

Angel David Nieves is Assistant Professor in the School of Architecture, Planning, and Preservation at the University of Maryland, College Park. His scholarly work and activism critically engage with issues of heritage preservation, gender, and nationalism at the intersections of race and the built environment in the global South.

Kimberly N. Ruffin is Assistant Professor in the Department of English at Bates College, Lewiston, Maine. She is working on a literary and cultural study entitled "Black on Earth: African-Americans and Ecological Insights."

Suzette A. Spencer holds a doctorate in African American Studies from the African Diaspora Studies Program at the University of California, Berkeley. Her research focuses on African American and Caribbean literatures and cultures and black feminisms. She is working on "Stealing a Way," a book about maroonage, slavery, and African American and Caribbean discourse. Her scholarship has appeared in *African American Review*, *Black Scholar*, *Macomere*, and *Women's Review of Books*.

Sonjah Stanley Niaah is the inaugural Rhodes Trust Rex Nettleford Fellow in Cultural Studies, 2005, and Lecturer in Cultural Studies at the University of the West Indies, Mona Campus. She is working on three book projects, including two edited collections on Jamaican culture – one on dancehall culture (with Bibi Bakare Yusuf, forthcoming, UNISA Press), and the other on the production of celebrity. Stanley Niaah has published on Jamaican popular culture in *Space and Culture*, *Discourses in Dance, African Identities, Social and Economic Studies, Caribbean Quarterly,* and *Small Axe*, and has presented conference papers in the Caribbean, Asia, United States, United Kingdom, Europe, and Africa. She is associate editor of *Wadabagei: A Journal of the Caribbean and Its Diasporas*.

James Tyner is Professor of Geography at Kent State University in Ohio. His research interests include political and population geography, black radicalism, and Southeast Asia. He is the author of six books, including *The Geography of Malcolm X: Black Radicalism and the Remaking of American Space*.

Rinaldo Walcott is Associate Professor at the Ontario Institute for Studies in Education of the University of Toronto. He is the editor of *New Dawn: The Journal of Black Canadian Studies*, an open-access online journal and is working on a collection of essays on the black queer diaspora.

Clyde Woods lives in Santa Barbara, California, and teaches in the Department of Black Studies at the University of California, Santa Barbara. His research examines the relationship between regional political economy and African American social and cultural movements. He also works on the blues as a central black aesthetic, social research epistemology, and development tradition. Woods is the author of *Development Arrested: The Blues and Plantation Power in the Mississippi Delta* (1998). His projects include manuscripts and development projects on Los Angeles, New Orleans, and blues/hip hop.

Index

About the Presses

Between the Lines and South End Press are committed to publishing books that promote social justice and radical social change. Both presses operate as collectives and were founded in 1977 – emerging from similar milieux, and with similar mandates. Both uphold principles of equity, diversity, and respect for human rights. As sister presses we work more and more closely together, through exchanges of information and ideas, to support each other's projects. Out of this growing relationship comes the publication of *Black Geographies*, our first joint edition.

To find out more about Between the Lines, visit:
<www.btlbooks.com>
To find out more about South End Press, visit:
<www.southendpress.org>